They pour from below and drain from above

Dark ravens of death and a lily white dove

They suck out my junk then they fill me with art

God I could use an inflatable heart

MY INFLATABLE HEART

A LEGACY BOOK
Published by
Koehler Books

© Copyright 2011 by John Koehler

For more information, please contact John Koehler
john@koehlerbooks.com
757-289-6006
210 60th Street, Va. Beach, VA 23451
www.koehlerbooks.com

Library of Congress Cataloging and Publication Data
Koehler, John - 1958 -
My Inflatable Heart

ISBN 978-0-9765932-2-5

Printed and distributed by Lightning Source and Ingram Books

Scripture is taken from: the New International Version (NIV), Copyright © 1973, 1978, 1984 by International Bible Society, used by permission of Zondervan Publishing House. All rights reserved; The Message (MSG) Copyright © 1993, 1994, 1995, 1996, 2000, 2001, 2002 by Eugene H. Peterson. Used by permission of NavPress. All rights reserved; and the Holy Bible. New Living Translation (NLT) copyright © 1996, 2004 by Tyndale Charitable Trust. Used by permission of Tyndale House Publishers.

All rights reserved. No part of this publication may be reproduced, stored in a retrieval system, or transmitted in any form or by any means - electronic, mechanical, photocopy, recording, or any other - except for brief quotations in printed reviews, without the prior written permission of the publisher.

The views and opinions expressed in this book come exclusively from the author and are based on his personal beliefs and opinions. They do not reflect the views or are they meant to suggest an endorsement by Young Life or any other ministry, organization, church, business or individual.

Edited by Tia Stauffer
Cover designed by John Koehler with help from Kim Nelson

CONTENTS

Introduction iv

Part 1: THE CALL
In the Beginning 6
Beach Bums 12
The Calling 22
Lake Champion 30
The Obstacle Course 36
First Club 42
Going on Staff 48
Rockbridge 2005 54
Rusty Missile 62
Tara, Tara, Tara 66

Part 2: SPECIAL PEOPLE
Special People 72
Bart and the Goat's Milk 78
Anna's Pearl 82
Jack's Back 88
Hamilton's Song 92
Melissa 96
East, North, South 100
Matthew and Peter 106
A Surfer Named Timmy 110
Ruben 116
Easter Lilli 124

Part 3: ME, MYSELF, AND I
I Wanna Go Home 130
The Dung Beetle 136
My Piehole 144
The Strangel 150
My Awful Club Talk 158
The Gates of Hell 162
Winning the Race 168
The Imposter 176

Part 4: HEART THOUGHTS
The Agape Myth 184
Theory of Forrest Gump 188
My Inflatable Heart 192
Crazy Love 198
Surfing Through Life 202

Marching J-Bots 208
Becoming a Made Man 214
Rabbit Holes 220
The Bark of the Forest 224

Part 5: OUT THERE
Motorworld 230
The Mayor & the Monkey 234
Griffon and the Idiot 238
Booker Beach Club 244
Locked Out in Norfolk 248
The Eyes Have It 256
Two Pastors and an Earl 260

Part 6: MAKE BELIEVE
Easter Eggs & Happy the Cow 268
Billy the Bully 274
Parking Details 280
The Execution of Mr. Nut 286
Sarah & The Heart Empire 290

Part 7: DEAR LORD
Ashley on the Side of the Road 298
When Anyone 302
Peter & Forrest 306
The Flight of Josh 310
Hofferbert Hill 314
My Second Allergy 318
Let Go 324
May Change 330
Ordinary Men 334
Mr. Speaker 338
Happy Happy Sad Sad 342
Josh the Supernova 346
Inside Knowledge 350
Cleaning Up the Unclean 354
My Three Sons 358
My Living Dream 362
Heart Surfing 366
Jasper the Amazing Dog 372

Part 8: NEW SONGS 378

INTRODUCTION

JOHN KÖEHLER

> Great crowds came to him, bringing the lame, the blind, the crippled, the mute and many others, and laid them at his feet; and he healed them.
>
> MATTHEW 15:30

Not long ago a friend of mine asked me when I was going to write my next book. I was quite pleased to tell him that I was working on not one but *two* books.

One book is based in part on the stories I had written over the past year on my blog, Köehlerville. These stories cover all kinds of things in my life and are basically journalistic and autobiographical in nature.

The second book is my second mental health book called Soul Crazy. It deals with the premise that since the brain is the home of the soul, we need to include the care of the soul in all mental health care. Sick brains equal sick souls, which equal suicide. Any questions?

I felt rather good explaining these book concepts to my friend, especially considering that he asked about one book and I told him I was thinking about two. What audacity to hope this way! What arrogance and pride. What a bloated ego.

My friend looked at me like I was crazy, which I suppose I am in some ways, especially when I'm off my meds. He shook his head with a disdainful look and said, "No, I'm talking about the book you need to write about Capernaum (a ministry for kids with disabilities) and all the stories you've told. I'm talking about *that* book."

It seems that everyone is a book editor, especially my friends.

Here I was thinking about two very relevant and worthy books (at least in my own mind), while my friend was thinking only about the book I needed to write, at least according to him. He didn't want to hear about those other books because in his opinion the book about Capernaum was the only book I should write. It was the book he wanted to read and—by extension—the one the whole world wanted to read.

I cogitated on this for a while and wondered if he was right. I had, in fact, also been thinking about writing that particular book about Capernaum but didn't think it was time.

My life with Capernaum has been a cauldron of experiences and living stories that continue to percolate inside of me, but I didn't believe I was quite ready to write the story yet. When do you say enough is enough, when the process and the stories never stop?

I had been writing stories about Capernaum from the beginning, since 2004. Stories about the kids, camps, leaders, clubs. Perhaps these were the minor league stories I needed to write to prepare myself for the major league book my friend wanted me to write. I don't know. But when is the right time to take the field as a major leaguer?

Who would call me up to the Bigs, to the Show?

I know, I know, you could argue that God was calling me up through my friend to give me the nudge I needed. The kind of nudge when you're out on the edge of the diving board, afraid of the water. A nudge from a friend to help you overcome your fear with that final push. Splash!

The water is cold, deep, and dark because your eyes are shut tightly in fear. Murderous thoughts consume you as you rise to the surface. But then you realize what just happened; your fear was overtaken by jumping into it, and by the time you surface, you are laughing with your friend. You still give him an Indian burn when you get out, but you also thank him for his help. He was a true friend for trying to kill you.

Many of the stories in this book are about my experiences with Young Life Capernaum, a ministry for kids with disabilities. I was called into this ministry by none other than the Big Surfer Dude in the Sky, otherwise known as God. I am not being cute when I say I was called because it is the truth.

There was no burning bush or choir of angels, yet it was as plain as day and as clear as a newborn's eyes. When asked to serve, I said no, but God said yes. Perhaps I should change my name to Jonah.

I was forced to do what my heart already knew how to do and the rest of me was learning. I was the right man for the job because God had been setting me up and training me all of my life.

Who knew?

I had never been trained nor did I go to school to learn about people with disabilities. I have never considered myself an expert about them, nor do I today. I believe that in many cases God does not really concern Himself with the training of our minds, but with the disposition of our hearts. He deemed me ready or not, 'cause here I come. I was willing for Him to use me whether or not I was ready to be used.

I was sent to help them find their way to the table of life, where a banquet has been laid out for them by the King Himself. I was not only sent as God's royal ambassador, but as His court jester.

Their lives are much too serious for me to bring them the Gospel and the favor and love of God wrapped in theology and religion. I was not called out at forty-five years of age to be their taskmaster so that I could demand their attention and point out their weaknesses. How droll that would be.

I was called first to light them up with goofy love, crazy agape, and ridiculous friendship. Then when their hearts open to me, when they accept me as their brother, their uncle, their father, their family, then I can drive the truck filled with God's grace and barbaric love straight into their hearts. Then I can teach them about Jesus and how much He loves them.

That is why God called me to this mission, to this purpose, to this ministry, and, by extension, to this book. It is as simple as that, and no matter how hard I try to find the theological or human reasons that would refine this for me, God's fingerprint is quite simple and clearly seen. No other reasons are needed.

Go and serve them, He said. Love them. Lift them up. Tell them that I love them just as they are because I made them just as they are. Tell them I expect them to work for Me and to open up their hearts to Me because I am coming. I am coming.

Tell them I'm standing right next to them, knocking on the door of their hearts, waiting to come in and eat with them at the table I have set. Tell them this table is Mine and they are Mine as are all people. There is only one table where all may come.

Tell them to come to My table of life.

Capernaum has flavored my life since May 2004. It has broadened my awareness of a God who I was already quite aware of. It has increased my potential as a ministry worker when I already had my own personal ministry. It has made me see things in ways that were unusual even for me.

Capernaum has added colors to the spectrum of my soul and made my heart beat a little louder and stronger. The truth is that Capernaum has completely changed my life, and that change flavors all the stories in this book, whether or not they are about Capernaum. The other truth is that God was with me before Capernaum, during, and He will be with me after.

I can't see the future, and I have no clue where I'll be when this book comes out, but I know that God will always be with me, even if I can't always see Him.

Many of the chapters with dates were taken directly from my Köehlerville blog. Most were written during 2007, a very good year in the end, in the middle, and the beginning. The rest of the dated chapters poured out of my head in June of this year, as a last rush of emotion, written in the Dear Lord style I used in my first book.

As these stories pour out of these pages and into your mind, I do hope you are blessed in some way. Bon apetit!

John Köehler, October, 2008

JOHN KÖEHLER

My Inflatable Heart
by John Köehler

Allen Nebrich (L) and John Koehler, moments after riding the zip line at Lake Champion, New York, in 2004.

For Allen

1974 - 2007

JOHN KÖEHLER

PART ONE

THE CALL

Allen looking happy down at the beach.

ONE

In the Beginning

for Lynda

> Go out quickly into the streets and alleys
> of the town and bring in the poor,
> the crippled, the blind and the lame.
>
> LUKE 14:21

In the beginning was Allen. God brought us together as brothers of different mothers and there was no mistaking it. We were as different as peas and carrots yet, as Forrest Gump points out, we're both vegetables.

God brings us together in spite of our differences and similarities. In spite of the physical, emotional, mental and spiritual comparisons we make about each other, we are called to find the very things that draw us together and unite us in the midst of the vast fields of separation in our lives.

I met Allen way back in 2003, in the atrium of Spring Branch Community Church. I was coming out of church after the service and noticed a big dude in a wheelchair just outside the doors, over near the windows. He was talking to a lady and I got in line to talk to him.

Why did I get in line, you ask? Well, I don't rightly know, truth be told. It just seemed natural. I wanted to know who he was and why he was there. I was simply curious and being a gregarious sort, I just got in line to fulfill the destiny of our meeting. The meeting that God had arranged and setup with a twinkle and a smile.

I looked at him as he continued to converse with the lady. He was one sorry looking sucker, I can tell you that! Now before you turn me into the police, or call the National Guard, you need to understand one thing: this book will be about honesty and telling the truth, no matter how much it might hurt your feelings or seem as if it hurt someone else's feelings. I am a truth teller, and while I do not go around trying to incite riots or upset folks, sometimes I do.

There is absolutely no question that I would be much better off by shutting my big pie hole and NOT sharing the words that just materialized in my brain a nanosecond before unleashing them on the world. Perhaps I would be better served if I ran the words through the filter of my heart.

But here's the deal. My heart is a cauldron, and the truth is that my SOUL lives in my brain. So all that I think and feel is mixed up in one place. All the good that God gives me, all the great stuff I read and hear and see is mixed in with all that is wrong with me.

All of my bad behaviors compete with my good and I don't always know which side is going to win out when I open the trap door to the dungeons that hold my treasure and my garbage. The trap door otherwise known as my mouth. Or, in this case, the fingers that are flying across the keyboards as these words spill out of me and across time for you to see.

Telling the truth about how someone looks or acts when I am good friends or family with them is not mean in my world. It is just accurate, and if I am to tell you the truth and invite you in to the world of Capernaum, you must hear everything. The good, the bad, the ugly and the beautiful. Remember: God made it all!

Back to Allen.

Allen Nebrich was one gnarly looking dude! If you could pull his big white butt out of his wheelchair (and I did many times) and unbend his crooked sinews and bones and muscles, he would stand about 6'4" or maybe an inch or two taller. He weighed about 175 lbs. soakin' wet and felt like a hippo when you were tired.

Now from a weight standpoint, that is not the largest man on the planet. But from the standpoint of having to carry him or lift him from his wheelchair or bed or a chair or even a zip line lift, Allen was a huge man and one sure to test the limits of your endurance if you aimed to care for him as I did in my complete stupidity and ignorance.

Allen was born with Cerebral Palsy. This is a condition that occurs at birth and usually affects the body and mind in some way. In Allen's case, by the time he was 20, he could not walk on his own and spent a good deal of time in a wheelchair.

His legs were pencil thing, his atrophied muscles fairly useless and under used due to the mixed signals between his brain and his lower limbs. He could move his legs some, as I quickly found out when after I had busted him for something stupid he had done, he kicked me. So much for the pity party!

His arms were also scarecrow thin. His right arm we affectionately named "the claw," because it was permanently bent backwards, stiffly reaching behind him like a huge cat's whisker. Quite useless to him and prone to bump up against doorways.

His left arm was his hero, and it gave Allen the freedom he needed to connect with the world, travel on his own and even shake hands. Allen would lean forward in his chair, reach across his lap and man the joystick and buttons of his wheelchair controller. This plus the weak muscles of his abdomen and back caused him to stay in a perpetual forward lean.

When he looked at you from this leaning position it was as if he could barely stand to look at you from the corner of his eyes. Allen would have preferred nothing more than to stand together with you and look you in the eye while you talked and laughed without a care or thought about your bipedal balance.

Allen wore glasses, held on by a strap that slipped and came undone. He couldn't adjust this himself and relied on the kindness and care of others to help him with that and many other adjustments in his life.

His wheelchair was his chariot, capable of going on road or off, as I came to realize later. Battery powered, it could attain speeds of 8 mph, twice as fast as a strong walker. Often Allen attached a fiberglass rod to the back of his wheelchair with an orange safety flag at the top.

I remember seeing him zipping along Great Neck Road or First Colonial on his way back home or perhaps to the video store. If cars were in the way of my sight, all I would see was his flag resolutely rolling forward, announcing to the world to watch out for the charioteer that was in their midst, fearless and strange.

At last the lady was done and I stepped up and announced, "Hey dude, my name's John. What's your name?" That is pretty much exactly how I would introduce myself to anyone. Since I'm from the oceanfront, "dude" is synonymous with man, and "chick" for woman. I called everyone dude. I call the highest ranking and most influential people I know dude.
And they like it!
So did Allen. He body started pulsing back and forth as he fought to answer me with his stuttering, popping and explosive method of speaking. This is from the palsy (Cerebral PALSY) that constantly washed over him in waves. From his difficulty breathing and speaking at the same time, and from weak facial muscles that just didn't connect to the nerves that waited on his cranial orders.
"Muh, muh, muh, my nuh nuh nuh namesallen."
I caught his name in the rush of the run on sentence and put out my hand to shake his. At first I thought he was trying to bring up his right hand, since that is the typical way guys shake, but instead he gave me his left hand, with its permanently bent fingers and wrist.
I asked him why he was in a wheelchair and over the next several minutes he told me about his CP (Cerebral Palsy). I asked him about his body parts because I wanted to know what worked and what did not work. I wasn't trying to queer or fresh, I just really wanted to know.
Here was a crippled man that was obviously capable of coming to church, carrying on a conversation and having rational thought. I was simply curious to know how he did it and how he overcame his ill-mannered and obviously deformed body.
My mother had always told my brothers and sisters as we were growing up, "If you are ever with someone that has something unusually or strange about them or on them, just ask them about it." Be nice about it but ask them. So I did.
Allen told me about being born and the problems involved. He told me about growing up and how he could walk with some help until he was a teenager. How he was main streamed into classes

because, while his body was crippled, his mind was not. This was of course not always the case, and Allen was on the cusp of a national sea change in thinking about how to serve people with disabilities.

He told me about his Mom, his advocate and provider. The woman who was always there for him, to care for him and provide for him. Lynda was a Mom that fought for her son, because if she didn't fight, he would be forgotten in a system and world that still wanted to put him away where we didn't have to deal with his kind. The kind of people we'd just as soon not have to look at and surely not have to treat like "normal" folks.

He told me that his Dad was a, "Duh duh deadbeat Dad."

So often in marriages that have a child with disabilities, the emotional, physical and financial strain of caring for the child is simply too much. More often than not, it is the father that leaves, leaving the mother to be the sole provider and defender of the realm that is their child's.

In the case of Lynda, her compassion and love for her son was balanced by her ferocity and sheer force to overcome and break through the old school mind-set of that time. In the case of Allen, that time started in 1974, when most folks thought of integration and civil rights as only something for black folks to fight for.

But as far as Lynda was concerned, Allen might as well have been black. I have noticed over the years the ferocity and tenacity of black mommas for their kids. Partly because in many cases the Dad's are deadbeat like Allen's was. Partly because they can see both the latent beauty and perfection in their child and the fact that society sees neither.

If I was a child put down by the world, I'd love to have a black Mom loving me and fighting for me. Or Lynda Nebrich, or any of the Capernaum Mom's I've come to adore over the past few years.

If you value your life, don't mess with the Moms!

Carrying "the package" to the beach.

TWO

Beach Bums

for Laura

> *"I tell you, get up, take your mat and go home."*
>
> MARK 2:11

God is the best matchmaker, and there was no mistaking His desire for Allen and me to come together as friends. And so we did. We did the normal thing that new friends do: we traded phone numbers and e-mail addresses.

If you looked at Allen's bent hands and stiff fingers, you would never expect that he could show enough dexterity to wave good-bye, much less use a joystick to race through traffic or a keyboard and mouse to compose e-mails. But he could and he did.

An e-mail from Allen was every bit as normal as any other e-mail. Well-written, logical, and to the point. Usually fairly short because what would take me two minutes to write would take Allen twenty minutes. He knew how to spell and to use spell check. His e-mails looked like they came from an educated man, and they did.

When I met him, Allen was attending Tidewater Community College. He was studying computer software, and it showed. Allen was pretty darned good around a computer. I used to tell him that he did pretty good for a crippled guy. He would do his Cowardly Lion laugh, and we would both laugh at the joke, which sought to lessen the sting of a word that the world used to limit him. Then he would try to run over my feet, kick me, or head butt me to get even.

That would make us laugh too.

As guys, our love was tempered by toughness and the need to give and receive barbs flung at each other whenever we were together. I know that this will bring some groans from many of you reading this, and I understand your discomfort with me treating a crippled man this way. But I knew instinctively that what Allen needed was to be treated like any other guy, and a sure sign of respect and acceptance among guys is the affection and love we extend by busting on each other. Let women mask their pettiness behind a facade of kindness. Men mask their love behind a facade of stupidity and machismo.

But truly, the mask was pretty thin between us, and the strong bond of philos (brotherly love) quickly transformed to the full-bred roar of agape (unconditional family love). We became brothers, and, as brothers, we expected a lot from each other.

I expected Allen to teach me how to care for him and—by extension—others like him. He expected me to show him my world and the things I did for fun. Though some said it was a wonderful thing I did for Allen, to me it was a good trade. They only saw the obvious in my helping Allen, and not the less-obvious joy and knowledge he was giving me. But we knew the truth. It was a good trade, as the Indians say.

Living at the oceanfront meant that during the summer my family and I—along with hundreds of neighbors and thousands of tourists—went to the beach on the weekends. Some of my friends and clients thought that I went there all day during the week as well and that my ears were constantly clogged with sand. Say what? The truth was that I worked hard during the week and played hard on the weekend.

One day at church I asked Allen if he wanted to go to the beach with me that day. If he had not been buckled in by his seat belt, I think he might have fallen out of his chair, so great were his excitement and palsy spasms. Yes, oh yes! His excitement only intensified when I told him that there would be thousands of hot chicks with oiled bodies wearing teeny-weeny bikinis. Guy talk of the normal kind!

He could not speak for a long while after I told him this, but just smiled and nodded his head, looking forward to his first trip to the oceanfront. We decided that I would pick him up from his home around noon, put him and his wheelchair in my van, and head down to the beach. Sounded easy.

Allen's "home" was a nursing home. He was twenty-nine when I met him and had been living there about ten years. After trying unsuccessfully to live on his own and getting into some trouble, Allen had no choice but to move into the nursing home. His mom certainly couldn't take care of him any longer, and even if she could handle his huge physical needs, she did not want to continue dealing with his emotional issues. She knew that he needed to learn to live on his own, regardless of his disabilities. She wanted it, and so did he.

The nursing home was a place for people to recover from accidents, illnesses, and surgeries. It was also a place for people to fade away and die. For Allen it was simply temporary housing because he had no intention of staying there forever. He always intended to find a place he could call his own.

I remember the first time I came in and saw the people living there. There were shufflers who walked slowly and were so weak that they could not lift their feet off the ground. They shuffled using a cane or a walker or the walls or maybe an imaginary aide. Some were in a paranoid world of their own. They talked to themselves and did not want to be bothered. Others just mumbled incoherent phrases in whispers and moans.

When I walked into his room, I had to pass the bed of his roommate, who was watching TV. He got up to greet me, and I asked him about the deep furrow in his face that extended from his nose to his forehead. I was thinking cancer or some kind of skin disease or perhaps a terrible burn. He couldn't speak much, so he pantomimed for me.

He took his right hand, extended his index finger, and placed it into his open mouth, pointing up. I still didn't understand what he meant and kept thinking surgery. Then he flicked his middle finger down while he continued to push his extended index finger up into the roof of his mouth. What was he trying to tell me?

Ahhhhhh, my heart felt so sad when I finally realized he was trying to tell me that he had attempted to commit suicide with a gun, and the bullet had blown a long, grooved furrow along the front edge of his face, removing part of his mouth, nose, and head and removing his ability to speak.

I hugged him and felt so bad for him. I remembered my own moments of suicidal thoughts when I contemplated taking my own life back in 1988. I had never considered a gun, instead imagining things like driving off a bridge or running into an unmoving object at high speed. Guns seemed so final, and I wanted a chance of redemption.

I wanted to wake up after killing myself and have everything put back together again; no more fire in my head, no more depression and horrific doubts gnawing at me like rats on a still-living bone. I wanted to be reborn into a new life of freedom and light and love with no more doubt and pain. But deep down I didn't want to die, and I couldn't go through with it, thanks be to God.

Yet here before me was a man who had gone through with it, pulled the trigger and lived to tell the tale, or at least to show the tale, since his frontal lobe had been partially removed by the bullet meant to remove his life. Imagine being unsuccessful in the last act of your unsuccessful life, only to be forced to go on with a broken body and mind.

I didn't know what to think or do or say, other than to feel a strong mixture of despair, pity, and deep sadness for this man. I was mildly repulsed by him, but I felt such love, the kind of love that comes only from God. The type of love Jesus taught His disciples to mimic when they went out into the world.

The kind of love a mother and father feel for their child. To them, no matter how disabled, no matter how ugly, slow, incapable, or displeasing their child is, to the parents their child is perfect in every way, beautiful beyond belief, amazing, and the very apple of their eye. God's favorite, beyond all right and belief. God's favorite.

I knew inside of me that God loved this man as His favorite, as He loves us all. I knew that there was some purpose for him to have lived and to be here at this exact moment and in the many moments until the bullet of his life stops moving, and his heart stills and turns to dust.

But enough with this buzzkill conversation. We were talking about going to the beach! There is no dust on the beach, but sand aplenty. There is no death on the beach, unless you count the shells that wash up on shore, given up along with the past lives of the inhabitants. There is life on the beach, and life lived abundantly. But first, I had to get my huge new friend out of his room and into my van. And this would prove to be a considerable undertaking.

There he sat, leaning over in his wheelchair, looking up at me with his eyes rolled up and a smile pasted on his face. He loved me, and I knew it. He loved me when we first met, and I knew it. He loved me because I loved him, and we raced across the finish line of brotherhood to see who would cross first. It was a tie!
In the race of agape, there are only winners.
I looked down at Allen and said, "Okay, so how do we do this?"
Meaning how do I get him from his wheelchair to the beach. The first thing I had to do (with his help) was get him dressed in his bathing suit. And to do that I would have to change him. He explained that it would be easiest if he were lying on his bed versus sitting in his chair. Very good, so how do we get him from his chair to his bed?
With a lot of humor we figured it all out. The process went something like this: he would explain what I needed to do, I would fail to understand him, and he would repeat it until I got it. He told me how to lift him from his chair, so I leaned down, grabbed him under his arms, and lifted up. This caused two things to happen: Allen started laughing at me and his upward momentum was halted. I had forgotten to unbuckle his seat belt. Allen was laughing, but then he helped my pain by saying, "Nuh nuh nice job, duh duh dumbass!" Which, of course, I was, but not wanting to be outdone by my new friend, I gracefully suggested that a huge mosquito had landed on his cheek and smacked him pretty hard across the face.
This made both of us laugh even harder.
I unbuckled his seat belt, grabbed him under his arms, and lifted him out of his wheelchair. He could carry some of his weight by using his legs, which helped a lot. Basically I was hugging him very closely, which gave him cause to try to knee me in the balls. We both

laughed even harder, until I threatened to drop him.

Allen then replied, "Go ahead. Yuh you'll have to pickmeup!"

Point, set, and match to Big Crip, my new brother. We shuffled our way slowly over to his bed, where I lay him down carefully, lifted his legs up, threw his blanket over him, and said, "Night night." Allen again laughed and so did I, proving once again that we both suffered from the same brand of slapstick Three Stooges humor.

After dressing Allen—with many instructions from the dude on his back—I got him back into his wheelchair and outside to my van. He rolled up to the passenger door, and we transferred him into the front seat. Not such an easy thing for a tall dude who has a tough time bending over and forcing his body into small spaces meant for bendable people.

Then I drove his wheelchair to the back of my van. I had already taken out the back seat to make space for the wheelchair. But since it weighed about three hundred pounds, I needed someone else to help me lift it up into my van. I found a dude walking in to visit a friend, and we lifted the chair together. Off Allen and I went, bound for the beach.

We made it to my house, and I threw a couple of chairs, a cooler, towels, and my yellow beach cart into the back of the van. Then we drove across the street and parked up near the boardwalk leading up and over the dunes.

I took the yellow beach cart with the oversized tires and placed it next to Allen's door. Then I carefully removed him from the van. He head-butted me on my chin when I was lifting him out, so I dropped him into a briar patch. Just kidding! I just promised to even things up later, and I did.

As carefully as I could, I lowered Allen into the cart that was never intended to carry a large, stiff-legged man. As soon as all of his weight was in the cart, it flipped forward. This caused Allen to laugh with great delight, while I tried out various words of, uh, praise. Okay, maybe not quite praise words, but I was starting to feel a bit frayed by all the attention I had to lavish on my friend just to do the simplest things.

Eventually we figured out how to balance him in the cart and headed up the wooden pathway. Man, he was heavy! We made it down to the beach, and I left him sitting there, inside the cart, while I went back to get the chairs and towels. I'm sure the folks down there wondered what I was doing and why the top of a man's head and his feet and arms were sticking out of my beach cart. But I was in a bloody hurry and did not have time to explain things. I knew I was not a cripple murderer, so let them think what they would.

After I returned, I set up the chairs and towels and took Allen for a spin in the cart. He laughed so hard as I drove him along the waves, as the spray splashed in. It was something I would have done for any child but had never done for a grown man. Even so I knew that he had never been able to experience this. Why should he miss out on the simple pleasures of life?

Turns out that Allen had never been down to the beach, probably because of the great difficulty of getting him there. The specialized Roleez tires weren't available when he was a child, and it was just too difficult and dangerous to get him down to the water. Not that Allen was too concerned about the danger; he loved the idea of being in dangerous situations. Whether rolling down First Colonial Avenue at top speed or splashing along the Atlantic Ocean in a cart certainly never meant to safely speed a quadriplegic, Allen defied the laws of nature and wanted to race and go fast.

After we finished, we drove up to the chairs. I dragged his big butt out of the cart and noticed the red welts caused by the exposed screws on the sides. I apologized to him, and he said no worries. Next time we put towels in, and ultimately discovered that a sleeping bag was best, providing both cover and padding.

After I placed him in my favorite beach chair, I cleaned off his glasses. How else could he accurately observe and compare the exquisite army of women that was obviously walking by solely for the sake of Allen?

The sun bothered him a great deal, so I took off my sunglasses and placed them over his glasses. This made things quite good for him, but I was not done. I set up my chair next to his, and from the small cooler I produced a miraculous golden treasure that men have sought for centuries and wars had been fought over.

Into the beer I placed a straw, and into his mouth I placed the straw. When he pulled on the straw, the golden nectar flowed up and then down into the pit of doom known as Allen's stomach. I felt quite good about giving Allen this beer, in spite of the fact that it is illegal to drink beer on the beach. My reasons were sound.

First, of the approximately 3,400 adults on the North End at that time, 3,000 of them were drinking adult beverages. Second, I figured that if a cop did see Allen consuming his beer in wanton disregard for the law, his oath to protect the laws governing the beach would be overcome by his pity for a crippled man.

He would probably arrest me for child endangerment in spite of my cries that the big buckethead was twenty-nine years old and I didn't even know how he got there, in my chair and drinking MY beer. Which would get me into even more trouble, even though I would change my tune and swear that Allen had brought the beer and was only faking being a cripple. He could walk. Really, ask him!

And the final reason the cop would never charge Allen? He was one scary looking dude, and no cop in his right mind would want to handcuff those arms together.

So we sat there and relaxed with Patty and her Mom, Laura, drinking Allen's beers. (I swear he brought them!) After a while, Allen kind of nodded over to the right and said, "Luh luh look at that!" And I'm like, what do you mean . . .look at a girl? And he's like yeah, that one over there. What an idiot!

I explained to Allen that because there were like four billion women on the beach, just pointing was not good enough. He had to use the time-proven system invented thousands of years ago when the first beach natives ate raw oysters, drank mead, and watched women as the waves washed in. Kind of like today.

The system was based on the nine o'clock to three o'clock rule, with the right-hand edge of sight representing three on the clock face and the left-hand side nine. Being an aficionado of all things military—meaning he was a full-blooded American male—Allen understood what I meant right away.

It wasn't long before he said, "Eleven o'clock!" And I would nod and pass my own judgment on the beautiful woman God had graced us with. We contemplated making up score cards, but the house was too far away, I was too tired, and I didn't want to get arrested.

Again.

What we did that day was something I had done many times: it was no big deal for me to hang out at the beach. But to Allen, who had never gone to the beach, it was a very big deal indeed. In order for him to fulfill that part of his life which had been withheld until then, I had to be his legs, feet, and arms.

I had to do for him what he could not do for himself. This seemed very natural to me and very obvious. It was like, "DUH!" Dude can't walk, can't roll down to the beach, can't crawl. He ain't gonna get there unless somebody takes him.

Another time we went to the beach, I took Allen out on a boogie board. This might as well have been a coffin, as I apparently tried to kill him several times when we rode waves in and he fell off the board. I must have taken the whole bottle of stupid pills that day! Then Rusty came out and helped stabilize the board, and it worked great. Until we had to get out of the water.

I was so tired that I dropped Allen several times. The problem was that he didn't really mind drowning because he was having so much fun, and he had already transferred his life and care into my hands. Plus he was laughing so hard that I kept laughing, which made me weak, and I would drop him again.

A truly vicious cycle.

We somehow managed to get back up to the chair after several friends rushed down to help carry Allen while I stumbled my exhausted self up to my chair. Why didn't they carry me?

We sat there, the two of us, with another hot chick in a bikini who I was lucky enough to marry many years before—my wife Patty, along with her Mom, Laura. We sat there as we watched the waves, watched the chicks, and drank our beer like men are called to do.

We were just a couple of guys. Buddies. Brothers spending a little slice of time together because, in the end, little slices of time add up to a lifetime of love and laughter.

Regina wearing a shirt and a smile.

THREE

The Calling

for Jim & Regina

She was bent over and could not straighten up at all.

LUKE 13:11

When I was first called to serve Capernaum, I said no. It happened one day at church. Regina Howley and her father, Jim, confronted me with whips and shackles and demanded that I do everything they told me to do if I wanted to live. Okay, not really. They didn't have whips or demands, but they did want to shackle my life and force me to march to the tune of their devious aims.

They told me about a new ministry for kids with disabilities called Young Life Capernaum. They were trying to get it started in the area and were looking for volunteers. Volunteers like me.

Why me? Apparently I had been seen in the company of Allen and other folks in wheelchairs like Regina. It was obvious to Jim and Regina that I was quite comfortable around them and their kind. I was therefore branded and put on a short list, a very short list indeed, of those who might be willing to help lead kids with disabilities to a better life.

I told them I would think and pray about it, which oftentimes for Christians is a euphemism for "There's no flippin' way I'm going to do this thing you ask, and since I said the word pray, you can't hold anything I do against me." But I really did pray about it . . . a little. I spoke to Patty about it, and she is a much smarter woman than me (not that I'm a woman). I talked to some friends. I already had my own personal ministry, my business, Oktoberfest, writing, a family, and many friends.

I had enough to do. I had been saying "yes" all my life. I am one of those guys who gets on the "yes" list. Not only the "yes" list but the "yes, he can and will accomplish what you ask him to do" list. This is a very dangerous list to be on, because soon the word gets out that you are an easy mark because not only are you capable, you are a Christian man. A simpleton in effect.

But not this time!

In the past I made most of my decisions with a huge dose of heartfelt emotion matched by what I hoped was significant logical thought. I would consider the options and the implications of my actions as well as how I felt about them. Sometimes I jumped into things based more on the positive vibes I felt about it rather than any rational thoughts.

Quitting my job, starting my own business, selling our home, and moving to a new home in Virginia Beach in 1994 was one such decision. I never doubted the outcome and could clearly see the solution stretched out ahead of me, an internal reality that was crystal clear and merely had to be reached in person.

What could be easier?

Being a visionary can mean many things, but for me the way I feel about something or someone is the key to my success and the decisions that I make about them. If my inner spirit is drawn to them, then I am ultimately drawn, even if my mind has some warning signs.

I am the eternal optimist, the man convinced that the world loves me. In fact, I know that people love me. Shoot, I have pretty much gone out of my way to try to win their love for a good part of my life by acting the clown and generally putting on the fool. It wasn't until later that I realized people love me because I love them first by the way I treat them and because of the fun I bring into their lives. I finally figured this out after nearly dying of depression when I was thirty years of age—my whole like stretching out ahead of me, and the vision that had created it whole and complete.

My vision came crashing down one fine day in 1988 when the

lights went out, the synapses started misfiring, and the doctors started consulting and doing the mumbo jumbo they call mental health medicine.

It is a wonder they did not kill me with their ineptness.

But God had other plans for me, and He helped me through this time of my life. He needed me to learn once and for all that I am nothing without Him. That all of the best of me is from Him. That my love for people and their love for me are gifts He has given me. And that even my crazy wild side is something that He will and does use.

I learned during those times that God does not want part of me, but all of me. I learned that He could and would use my weaknesses as well as my strengths. I learned to crawl again, both mentally and spiritually. Eventually I started walking and then running.

After a while my walking and running days were over, and God was strapping a jet pack filled with His spiritual jet fuel to my back, and I was off again. Flying high and low, I was no longer afraid to die, no longer afraid of where I would go. I knew.

But alas, my ego knew no bounds and fought to outrace the angels who had been assigned to me. My pride soared, and I took great delight in the things that I did and the world I lived in. It was so easy to convince myself that I was an amazing man because—truth be told—I was pretty amazing. I excelled at most of what I tried; I was good with people and good at doing things. Except for golf and cooking, may they both be cursed.

I'd like to take back my curse on cooking since I love to eat, and we need good cooks to satisfy our cravings and culinary desires. But as for golf, pah! I spit it out of my mouth and dust it off my feet as I walk my way to the next green. Huh?

Being a successful man of God does not relieve you from the temptation and stupidity of pride, arrogance, and a bloated ego. Fortunately I make up for it by being awesome at humility. That's a little joke from my Friday Morning Men's group. We studied a book that dealt with pride and humility, and we decided we rocked at being humble. Funny.

I called and left a message at the Howleys on the night they were having a meeting for volunteers. I told them all that I had done to make my decision and that I was not going to be able to get involved. It was my choice not to get involved.

I felt pretty bad about this choice, probably because in my heart I knew that I wanted to do it. Truthfully, my decision was based more on what my mind thought than what my heart felt. I wanted to be smart about this decision and not jump to conclusions based on the way I felt. I already knew I made impetuous and hasty decisions. Not this time!

Perhaps I felt it was time for me to grow up and stop wearing my heart on my sleeve. How could I possibly make headway in life if I allowed myself to get caught up in every little thing that made my heart go kerplop? I would be much better served and much more productive if I just concentrated on the things I had and used my head (not my heart) to lead my life. Sounded smart to me.

Maybe it was a smart choice, and no doubt many of the reasons that helped make my decision were true. Yet my heart gnawed at me, and I kept looking at the decision from the side of my memory and wondering what had just happened. Did I do the right thing?

Then things started happening that proved me completely wrong. I call them alignments and happenings. I believe that God used the world to show me the error of my ways. Sometimes it seems that God shoved me back into Capernaum, but I think He merely showed me my world and the world He wanted me to have. Once I saw the true beauty of that world, I let go and fell in.

I continued to hang out with Allen, and our friendship grew. I continued to see Regina and Jim at church, and in spite of my rejection of their new cause, our friendship grew.

Regina was easy to be friends with. She was pretty to begin with, and for me, that always put a good spin on things. Call me a sucker, call me old school, call me a chump, I don't care. But a pretty girl tends to open up my heart from the start. Regina was pretty through and through, inside out and true as blue. Long dark hair and eyelashes as long as a butterfly's wings.

Her CP had rendered her incapable of walking but had not affected her speech in any perceptible way. A minor dose of learning disability that showed up in her spelling was pretty much the only sign of the effect the CP had on her brain. She was delightful to speak with, charming and fun, a young woman I delighted to be around.

Her father, Jim, was just about the polar opposite of his daughter! Jim looked like a biker (and he was!), with long hair and sometimes biker leathers. He wore cross earrings and had a smoker's hack that rumbled in his chest in a frightening way. He was flat-out one ornery-looking hombre on the surface until you got up close and saw his smile and twinkling eyes radiating the love of God.

I loved him right away and recognized another barbarian brother. He was about as strange and unusual a specimen as I was. The things we held in common were our oddness, our love for Jesus, and Regina. Regina was the glue that bound us together.

I remember the day that my world shifted like it was yesterday. I was taking Allen to the Spring Branch church picnic, and we were hanging out in the foyer. I was busy throwing doughnut holes into Allen's ginormous mouth, which would later earn him the nickname "The Black Hole." I would toss the doughnut hole in from a distance of several inches, careful not to get my fingers too close to his chopping teeth.

This was quite funny for both of us, and we wound up laughing loudly as Allen choked while trying to eat his airborne breakfast. No doubt many people looked at me akin to an ax murderer for taking advantage of Allen in this way, but I was not doing that at all. Shoot, I was feeding the boy, and he was happy as a clam. Or a clam-flavored doughnut.

So there we stood and sat like peas and carrots, when up rolled the queen of the roller derbies herself, Miss Regina. She rolled right up to me and said, "My dad's sick; can you take me to the picnic?"

I looked down at her and then over at Allen, then back at Regina. My heart kind of glowed inside of me, and I started laughing because I knew that God had won and here was the evidence. Her dad was sick! I mean, come on . . . that God would sink to such a thing as a sick man to have His way with me. Do you think He would do such a thing? Why, sure He would, and He did, just as sure as turkeys can fly.

Now I was in it deep. I was responsible for not just one wheelchair-bound human, but two. Allen and I drove over to Regina's, and we all piled into her wheelchair van, which was a whole new concept for me; my back was very grateful. Whoever invented wheelchair vans should get an Oscar or Nobel Peace Prize or a box of Girl Scout cookies or something. That van rocked!

They were both hungry as soon as we got there. After all, it was a picnic, and Allen was pretty much always hungry for food other than the institutional glop he got back home at the funny farm. I led them over to a picnic table and got in line for food. It was a challenge to balance two plates while piling food on them.

For Allen I concentrated on mass quantity, but I tried to be a little pickier for Regina. I was so overburdened that Michael Simone, the senior pastor at Spring Branch, came over to help me. I don't know how he figured out that I was helping those two, but I reckon it was pretty obvious.

I will never forget that simple act of kindness he showed me that day. We brought the food over to the tables, and I got between Regina and Allen and started shoveling food into their mouths. Feeding an adult with a physical disability is not hard. If you can do it for a baby, you can do it for an adult.

Allen could take three times as much food per bite as Regina, so I had to regulate how I fed them. Soon I was overwhelmed and had completely forgotten about feeding myself.

Then an angelic voice asked me, "Can I help?"

Her name was Jenn Paugh, and God sent her to help that day and to get involved with Capernaum. She took over feeding Regina, and soon those two were jabbering away like two blue jays while Allen and I did our best to render the other useless by way of bad jokes and poor manners. I'm pretty sure I won.

Later I took Allen over to the softball field and helped him run the bases. Naturally he cheated and stole when he should not have, knowing they would break the rules for the poor crippled man. I wanted them to call his sorry self out, but, of course, he made it all the way to home base and scored. He was relentless.

Come to think of it, so was I. That was another thing we had in common. We both were bound and determined to do a thing once we had made up our minds to do it. For Allen to realize his dreams, it took extraordinary courage and commitment, plus dexterity and discipline.

Toward the end of the day I saw Scott Hamilton, the top-dog Young Life dude, talking to Regina over near some swings. Allen and I walked and rolled over. I told Scott that I had changed my mind about Capernaum and that I was in. I was all in.

He invited me to come to a meeting soon after, where he asked everyone to say why they had come. When my turn came, I said, "My name's John Koehler. I'm here because I'm following orders. I have been ordered to be here, and I have no clue why. But I'm here."

That was the absolute truth, and I wasn't trying to be cute. God had clearly ordered me to come and had put everything in place for me to come. He had made all the arrangements and pulled all the strings. He is the best matchmaker I know, and I know a few. He is a jealous God, and He clearly wanted me in this new thing called Capernaum.

Who was I to argue?

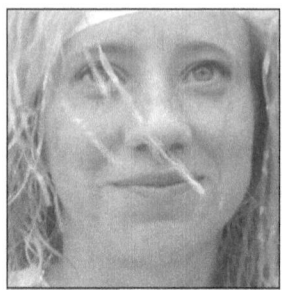
Jenn before her haircut.

FOUR

Lake Champion

for Jenn

JOHN KÖEHLER

A champion named Goliath, who was from Gath, came out of the Philistine camp. He was over nine feet tall.

1 SAMUEL 17:4

Scott Hamilton (may his beard grow long) sent Jenn, Regina, Allen, and me to Lake Champion, a Young Life camp in New York, in June of 2004. This was a rather obvious move, considering we needed to learn how to do things in Capernaum. He lined it up for us to work with and hang with the Capernaum crew from Baltimore, led by Suzanne Williams and Carissa Mortenson.

So off we went, completely ignorant about what was to come, without a clue as to the magnitude of our adventure. We just knew that we were on God's path and that it would be amazing and fun, a combination I'm personally in favor of.

I remember going over to Allen's place and meeting his mom a week or so before we left. She wanted to meet the crackpot insane enough to take her son away for a week. (That would be me.) She wanted to make sure I knew what I was getting into. I knew that she was talking about taking care of Allen. I said I'd been with him long enough to get a sense of it, that I knew how to help him go pee, and the rest would just be learned.

She must have thought I was either stupid or insane. Or both.

And maybe she was right. Because she had cared for Allen for the first nineteen years of his life, she knew how much work was involved. She still cared for him at the ripe old age of twenty-nine, even though he lived at the nursing home. He still needed her help, and she gave it constantly.

She looked at me like my head was one size too small for my

body (think shrunken-head man) and asked me, looking at Allen, "Do you have any idea what you're getting into?"

I looked at her and laughed, the laugh of a completely ignorant man. The laugh of one who really has no clue at all. She just shook her head at me and chuckled because she knew the truth of what it took to care for her son. She relented because this was not about her; it was about Allen, and—no matter her concerns—he had to live his life as fully as possible.

I was the lunkhead stupid enough to be his cartoon warrior and take on the reality of the man who was Allen. I was the guy positive that no matter what, I would figure it out. We would figure it out no matter what bumps the road held. What bumps?

Taking care of a wheelchair-bound person is no cup of tea. It is not for the squeamish or the faint of heart. Taking care of Allen provided enormous space for humility and zero space for pride. It would become a test of endurance, patience, and all the fruits of my spirit.

But for some reason I was not concerned about it. I was confident that God would provide and that we would figure it all out together. Oh ignorant and faithful man!

The first night at Lake Champion was chaos. Fearful campers who missed their parents and had just completed the obstacle course, leaders still learning where clothes were and the routines of their kids. It was crazy. I learned quickly the art of changing a pair of briefs (a diaper) on an adult unable to do so for himself. I learned the fine art and beauty of the piss jug, a tool we could not do without.

And then . . . Allen needed me. He needed to be changed from the nasty clothes he had worn through the obstacle course. In fact, he needed a shower. Sounds easy, right? Imagine having to move a quadriplegic 170-pound man from his wheelchair to the shower. Now, add some swamp slime so he's really slippery, and make him so tired he can't really help you. Oh, and did I mention that I was forty-six years old! Dude, all the other leaders were in their twenties.

Maybe Allen's mom was right about me: I was an idiot.

I had to do everything for Allen. I had to feed him, clean him, shave him, dress him, comb his hair, put on lotion, put crap in his hair. I had to drag him out of the water, throw him in the water, dry him off, shower him. And, of course, I had to encourage him, talk with him, cajole him, teach him, joke with him, love him, make fun of him, and hang out with him. Once we got outside and he was in his chair, he became pretty independent, except for at meals. But in the cabin, I was constantly on call for him. I was his care partner, his companion.

Working with Allen and caring for him taught me true humility. I had to put myself down in order to lift him up, literally and spiritually. While this type of work is saintly, I am far from a saint and had moments where I got bitchy or lost my temper. I discovered that in order to take care of another human being, I also had to take care of myself.

Giving yourself completely to someone else and forgetting yourself in the process is a sure way to fail. You have to find the right balance. Feed them a little, then yourself. Brush their teeth, then yours. Take turns with your care. They will understand, and you'll both be happier than if you let the resentment build as you completely forget about yourself.

Allen went to Lake Champion as a leader but—in truth—he was really there as a camper, a young person at least in his mind, there to live life to the fullest and have the best week of his life. It was an experience that he would never forget, and I am happy and thankful that I could help make it possible for him.

Allen was fastidious to a fault about his physical care and dress. After only a day of having to dress him, bathe him, clean him, and care for him, I was calling him a sissy girl. The process of preparing him for the world in the morning was ridiculous.

First, I had to deal with his intimate physical needs, which meant dealing with his diaper. Allen preferred the term brief because it conveyed more dignity than saying diaper. Even though he could do very little for himself, keeping his dignity was important to him. He knew what men were supposed to do and how they were supposed to be around each other.

I would pull off the plastic tabs on the top and bottom of each side of his brief and pull down the front piece. Then I would bend his legs up and plant his feet on the bed. That would give me the space to expose whatever awaited me on the nasty side of the brief. Welcome to the dark side!

Some days there was very little, but most days there was a surprise waiting for me, one that rhymed with voodoo. We used humor as the best way to deal with the stinky situation. To show me grace and his appreciation, Allen would say things like "Good luck with that."

And in return I would say encouraging things like "Hungry?"

We were pretty disgusting, but I'd much rather work through stuff like that while laughing than in all seriousness. That just wouldn't work for me or for him. So we laughed and busted on each other, and eventually Allen was cleaned up and ready for clothes.

Imagine trying to dress a large scarecrow that has stiff limbs on hinges that move at the most inopportune moments. It was best to put on Allen's pants or shorts while he was still in bed after a new pair (or two) of briefs had been installed.

It sounds like I'm talking about working on a NASCAR vehicle, and in a strange way I was. You had to do certain things to get that sucker ready for racing.

After I had his shorts on, I would put on his socks and shoes. Then I would slide his feet and legs out and over the edge of the bed, into a position so that I could sit him up. Then I would reach over and under his arms and lift him up so he was sitting up on the edge of the bed.

Now came the tricky part. Transferring him from the bed to the chair. With a one-two-three count, I would lift Allen up from the bed using the hug hold. He had a certain amount of strength in his legs, and this helped a lot. When a quad or a paraplegic can support some of their weight, your work is significantly reduced.

Because Allen could take some of his weight, I would pivot off his feet and turn him around me, or I would circle and spin him around. Whichever worked best at the time, that's what we did. It was not like he didn't help. He would guide me through various moves as needed, variously laughing with me and at me depending on the circumstances.

I would back him up to his chair and say "Going down." He

would stop holding himself up, and we would let gravity do its work and drop him into his seat. Then I would put on his T-shirt, being careful to let him pick out what he would wear for the day. The boy did have some style, whereas my fashion style was completely crippled. No kidding.

After we finished dressing him, we'd buckle him in the chair and roll into the bathroom to take care of his shaving kit stuff. He had goop for his hair, plus stuff to put in it that would stop the itching. Not like he could just reach up like you and me and scratch it. Even so, I stopped using that stuff on the little girl after only a day. It was just too much, and I told him we had to cut down on the time it took to get ready or I was going to start calling him Alice. He said, "That's fuh fuh fine, you buh buh big duh dumbass!"

Getting a tongue lashing from a cripple is kind of fun.

After Allen was ready, I had to get myself ready. I learned after the first day that I needed to get myself ready first; otherwise I'd be left behind while he set out for the dining hall in his electric chariot. After he was made ready, gassed up, tires rotated and balanced, Allen was a lean, mean racing machine and could do a lot for himself.

Unless it had to do with eating.

Allen was in love with Jenn, and everyone knew it. He threw himself at her (as he did with many women) and made it clear that he was the man for her. She laughed at him as she would any guy.

One day after lunch the four of us were sitting around the table laughing and talking about the day. I picked up a chocolate pie with thick whipped cream on top, held it up next to Allen's face, and smiled—the threat of pie obliteration clear to him and the others.

He started bobbing back and forth, the way he did when he was excited and about to speak. "If you duh duh do," he said, "you'll have to clean me up." Dang it, not fair!

Not to be outdone, I asked Jenn if she would clean up Allen after I pied him. "Sure," she answered. No sooner had I said that, Allen buried his face into the pie that I was still holding in position. The boy was so anxious to be cleaned up by Jenn that he pied himself.

Very impressive. In his position I might have done the same!

Allen and some of his 16 carriers.

FIVE

The Obstacle Course

for Pam

> Therefore this is what the Lord says:
> "I will put obstacles before this people.
> Fathers and sons alike will stumble over them;
> neighbors and friends will perish."
>
> JEREMIAH 6:20-22

Allen, Regina, Jenn, and I had been sent by Scott Hamilton (may his putter's aim be true) as leaders with the express purpose of learning how to work with and serve kids with special needs. All four of us were 100 percent behind this idea and agreed to it in every way.

But truth be told, the magic of Lake Champion soon had her way with Allen. Shoot, it overcame me too, and I had already experienced so much cool stuff in my life. But for Allen it was simply paradise, and he aimed to enjoy every single bit of it. Especially now that he had a new lunkhead friend (that would be me) who was willing to take him high and low, up and down dell and whatever it took to live it big, baby, totally big. Allen's favorite line was "All the way," meaning that we would not hold back, that we would not let his wheelchair or his stiff arms or any of a number of things prevent us from potentially enjoying some aspect of the camp.

We spit on adversity, we laughed at hurdles, and we launched ourselves at things in ways that soon earned us the title of "complete idiots." We were so proud of that title and felt that we deserved it.

Even the meals were amazing. Dinner was our first "event" at Lake Champion. I remember walking in and seeing the lake of tables and chairs and high-school kids banging their fists down in unison for the work crew to come out. And soon they did, carrying trays piled high with great food, serving with smiles on their faces.

I remember thinking to myself, "These are my people!" I might even have stood up and shouted it, but no one could have heard me in the din and bedlam that was the dining hall. I proceeded to throw food down the bottomless pit of doom known as Allen's mouth.

He was quite simply an eating machine. Compared to the slop he got at the hellhole that was home for him, Young Life food was a little piece of heaven prepared by the finest French cooks money could buy. Allen didn't care that they were plain old tried and true American chefs and recipes. It would be like telling a man dying of thirst that the Dom Pérignon you just gave him was in fact just a liter of water. Plain water.

The rhythm of eating was eventually established and quite simple. I gave him a bite, then I took a bite. I gave him another bite, then I took one. I gave him a sip, and then I took one. Sometimes just to mix things up I would take a forkful of food from his plate, aim it into his mouth, and at the last minute dump it into my mouth. This may cause you to think me cruel, and the truth is you would be right. But Allen would laugh hard; we both would. And he would try to kick me under the table. Eventually I was able to judge those moments when his foot would swing forward, but I never knew when the next head butt would come.

After dinner we changed into our grubby clothes and got ready for the first real activity: the Obstacle Course. Allen was all over this puppy, and I was too. Of course, some of the important details like how would we carry him without killing him had not yet been worked out. But I figured, what could happen? He was already a cripple. In fact, I told him that, and we both laughed until we cried. That is very tough humor between a crippled dude and the brother he loved. You don't have to approve of it; just accept it as the way that men can be with each other. Disability or not.

The Obstacle Course. There is no gentle warm-up activity at Young Life camp. You go hard-core pedal to the metal from the first day. We headed over to the start and waited at the top of the hill, listening to the sounds of laughing and screaming coming down below, where the various groups were going into the grip of the obstacle course.

This course was not a pushover for "regular" kids. It had spiderweb rope courses, mudpit crawling tunnels, ladders, crossovers, slides, and more. That sounds great for most kids, but how were we supposed to take kids through who were scared to death, crying, unable to follow the path, and many who could not walk?

I learned that there is no such thing as "No I can't" at Young Life camp. From the leaders to the cooks to the signs to the music, the attitude is "Yes you can!" And so . . . we did.

Leaders teamed up with kids who needed help. The entire course was lined with work crew kids whose job it was to encourage those going through the course. It was simple and completely beautiful for them to be doing that. They were following orders to do so. We have all been given orders by God to encourage and love one another, to exhort each other as we go through the obstacle course called life.

Those who could not walk were carried. Allen was carried by a team of four young, studly leaders. It was horribly amazing watching him go through the spiderweb. I looked and said, "No way, they can't take him through that." But they did. I know because I was there, capturing it all on videotape, using the night vision mode.

We went through the entire week of camp doing all the things that the other kids were doing. We did the zip line. Allen and I went together. I am afraid of heights and he is not, so he mercilessly ridiculed me as we were being harnessed. We went down together on two tandem lines about ten feet apart.

Among the most amazing stories is when we did the rafts together. They towed two round, inflatable rafts behind a jet ski. Remember that Allen can only hold on well with his left hand. We got it into position, and then we managed to get his claw onto the other side. We were ready for takeoff. The driver—overcome with cripple pity—asked Allen how fast he wanted to go, and Allen said, "All the way!"

Wonderful. Allen was not interested in any kind of cripple pity and wanted to show the world that he was tough as nails and capable of doing it all. Did he care about the old-as-crap caregiver who came along for the ride? No, he did not.

After we started bouncing over our own wake, I remember

thinking, "Dear Lord, please don't let me fly off before the crippled guy." Amen. I didn't think my pride could survive if the entire camp knew that I was the man who hit the water before the quad dude. That would be a most horrible fate, even if Allen were in heaven due to drowning caused by laughing at me, which caused him to foolishly try to breathe water.

I nearly fell off before Allen did, but eventually he went flying off because the claw got tired! I jumped off and swam over to Allen as quickly as I could because by now he was floating face down in the water with only his helmet and the top of his life vest showing.

It took me about twenty seconds to get over to him. I grabbed his helmet and yanked his face out of the water.

He coughed, spit out some water, and started laughing!

He knew he was going to be saved, and his faith in me was huge. That's what happens in Capernaum: When the trust does finally kick in, it can be profound, strong, and complete. When people with disabilities decide to trust you, it could be with their lives, and there's no fooling around.

Capernaum is like betting high at Texas Hold 'em. If you go in, you go all in.

Every night before lights out, we had cabin time. We talked about the day, laughed about the day, and also talked about the club talk we had heard that had to do with Jesus and His teachings for us. Adam was our preacher, a man who could be counted on to pull Scripture out of his head or from the Bible he carried with him. Adam realized the simplicity of the love that Christ has for us and commands us to have for each other.

Adam has Down syndrome, and no one cared.

His love for the Lord was so complete, so profound, that we all loved to hear him speak about anything because he always managed to bring a beautiful simplicity and directness to the subject. The part of his disability that reduced his intellectual abilities increased his discernment of things of the spirit.

He came to the Lord with the spirit of a child, exactly the way Jesus exhorts us to. Not childish, but childlike in the way he showed his faith and beliefs. He was so focused on the Word of God that nothing could stop him for long. One night before cabin time, we began one of the classic competitions that boys and men enjoy: a farting contest.

Now most of us were able to control our, uh, internal desires when we began cabin time. Except for Eddie. Eddie was profoundly mentally and physically challenged. He couldn't speak, and his communication skills were nearly nonexistent. Not that night! Eddie communicated quite loudly and profoundly to the entire room and continued to do so for most of cabin time. Adam began speaking during a lull in the Eddie bombing raid, but apparently Eddie dropped a SBD (Silent But Deadly). When it hit Adam in the middle of his discourse, he stopped talking, looked over at Eddie, and said, "That really stinks." And then he went on talking without missing a beat.

Adam is also very strong physically and an excellent wrestler. Guys with Down syndrome aren't always very big, but they can make up for their lack of size by being extremely strong. Every night he would wrestle Aaron, another camper with Down syndrome. Throughout the day they would trade friendly verbal taunts, and then at night they would wrestle.

The word got out. By the end of the week, we had other cabins coming in to watch the match. We could have taken bets on those two!

John & William the weatherman.

SIX

First Club

for Suzanne

JOHN KÖEHLER

> "Lift your eyes and look to the heavens:
> Who created all these? He who brings out the starry
> host one by one, and calls them each by name."
>
> ISAIAH 40:26

After Lake Champion we four fearless leaders were fired up and ready. Clueless still, but now we had a taste of what could be. For me the taste became a vision, and the vision became a plan. The plan was to start a Capernaum club in the fall of 2004.

Scott Hamilton (may his skates be ever sharp) was as usual way ahead of us and had made arrangements for us to start club at the Landstown High School cafeteria.

Since I had seen Young Life club at Lake Champion and had been told that club at camp was usually the highest level, I immediately decided that we would set the highest standard for our club.

Who put me in the position to make this decision, you ask? Well, the truth is that I did not seek permission or the authority to do this. I assumed it. All I knew was that, based on experience, I was the most qualified to put together and run club. It wasn't a case of me taking over and leaving everyone else on the team in the dust; it was more about me just taking charge, and then including the others to help develop and execute the vision. It was—after all—their vision too.

The argument could be made that this was not about executing our vision, but God's vision for Capernaum. But I'm a practical and pragmatic guy and have always known that God relies on us to fulfill

His visions. We had to put shoes on His dreams (to borrow a line from my friend Mike Burbage). The dream was to bring the Gospel of Jesus Christ to kids with disabilities. The method was to use the Young Life system of reaching kids as appropriate to the culture of disabilities.

This meant we had to have pumping hot music, food, fun games, and a talk at the end about Jesus. The pumping hot music turned into songs on my computer and Scott leading a sing-along. The food turned into pizza and soda at the beginning of club. The fun games turned into, uh, fun games that everyone could enjoy and laugh at. And the talk turned into the truth and the beginning of hope for these people who had been refused hope for so long.

The cafeteria was a cavernous space and the center of activities at night, so we stood out like a sore thumb. A crippled thumb in fact. We claimed our corner, set up the sound system, laid out some funky hats, wigs, and other fun things to wear, and waited for the mob of kids to rush the school.

About eleven kids showed up that first night. I was, of course, expecting twenty-five even though I had been warned by other Capernaum leaders to be prepared for three or four. Pah! Why think or dream small?

Club started at seven, and we spent the first thirty or forty minutes eating pizza and hanging out, meeting people, and showing and telling them that we loved them—for no particular reason other than God told us we are supposed to treat everyone that way. Everyone meant everyone, regardless of how they looked, acted, smelled or whether they could talk, walk, or roll.

I remember that later I apologized to some of the parents for the pizza time going so long and let them know we would try to shorten it in the future. They simultaneously said, "No! Don't change a thing!" They explained to me that the simple act of breaking bread and hanging out with friends was something their kids didn't get to experience much.

This was only the beginning of the vast shift in thinking I would go through. All things that I took for granted I could no longer forget. I had to look at my world and think about the things that were important to me, no matter how small. I had to look at the little things that brought me joy and find a way to bring these things to the table that was Capernaum. Capernaum kids just didn't get chances to experience what we would call, in adult speak, a cocktail party—the time before an event begins when you socialize, talk, and laugh with friends and meet new people.

This happens in a setting meant to put everyone at ease, with some food and drink on hand. The hosts introduce newcomers to those who had already come and set the tone of loving hospitality for all to follow. All are welcome, and the welcome is everything.

I already knew what to do because I had been doing it all my life, at parties Patty and I hosted and at events I had thrown with various organizations I belonged to. Whether an Oktoberfest at our house with several hundred people, an intimate family gathering, or a black-tie banquet for four hundred, the goal was the same: help people feel comfortable and welcome.

The key to feeling welcome is to feel loved.

This cannot be overstated or glossed over. Perhaps the better translation would be to say that the key to helping someone feel welcome is to treat them as if they are in your family. We tend to treat people differently depending on how close we are to them. Family receive the most personal and loving welcome, and we lavish our affection on them with hugs, kisses, smiles, and radiant love. Unless we're not speaking to them!

Imagine how people would feel if you treated them as if they were in your family. Gross! Imagine how they would feel if you greeted them as if you had known them all your life and theirs. Imagine how they would feel if you acted as if they were the most important guests at the party and their arrival the most important event of the party.

I had no trouble imagining this at all because I could easily picture how I wanted to feel when I went to a party and was treated well. I knew instinctively the right way to treat people upon their arrival.

This is not a religious conviction at all. I know about agape love and how Jesus told us to love one another as He had loved us. I know that loving our neighbors as ourselves is key to actually fulfilling our destiny as God's children. But I don't think God wants us to take actions merely because it is what He wants us to do.

Perhaps at first when we are trying out a new method that God wants us to do, that is okay. Kind of like a new habit we're trying to take on and add to our life. Whether a diet, exercise, or a new philosophy of loving people, we have to work at it and believe it and try it and practice it. We do this with sports, and we do this with school and work.

We dedicate ourselves to becoming as good as we possibly can at whatever thing we are learning to do. If we really study it and learn and practice, a moment will come when we transcend the practice phase, and the thing we have learned becomes the thing we know. It becomes part of us, as natural as breathing.

For me, welcoming people in love and joy is as natural as breathing, and I knew that it worked because I had been doing it all my life. My life was filled with friends, and our parties were successes where people left feeling important and loved.

When you stop and think about it, hospitality really means love. Love really means bringing someone close and opening the doorway of your heart to them. Opening the doorway of your heart means exposing yourself, offering yourself as a sacrifice and a place where they can rest for a little while, there on the shores of your sandy beach where the seagulls cry and the waves lull you to sleep.

Eleven kids came that night, along with their parents. At regular Young Life club, parents do drive-by deliveries of their kids and push them out of the door and race away, hoping to never see them again. Okay, so maybe it isn't quite that bad! But the parents have no intention of coming into the pit of doom known as club.

Nor do the kids want their parents to come and embarrass them in front of their friends and, even worse, in front of the upperclassmen and women they wish they could hang out with. For typical kids at typical clubs, parents don't exist at all.

But for Capernaum kids, parents are their everything, representing them with fierce solidarity and protection. They came in and checked out the club and made sure that the people and the place were capable of delivering the kind of care their kids deserved. Parents of kids with disabilities are both incredibly strong-willed and thankful. They are strong-willed about their dedication to helping their child receive all that he or she must. They are thankful when they realize you feel the same way.

We welcomed them, we signed them up and got their contact information, we ate pizza and hung out. Then we started playing games. I had brought some long clown balloons, the kind used for making animals. We blew up a bunch of them and turned them into swords. The stupidity began.

Then we made two teams and told the teams to try to pop the balloons of the other team. At the end of the time, whichever team had the most balloons would win. The stupidity continued.

I mean, seriously, who would ever be so stupid as to create a ridiculously competitive game for kids, much less kids with disabilities who might not get the nuances of the game and could completely miss the fun in the humiliation of losing. It was me!

Yup, I was the idiot who crafted the game. Truth was, it was fun, and people were running around, holding up balloons, popping them, and laughing. Some of the kids popped their own balloons in huge offers of ritualistic sacrifice.

William had autism. He was a big dude. He was also very intelligent and got the game. He knew he had to destroy balloons, so he did exactly that. He was an automaton, marching around like Darth Vader, grabbing balloons, and killing them with nary a smile. This was serious business to William.

Then he came to C. R. and tried to grab his balloon. But C. R. wanted nothing of that and pushed William away. William came back and tried to steal the balloon. C. R. slugged him in the nose, and blood gushed out. We heard the commotion and ran over. I grabbed William, who had grabbed C. R. William's blood dripped onto my hands and arms as he held on to C. R.'s torn shirt. He was enraged.

The parents were in the back of the room talking with Scott when it happened. They turned and watched us handle the situation, then turned back and continued talking to Scott.

Our first club was a bloody success!

Bergermeister Johann at Oktoberfest.

SEVEN

Going on Staff

for Scott

JOHN KÖEHLER

A voice of one calling: "In the desert prepare the way for the Lord; make straight in the wilderness a highway for our God."

ISAIAH 40:3

John the Baptist was a man of great power and passion. He was also kind of crazy and wild and even scary to people. They were drawn to him while at the same time being somewhat repulsed by his person.

I confess that I have always felt a certain affinity for John, partly because we share the same name and partly because I too see myself in a similar way to how folks saw John thousands of years ago.

Certainly the wild and crazy part fits. Not only am I seen as crazy in the sense of being a person who acts and thinks outside of convention and the box of society, but having bipolar syndrome gives me the medical right to proclaim my craziness. And I have the meds to prove it!

Passion is my middle name it seems. This is a boon and a bane for me. A boon in the sense that I throw myself into life and into lives with utter abandonment. People tend to respond well to that when they aren't afraid of me. My passion is real and complete and takes me to places less passionate men will never go.

My passion is a bane because it can make me intemperate and impulsive. I sometimes react quickly instead of thoughtfully responding to events and situations. Clearly God wants us to listen to our hearts when we have to use judgment, but He also wants us to use the wisdom of our intellect. Our heads.

Yet my passion and craziness give me power to blast through and quickly find solutions to things that some folks would waste hours, days, or weeks worrying and whining over.

John the Baptist was a visionary and could clearly see the endgame that God wanted him to reach. He knew that Jesus was coming, and he had to prepare the people and get them to change their ways and turn around to God. Go the other way, he said. Turn around and see God. Turn around and look for the One coming down the road, inviting us all to the table of His life.

I am a visionary too. Not in a prophetic way, but in a natural and simple way. Sometimes I look at situations and simply see the solutions, plain as day. To me it seems so obvious, and I am always amazed when others do not see it too. Leadership is about not just having a vision for something, but being able to show that vision to others in such a compelling way that they, too, would see and grab hold of it.

My passion combined with a vision for Capernaum—the vision started by Scott and others before me and anointed by God—created a force and momentum for Capernaum. Combined with the other amazing volunteer leaders, parents, and kids who happily bought into our vision, we created a force to be reckoned with.

The club grew. What started with eleven quickly grew to thirty. We got better at running all aspects of the program, leading the music, giving talks, and going on excursions. We bought sound equipment and gear. In my mind, even back at Lake Champion when we first dreamed about starting club in the fall, it was already real, already successful. All we had to do was fulfill the vision. We did.

Meanwhile Capernaum in Hampton Roads continued as an all-volunteer force of nature, and Scott Hamilton (may his terrapins never sink) decided it was time to change things and bring on someone to run the show. That would be me!

Shoot, I was already running the show. But now he wanted to bring me into the fold and put me on staff with Young Life. He wanted to hire the crazy, wild, passionate guy to do something he was already passionate about . . . but this time getting paid to do it.

It was as if he had opened a door for me, and on the other side was a vast land called Capernaum. I ran through the door screaming my head off with joy and passion. My dream was coming true, and now I understood what was happening and why God had waited until I was forty-five to drag my white butt into all this.

When I finally calmed down, I turned to look back at the door, a long way off. There stood Patty, my wife, weeping and looking the other way. She did not want to walk through the doorway that Scott had opened for me. She was afraid and thought that I was leaving her.

Reluctantly I walked back through the door and back into my old life. I had to show Patty that this was the right thing for me to do, the right thing for us to do. I needed her support, so I had to show her the way and answer all her questions about money and change and time and what would happen to her in all of this.

I decided that I needed some good advice, so I met with several pastors from various local churches, along with friends whom I trusted to give me good advice and tell me the truth. Every pastor I spoke with told me to keep my wife in the middle of this and allow her to help me with it.

Perhaps they could see and feel my passion and were worried that I would take a unilateral stance and block Patty out of the decision. I confess that I felt called and did not completely understand why she did not automatically run through the door with me. Run? Shoot, she was backing away from the door and had no intention of even walking through it.

Not until, that is, she had satisfied all her questions and needs.

What about money? Could I afford to quit my job running Koehler Studios and concentrate solely on Capernaum? That would have been my preference at the time, as my commitment to the studio had been eroding over the years. But the reality was that Young Life could not pay me enough to afford our lifestyle. We lived at the North End of Virginia Beach and had just bought the lot next door by way of refinancing and home equity. Plus we had two girls about to start college. Every bit of my paycheck was going to our mortgage and expenses related to the house and family things.

I set out to craft a hybrid solution. I worked it out on paper and in my head. The plan was to reduce my time with the studio by a significant amount and to cut my salary in half. We would then take that money and hire a designer to pick up my slack. Young Life would then make up the difference of what I had to pay the designer. This brilliant solution meant that I would have two full-time jobs for the price of one. Somebody was getting a good deal, and it wasn't me!

But this wasn't about getting a good deal; this was about fulfilling God's plan for me in a way that would lift up my wife and my family, continue my business, and grow Capernaum. It made sense on paper, just barely, but it put a tremendous amount of pressure on me to make it work. And I could not do it on my own.

I laid out the plan to Patty and took a lot of time to explain it and show her how it would work. She bought into it over a series of days. I knew it would take her a while to wrap her mind and soul around it, and it did.

Then I showed the plan to Kim Nelson, my creative director for the studio. She was effectively acting as the chief worker bee, doing most of the work, and so the plan did not surprise her. I told her that if we were able to pull this transition off and keep the business afloat for a year, at the end of that year I would put her name on the letterhead and make her my partner in the firm.

This would mean—in the words of Mark DesRoches, my CPA—that Kim would be my profit partner, not my equity partner. She would share in any profits we made, but I would retain legal ownership of the business as well as financial responsibility. If any actions had to be made to fill any temporary money gaps, I would continue to be the man. Kim got a good deal!

I also shared the plan with many of my key friends, accountability partners, and advisers. Once again I only wanted guys who would tell me the complete truth and give their honest opinion. Since they already knew I was patently and completely crazy, my plan came as no surprise to them.

But I also think that they could clearly see the hand of God written all over this new way I was choosing to go. Seriously, what kind of idiot purposely chooses to add a second job without making more money? I don't know if being called by God makes you an idiot or not, but it does make you relentless in your pursuit to find a way to get 'er done for the Big Surfer Dude in the Sky.

    Aka God.

MY INFLATABLE HEART

Billy Ray and his twin brother Billy Ray.

EIGHT

Rockbridge 2005

for Win

I press on toward the goal to win the prize for which God has called me heavenward in Christ Jesus.

PHILLIPPIANS 3:14

After we established that first club at Landstown in the fall of 2004, we realized not only that we could do it, but that God had His hands on it—and therefore us—and by golly, we had us a bona fide success story. All we had to do was grab ahold of its tail and go along for the ride.

It wasn't long before I could really sense that this thing was much bigger than just me and the other leaders, parents, and kids. Something huge was happening, and as the weeks wore on, I realized that God had picked me to be the engineer on the train we called Capernaum. As I told our leaders, "The train is leaving the station, and you'd better hurry up so you don't miss it. Get on the train!"

It wasn't until much later that I realized I was not the engineer at all, but merely a member of the work crew. Shoveling coal, serving customers, or cleaning windows, it didn't really matter. In fact, I figured out after a while thatI could even be like a dog in a car with the windows down—head sticking out, biting the breeze, tongue flapping back against the wet window. Pure happiness!

Dad was driving, and that dog did not have a clue or a care in the world about where dad was taking him. All he knew was that dad loved him, and the window was down, and the wind felt so good on his face. The river of smells floating by was the most delicious thing he'd had to eat since breakfast, when he'd cornered Mrs. Ailstock's cat in the tree, oh yes! Cats are bad, but cars are good, and Dad loves me, and I love him. I don't care where I'm going.

Let's roll!

When Scott hired me to fulfill what God wanted me to do and had prepared me to do my whole life, I really did think I was the engineer and that the train belonged to me. It was mine, and I was jealous of it. My aim was to guide that engine out of the station and onto whatever track God wanted. But the truth was I didn't always know if I was taking the right way or my way. Back then it all just melted together into a blur of passion and pride. Not to mention ignorance.

Normally Area Directors (my Young Life title) go through a two-year intern program, where they are taught how to effectively run a Young Life area. This includes spiritual, mental, emotional, and practical training; methods and logistics and systems and services; ways to get things done in an effective manner; ways to win donors; ways to win kids and leaders; how to train leaders in a way that gives them both practical methods for reaching kids at club and school as well as ways to deepen their own spiritual walk; how to run a banquet and handle the financial affairs of an area; and how to plan and execute a camp trip.

I never went through the Young Life intern program. I was an Old Guy in Young Life. Shoot, I had run a successful business for more than ten years, not to mention working at large ad agencies, traveling around the world, and hosting large events for hundreds of people at a time.

I was forty-six years old, not some wet-behind-the-ears, little bitty twenty-three-year-old recent college graduate. Scott Hamilton (may his kilt never falter) wasn't going to send me into a training program with little kids. I would have eaten them for breakfast. I would have powdered my face with them and then played soccer with their heads. Is that legal?

Nay, Scott was not stupid, at least not to my face. He said that I was in the Second Wind program. Basically that means anyone who has had significant life experience (aka age), business experience, and a strong entrepreneurial nature. I laughed at the title and quickly renamed it "Suckin' Wind." That's because Young Life expects us to figure it all out on our own for the most part, and if we can't then we can just suck wind. Oh, Scott was there for me plenty, but I knew I could not keep going back to him for answers I could figure out on my own. Even if it took me years to do it.

If I could not figure it out through my growing network of Young Life friends and colleagues, I would do whatever made the most sense based on my many years of working and my endless life experiences; but sometimes all my experiences still didn't work. In other words, I sucked wind! Kind of like a big Hoover vacuum. But that was not the expression most used in the ministry for newbies like me. They said I was sucking from the fire hose. Now there's a buzzkill.

Scott had warned me that a lot of information would be thrown at me as I learned the intricacies of Young Life. Young Life is a large corporation, and as such, it is populated by many people and many systems. According to the The Book of Stupid Human Tricks, there will always be a certain number of stupid systems in every corporation, no matter how small or large.

Young Life is no different in this regard. For the most part the people are amazingly friendly and extremely capable. The systems and services are also quite effective. But as I expected, there was a tremendous amount of what I would call unworthy information and things to avoid.

Scott said I would be sucking from a fire hose, and he was right. A huge amount of information and systems and ideas and "really important" stuff was thrown at me. More than could be consumed, even with a fire hose. I learned what to take in and use and what to let flood by me to join the flotsam and jetsam of rejected fuel. I simply did not have time to check out everything thrown at me. Especially if I wanted to run my business while I ran Capernaum. Ack! I had to let it float by me, regardless of the presumed importance or value.

I'm thinking that some of the stuff I rejected had to do with camp because I managed to muck it up so bad on our first trip that it has become an epic story of stupidity (my own) as well as bravery and resounding love (our leaders).

MY INFLATABLE HEART

In the spring of 2005 Scott Hamilton (may his sideburns grow long) and I agreed that Capernaum would take a trip to Rockbridge, another Young Life camp in Virginia. I contacted the camp and talked with the intern there about our trip. She asked the age of the kids we were bringing.

When I told her that some of the "kids" were in fact in their twenties, she explained that this was a high-school camp and that only people who were "of high-school age" were eligible to attend. She became the first Young Life intern that I would consume live, bones and all. Luckily it was over the phone and not at all painful for her; it was over quickly.

I explained that Capernaum was ageless and that some of my over-twenty-year-old folks had the mental and emotional capacity of teenagers or even younger, heaven forbid. I'm afraid I did not ask for her permission in this matter, but merely told her the way that it would be in no uncertain terms.

By now I had already consumed her entire head, sucking it up through the phone lines. Since her head was missing, she was unable to argue with me and agreed to our trip—she even managed to sound excited about it. Because of that show of support, I regurgitated her head, sent it back over the phone lines, and allowed her to continue with her temporarily interrupted life. To this day she's really not sure what happened. Yet she lives.

The first issue of going to camp was getting campers and leaders there . . . otherwise known as transportation. This was my greatest mistake on the trip. In my magnificence and complete brilliance I decided that we did not need a bus. We only had thirty-four people going. Why waste all those empty seats?

I managed to consume the entire bottle of stupid pills and decided that in lieu of the bus, we would take eight vehicles. And into those eight vehicles we would stuff the twenty-some campers with special needs and the dozen or so leaders without special needs.

By the end of that trip we would all have special needs.

The first thing we learned on the trip was that toilet needs are not, uh, normal for people who are, uh, not normal. We were so unfamiliar with the reality of their needs that we simply reacted to every single need they had. This fact alone turned what should have been a five-hour trip into a seven-hour trip.

We communicated by cell phones or, in the case of the lead car, by pulling over onto the shoulder of the road. Doing this on I-64 with one car was probably not a great idea, especially if a cop came along and found out you had stopped to take a pee. Doing it with eight vehicles took us so far past illegal that we were borderline psychotic. The real problem was not that one particular person had decided that she could not wait until the next rest stop. The problem was that as soon as we stopped, some of the other male campers decided they also had to get out and pee, and we let them! Chaos.

Since we were without a clue to the best way to handle this problem, we let them all out of the car and told them to go into the woods to pee. We started herding them in that direction, but Bart decided he was ready to pee right then and there, halfway between the cars and the woods.

He dropped his trousers before we could do anything and started peeing. In broad daylight. In front of the girls, the guys, the leaders, and the hundreds of people driving by. His white ass was like a beacon, and at once four male leaders ran to Bart and formed a human shield to protect the eyes of the innocents.

Bart was just doing his duty, and we held no grudge against him. In fact, we started laughing at the utter stupidity of the situation. Making a human shield so a man with disabilities could pee along an interstate highway was actually quite funny, if you stepped back and looked at it with the right kind of attitude.

It was during one of these stops when I first said to myself, "Dear God, what have I done?" I realized front and center that we should have taken the bus, but by then it was, of course, too late. The deed was done, the train had already left the station, and the conductor was completely insane.

We stopped for lunch in Charlottesville where half went to one fast food joint and half to another. More chaos. By that point I was sure that God hated me with Old Testament vengeance and was, in fact, torturing me. Yet even in the midst of the stupidity and idiocy of the entire trip, there were moments of amazing clarity where I could see what could be and feel things that God wanted me to feel in the crazy maelstrom that was Capernaum.

We really weren't supposed to bring so many people with disabilities to a camp, but we did it anyway. We certainly weren't expert in all their various problems, but that didn't stop us from coming. We had no clue what to expect at any given moment, yet we marched forward in faith and the assurance and hope that we would be able to figure things out in most cases.

Or . . . we would not. Either way we would get through and get by, until death or the end of the trip do us part. Before we even got to Rockbridge I was longing for the end of the trip so I could disappear in obscurity, resign from my position with Young Life, and perhaps find the job I'd always wanted: sanitation engineer.

Eventually we made it to Rockbridge. They make a big deal when campers arrive, but usually the campers arrive in buses. Everyone piles off the bus and goes to a welcome area. Summer staff and work crew kids take the luggage to the assigned cabins, so that by the time you finish the welcome and walk over to your cabin, your stuff is already there. Very nice!

But we had eight cars, and they didn't know what to do with us. Finally we agreed to walk up to the welcome, watch the whacked-out program guys act stupid (they were our kind of people), head back to our cars, and drive them over to our cabins.

The cabins were very nice, and I quickly claimed a bottom bunk and helped campers find a bunk, put their things away, and get used to their new home. Day one for typical campers is chaotic, but for Capernaum campers you must add bedlam, panic, and terror into the mix. By the end of the week the terror was coming from the leaders as well as the campers.

We ate dinner, and our campers and leaders had a blast. We did the obstacle course, and no one died. Amazing. By the time we returned to our cabins, it was midnight. Many of our campers were used to going to bed by nine, so you can imagine what kind of shape they were in. Somehow we got everyone ready for bed, quieted down, and then they fell asleep.

That night Rusty, Nate, and I met on the porch of the Spring Center for the first of many sessions which would become epic and huge over the years to come—so big we would get shut down in 2007 by the wicked mean people of another Capernaum, who shall remain anonymous to protect their innocence. They shall receive wet towel snaps when they least expect it. Or TP their houses. Or both if they're not careful.

Sitting in those rocking chairs, sipping sodas, and laughing about the day saved my life. No kidding. We were absolutely exhausted in every possible way: physically, mentally, and emotionally. We were burnt toast, wasted and worthless. Dead men rocking.

I told them my life was over and that I was a complete moron. They laughed at me. They did. They laughed at me. And the laughter was one of the things that saved my life because it reminded me that I was not in this alone. They were in it with me. And even though I was the idiot who had taken the stupid pill, they were still with me. They gave me hope.

The next morning was Field Games. I had rallied a little by breakfast and now believed that God would not kill me at camp but would wait until I got home so I could be tortured for the entire week by having to take care of my campers and leaders. He wanted me to be strong for them even though I felt so weak, so amazingly weak and ignorant. So stupid. Idiot!

While we were there, hanging out and actually having fun in spite of my own mortification, my friend Win Levis showed up and saved my life again. Win was the Virginia Beach area director, and he already knew some of our campers and leaders.

Win hung out with us and loved us, and doggone if that boy didn't take some of the pressure off me. He told me I was okay and it would all be okay. He loved our people and, by doing so, loved me. I will never forget what he did for me and my people. He helped save our lives. The whole camp did.

Then Tara showed up and saved our lives again. She saved everyone's life, especially Rusty's. Game on!

Rusty and Bobby share a moment.

NINE

The Rusty Missile

for Tara

JOHN KÖEHLER

"Here comes that dreamer," they said to each other.

Genesis 37:19

I met Rusty at the Bayville disc (Frisbee) golf course in Virginia Beach. He was a pro-level golfer while I was just getting back into the sport. I got to know him in the course of buying some discs from him.

I started going to the Monday night weekly tournaments, worked my way up to the intermediate division, and started hanging out with Rusty before, during, and after the events or casual rounds. One Monday night it started raining cats and dogs. I ain't talking little Chihuahua rain, but full-size Sainat Bernard rain. It was coming down!

Rusty and I wound up sitting in my van while the rain came down. We got to talking, and somehow he started telling me his dreams. He wanted three things: a house, his own business, and a woman—as in a wife with whom he could start a family. He was really clear about it. Those were the three things he wanted.

He was not interested in finding God at that point, but God had already found him. I believe that God was all set to give Rusty his dreams come true, but first He needed him to jump in and get on the runaway freight train because it was leaving the station.

I was the man sent to take Rusty to the station.

We started talking about God, and then Rusty started coming to

Capernaum. He was the kind of guy who wanted to help set things up and then watch from the back. I tried to get him involved with the skits and games, but he wanted nothing to do with that.

"John," he said, "I'm a backstage guy. I don't want to be up front. I'll help you from the back." Yeah, sure you will, Rusty.

I invited Rusty to come to camp, and he started shaking his head no. I kept after him, and he kept saying no. Unfortunately for Rusty, the kids were already changing his mind. He was drawn to them though he would not admit it. He was falling in love with them though he thought he was just doing good community service and helping me out.

He was, but it was much more than that.

With a month to go, I changed tactics and started telling Rusty that he was going to Rockbridge. He said he wasn't. I said, "Rusty, you can whine about anything you want; you can stay home from the next three clubs; you can do whatever you like; but you are going to camp!"

With two weeks to go, Rusty gave me a check for camp and said, "John, I'm doing this under protest."

I had already met Tara Lundy at Lake Champion in 2004. She was a young college leader for Baltimore Capernaum. Dedicated and capable with the campers. Selfless, humble, and one of the most godly women I have ever met. I remember thinking I was nothing like her and did not deserve to do the same things she did.

Tara had heard that we were going to Rockbridge for our first camping trip and could probably use some help. To this day I do not know how she knew this. My guess is that the powers that be in Capernaum (Carissa Mortenson, Suzanne Williams, and Pam Harmon) knew about our trip, and that we were in way over our heads. Women!

Who were they to decide we were in over our heads? Of course, we were in over our heads, so a cry went out across the land, and Tara answered the call. Thanks be to God!

Tara arrived at Rockbridge like an angel coming down from on high. She was such an asset to our women leaders and brought a calm assurance that helped us immeasurably. We all noticed her and were thankful. Rusty noticed her and was *very* thankful.

Rusty met Tara and transformed himself into a heat-seeking missile—a guided missile with only one purpose: to change Tara's last name to Criste. It was beautifully, amazingly pathetic, yet also powerfully direct. He threw himself at her, and she simply did not know what to do.

Never before had a man pursued her in that way.

Rusty came to me and said, "John, I think I've found the one!" The last time that was said, it was about the Messiah, but Rusty didn't know the Messiah yet. He was talking about Tara. I was like, "Dude, she's half your age or something. Are you really sure about this? Does she even know you?"

Tara came up to me after a few days of dealing with the guided missile that was Rusty Criste. "John," she said, "who is this guy? I don't even know him, and he's following me around like a puppy. It's a little creepy. Should I trust this guy?"

I remember looking at her and feeling kind of sorry that she had to deal with some old dude throwing himself at her because he thought one of his dreams was going to come true.

"Tara, he's pretty crusty on the outside, but he's got a heart of gold."

Game over, dude. Rusty may have found out I said that to her, probably because he beat it out of me over root beer that night on the porch of the Spring Center. He doubled his efforts and relentlessly threw himself at her like a love-starved juvenile.

On the day we left, Rusty managed to get her cell phone number, but she made him promise that he would only call her in an emergency. He agreed. After we had some trouble with Jim Howley's van, Rusty agreed to drive it back by himself. Then the van broke down, and Rusty had his emergency. He called Tara.

Long story short, they are married now and expecting their first child in October of 2008. Rusty also started a painting contractor business and bought not one but two houses in Suffolk. And also—by the way – met a friend of mine named Jesus the Christ along the way.

Rusty jumped on the runaway freight train and now all his dreams are coming true.

John and Tara walking and rolling.

TEN

Tara Tara Tara

for Rusty

> "Well done, good and faithful servant!"

MATTHEW 25:21

As soon as I re-met Tara at Rockbridge, I knew that she was mine. I know, I know, that sounds bad. Throw the book at me and call me a sinner, but you would be wrong. Tara was and is beautiful in every way and lit up my radar like lightning in July. But remember that I react to just about all women that way! Besides, if I had pursued Tara for the wrong reasons, Rusty would have killed me slowly with a rusty spoon. A dull, rusty spoon. An old, dull, rusty spoon.

I wasn't interested in Tara for the wrong reasons, but for all the right reasons. She is everything that I am not. She is truly a godly person, devoted to God and completely molded to His ways. She is kind and caring and skilled in the ways of special needs folks, knowing what makes them tick from experience. She is humble and walks softly, with a certain grace in her bearing. Her pride is in God and His works. She knows the Bible and has eaten so much of it that it is in her blood and bones. The aroma of God is around her, and it (she) was pleasing to me.

Where I am loud and obnoxious, Tara is quiet and unassuming. Where I am old and mean, Tara is young and loving. Where I am the voice of passion and force, Tara is the voice of compassion and care.

She is the polar (not bipolar) opposite of me, and I knew

instinctively that I needed her, that Capernaum in Hampton Roads needed her to help us become better. So I set out to steal her away from Baltimore. Amazingly enough, Rusty supported my desire. Wasn't that thoughtful of him?

Tara was in her senior year at Towson State University and had to make a decision about where to go after she graduated. I suggested that she should move down to the Beach and work for Capernaum. I had no clue where the money would come from to pay her. I didn't even know if this would be approved by Scott, yet I instinctively knew this was exactly the right thing to do.

So I carefully and subtly began wooing her.

"Tara, you need to come where Capernaum is fun!"

"We have a brand-new area, and you can help build it!"

"You can do what you've always wanted to do!"

"Come to the dark side of Capernaum and live!"

Okay, so maybe it wasn't so subtle, but it was effective. Between me telling her about her career choices and helping her figure them out, and Rusty telling her what a great catch he would be, Tara was overwhelmed by the desires of two old guys. Unfair? Of course it was unfair, but in the end we were only doing God's will. At least that's what we kept telling ourselves, though the lines between God's will and my will sometimes get blurred. Or disappear completely.

I've always been the guy who figured out roughly what God's will for me was or what His general plan for Capernaum was. I knew He wanted it to grow. Therefore I was called to help achieve that growth, using whatever methods I could.

Now some folks would say that was more about me than about God, and in some ways they would be right. But I am always more interested in moving things toward the big prize versus arguing about the little movements we made marching toward the prize. Some folks would rather pray about each and every move they intend to make or hope to make, and wait on an answer from God to show them the truth or the lie of their plans. But I am not some folks, and I do not like to wait on God. Sue me!

God clearly intended for Capernaum to grow, and I knew we would need help to achieve His stated desire. Tara showing up at camp was no accident in my way of looking at things. She was a gift from God, all wrapped up and ready to go. All I had to do was figure out how to get her there.

God provided Rusty to help with that.

Tara had never been pursued by a man in that way, and the feeling was very strange for her. She was attracted to his desire for her and also repulsed by his direct intensity. Not to mention he was like a billion years older than she was. Or maybe it was sixteen years. Don't know.

Point was he was from another generation. Where Tara was comfortable with the Internet and e-mailing, Rusty thought the Internet was a European police agency and e-mailing was for the birds. An e-mail sent to Rusty was sure to be returned to sender due to either a full mailbox or an out-of-service account.

Tara could teach Rusty about God and the Bible and the softer, more important things in life according to her world. Rusty could teach Tara about beer and the proper methods of partying and having fun in a walk on the dark side. She brought Rusty the lightness of God, and he brought Tara the darkness of men. A match made in heaven!

Eventually the planets aligned, which means God got fed up with all the delays, and Tara moved down to the area and lived with the Jensons. She came on staff as our intern in the summer of 2006, and we became immediately better for her arrival. She was a breath of fresh air and an instant blessing for our growth and our souls. She showed me how to be more careful and loving, and I taught her how to get things done, how to be relentless. How to ask for forgiveness after the fact rather than asking for permission before.

We opened up Chesapeake, and she made it hers. She fell in love with Rusty and made him hers. She fell in love with our kids; now they are hers, and she is their older sister.

Tara has always been a part of my family, and our meeting was simply to do the obvious and fulfill what our heavenly Father had determined before we were even a twinkle in our earthly Daddy's eyes.

Capernaum's Hampton Roads staff (L-R) First row: Tara Criste, Angela West and John Koehler. Bottom row: Rece Criste (in Tara's tummy). Photo by Glen McClure.

JOHN KÖEHLER

PART TWO

SPECIAL PEOPLE

Neal having a happy moment at Club.

ELEVEN

Special People

for Mommy Gail

JOHN KÖEHLER

She replied, "Do me a special favor.
Since you have given me land in the Negev,
give me also springs of water"

JOSHUA 15:19

There has never been a question in my mind whether or not Capernaum people are special. We are. And yes, I do count myself as one of them. Partly because of my own disability: bipolar syndrome. And partly because I have always considered myself special and unique in many ways, set apart by God. Wonderful and amazing and absolutely one-of-a-kind. What foolish pride!

We are all made in the image of God, and last I checked He is pretty wonderful and amazing. He did not make us to be mildly amazing or kind of special. He made us to be like Him, absolutely amazing, to please Him and for His personal enjoyment.

Shoot, even dog breeders take great joy from the puppies and dogs that spring forth under their care and love. They coddle them and train them and feed them, and then they receive canine love in payment for their efforts. They do all this, and the dogs are not even made in their image—though some owners do bear a striking resemblance to their pets! The dogs do not come from their loins, nor do they create the dogs in their own image. Yet they adore them as their own.

Closer to the mark are new parents. They plan and pray and hope and try their best to make a baby, a baby that will, in fact, be in their own image and that is made by them, through them, and in them. This is an act of love far greater than the dog breeder, though some would argue the point, especially childless dog breeders.

Parents look upon their own children as acts of creation that they participated in and controlled to a certain extent. Whether or not they believe in God, they recognize the inherent miracle in the birth and in their child, and they are oh-so-thankful for the miracle and act of creation: thankful either to God or to each other.

Or both.

Parents consider their children absolutely special in every way and will do everything they can to nurture their children so that their gifts can bloom and reach full potential. Parents know their children better than anyone and will gladly recite their gifts and talents whether or not you care to listen.

And then there is our Big Daddy in the Sky.

God created us in His image and for His pure enjoyment. He created the world for His enjoyment and for our enjoyment. All the animals and the plants and the wonders of nature He gave to us and said, "I made this for you to enjoy. Take care of it and love it as I love you." We do enjoy the world He gave us while we do our best to destroy the gift of life He gave us.

I find it amazing that some churches and religious groups are just now realizing that since God made the world and gave us the responsibility for it, we should probably try to take better care of it. Bravo! Welcome back to the table of life. Welcome back.

If God did, in fact, make us in His own image and for His own enjoyment, then that makes us His children—not just spiritually but physically as well because whether or not you believe in creationism or evolutionism, you better believe that God made it all work.

Personally I do not care one whit whether God had us evolve from a protozoan to a newt to a monkey to a humanoid and at some point—poof—He gave us His spirit. In fact, I find humor in that and a reminder that we all were made from the earth and mud and the nasty bits of the world. From dirty clay a sculptor can make the most beautiful objects, and certainly God is the finest of sculptors and we His works of art.

But what about a child with disabilities?

Are they not also made by God and in His image? How can you say a child with deformities is made in the image of God? For that matter, how can you say that any living thing with a deformity is an act of creation versus a mistaken act of sin?

Many people think this is the case, and they are not the first to think so. Two thousand years ago when Jesus walked the planet, people thought that any child with a disability had sinned against God or else his parents had sinned. This belief system is alive and well in the present day, in spite of what folks profess to the contrary.

They say that they are okay with the concept of people with disabilities needing a place to stay, as long as it is not in their neighborhood. They say that we should include special needs kids in schools as long as they have their own classrooms. They say we should all accept the disabled as long as they do not have to do it personally. They say that we should allow them to worship in our churches as long as they follow the rules and are not disruptive. They say that society should take responsibility for the weak and broken as long as they remain out of sight and out of mind.

They say many things with their mouths, but their hearts and minds prove the lie of their words when they take actions diametrically opposed to the words they speak. The good news is that finally a conversation is happening about including people with disabilities. The bad news is that it takes a long time for society to move from talking about a possible solution to actually doing the things that need to be done. Whether the subject is civil rights, women's rights, or the rights of disabled people, the pattern is always the same.

One does not change a society overnight. Inbred thoughts and belief systems take centuries and in this case millennia to create and a long time to alter course, much less turn around and go the other way.

Which is—by the way—precisely what repentance is all about. Repentance is not just stopping what you are doing; it is actually doing the opposite of what you are doing. John the Baptist told folks to turn around and go the other direction, but they merely wanted to dip their heads into the waters of the Jordan and keep doing the same things they had always done.

That is why he called them vipers from the pit, because he knew they merely wanted temporary absolution for their sins but were not at all interested in changing their behavior. These behavioral patterns traced back to their ancestors, all the way to the time of Eden.

John screamed at them, "You're going the wrong way! Turn around and go the other way. Go God's way, and you will truly be baptized in the waters of His Spirit, symbolized by the dunking I will give you. Continue to go your way, and this water will only clean your body for a day or two, until the dirt of your sins makes you unclean again."

For the record, John did not say these precise things, so I'm asking the righteous Pharisees to withhold their judgment of me. They do not like it when I suggest words that Jesus or other biblical figures might have said but were not recorded. Sinner! Heretic!

I really love Pharisees . . . from a distance.

So what is the deal with the Disabled? Capital D.

Why do we call them Special People? Special Olympics. Special Education. Special Camps. Special Places for Special People.

If they are created in the image of God as we are, then we are all part of the same family. Since God made us all very special for His enjoyment and since God does not make mistakes, then logic would say that people with disabilities are no more or less special than the rest of us. What? How can this be? How can I be in the same gene pool and the same family as a kid with Down syndrome or cerebral palsy? Why should I have to share the same table with them or the same school? Why should I have to share the same church with them? Or the same God?

The answer is amazingly simple. We are all created in the image of the Lord, each and every one of us, regardless of our beauty, our abilities, or our disabilities. Regardless of our obvious or hidden gifts, we were sent here to please God, and no one can refute it or deny it. No man or woman can reject something that was created by God, especially something created in the image of God. That would be us. All of us. To do so would be to reject God Himself.

We look for perfection in ourselves and wish to present only our very best to the world and perhaps to God. This makes sense. But God wants all of us, including the best and the worst of us. He wants our abilities and will use them for His sake, but He also wants our weaknesses and disabilities to use for His sake.

Perhaps He wants our weaknesses and deformities to prove to the world that He can do great things with anyone, regardless of whether or not he or she meets any ill-conceived benchmarks set by the world. Perhaps they are to bring out the best in others who are reminded of how lucky they are in their own strengths and weaknesses. "There but for the grace of God go I," they say, completely missing that God's grace is shown through the disabled person they pity. It is the grace of God that makes them thankful and think of God.

We are all special people because we are made by God who—last I checked—is a most special Creator and Father of us all. We are all part of the one Father, and regardless of the dysfunctions and weakness within us, we are beautiful and perfect according to God, the One who made us.

He does not see your disabilities and weaknesses when He holds you in His lap of love and whispers that you are His favorite child. Just as my momma did to me and my siblings so many years ago.

It is only through agape that we can become blind to the disabilities of all the members of our extended family. When you see through their weaknesses, then you will see God. But you must look through the eyes of your heart. Then you will see the truth.

Bart wondering what's next at camp.

TWELVE

Bart & The Goat's Milk

for MJ

"Do not cook a young goat in its mother's milk."

EXODUS 34:26

May 8, 2007

Bart was born with a disability that is so long you can't rightly say it in one breath. Now his mom, Miss Mary Jane (MJ to her hiphop friends), she can say the whole thing without thinking, but it took her about twenty years to memorize.

Bart almost died when he was born, and the doctors couldn't tell what was wrong with him. Eventually they found out it had something to do with the way his body processes food, or doesn't process it, and enzymes and all kinds of tricky things. Bottom line, he was dying until they found out that his body sure did like goat's milk. Shoot, those goats saved his life.

Funny thing about goats. In the Bible they talk about separating the sheep from the goats because goats were not held in high esteem. Sheep could give wool and lambs and blood and skins that could keep you warm during the cold of winter. Sheep were high class but goats low. Sheep were valuable and sought after, while goats were just... goats.

But the sheep didn't save Bart. The goats did.

The first time he came to Capernaum was pretty cool. At first take, you might think that Bart doesn't really know what's going on.

Oh, but he does. He knows exactly what's going on, just not in the same way that we do. Bart wasn't so sure about Capernaum at first, and shoot, I don't blame him at all. We're a right noisy bunch of folks, everyone jumping around like spastic monkeys, playing and laughing and carrying on.

And those are the able bodied leaders I'm talking about!

So old Bart, why he just walked by us for the first couple of weeks. He was processing us, paying attention, holding his toy walkietalkie, wearing his trusty New York Yankee baseball cap, glasses down on his nose, and talking quietly to himself. Once again, some folks would say, "That guy is out of it." But no, he wasn't out of it at all. He was just trying to decide when he was ready to get with the rest of the strange folks of Capernaum.

After a couple of weeks, Bart had a breakthrough and started walking right through the middle of club. It was his way of saying, "I think you folks may be okay, so I'm gonna just slip on by and give you a feel for me and me a feel for you."

Didn't matter much what we were doing: dancing, doing a skit, eating pizza or even giving a club alk. Shoot, we could be right at that point of the club talk where Jesus is being lifted up, and here comes Bart, right on through and out the other side, to continue making circles around us as if to churn us all into spiritual butter.

A few clubs later, we were playing Beach Boys music. Bart was walking right through and then he stopped over near the speakers. He stood there for a while, and then he started dancing. Kind of leaning forward and back, bouncing up and down. He sure did like the Beach Boys. Well, needless to say, we all noticed and had us a little celebration and from that moment on, we made sure to play Beach Boys and had the Bart Sufficool Dance Fest at every club.

And that's how God snatched Bart into Capernaum.

Once at Norfolk club, Bart was being an A Number One Pain in the Keester and would not leave. His staff person couldn't get him to budge from back in the kitchen area near some tables, so she asked me if I'd try. Now normally I can do this with no problem, as I've learned a few things from MJ.

But Bart wasn't having any of it, and just kept bouncing a little and looking down at the floor, saying something. I tried pushing him from behind. Nothing worked. So then I actually paid attention to what he was looking at: my power strip had fallen out of my bag. He wanted me to know it was there, and though he couldn't tell me, he could show me. Then I figured we were ready, but no. Bart stopped at a table and stared. There was my pen and a DVD cover. He knew they both belonged to me, and he wanted me to see them, to take them home with me.

You know, it sure is a good thing that God put Bart into my life to help me with my forgetfulness and to remind me that everyone on this planet is just about finer than Caroliner and can speak to you if you just care to listen. And listening isn't always with the ears, but with the eyes and nose and mainly, in the end, with the heart.

Thanks Bart. I needed that power strip. Good thing about those goats, little brother. Good thing you stuck around.

The other Anna ready for weather.

THIRTEEN

Anna's Pearl

for Susan & Doug

JOHN KÖEHLER

"Again, the kingdom of heaven is like a merchant looking for fine pearls"

MATTHEW 13:45

May 9, 2007

When God made the heavens, He laughed, and pieces of His Spirit flew up into the sky like a billion lightning bugs. There they became stars, each one a small pearl of His laughter and joy, little love babies ready to be born. When a child is created in the belly of her momma, God plucks one of His star pearls from the sky and drops it into His new love child so that she will have a small piece of Him, a small pearl of love and joy just growing and glowing and shining and defining how much God loves His daughter, His most favorite child in all the universe.

We had club at Chesapeake last night, at the Church of the Messiah. Pam Harmon, the acting national director of Capernaum (I think this places her just below the disciples or the pope, but I never get that right) was there again, as she was in Norfolk the night before. She gave an awesome club talk ... again.

There were twenty-one people with disabilities in Norfolk, and Pam thought that was "just right." We had about thirty-one in Chesapeake, and Pam thought that was a bit big. Well, thank God Almighty that she's not coming to Virginia Beach on Thursday, where we get close to sixty people with all kinds of disabilities of the mind, body, spirit, and heart.

Shoot, if we're counting disabilities of the heart, then I reckon we're all disabled.

It seems that our awesome senior leader, Miss Angela West, has not quite figured out that she may not be able to do all the things that God wants her to do on account of her having cerebral palsy (CP) and all that it brings. I mean, come on, she has a hard time getting folks to rightly understand her, she can't drive herself anywhere except in her wheelchair, she takes an awful long time to "hunt and peck" her e-mails and do any work on the computer. Why would anyone want to work through those deficiencies?

If you asked Angela, she'd tell you she's just trying to please God and to fulfill the promises He put in her. She's trying to do everything she can to love all God's people. And she's proving that God can use anyone, no matter what holds them back, no matter how smart or slow, no matter how cute or ugly, no matter how strong or weak, no matter how rich or poor. Walker or talker, smeller or feller.

Angela invited a friend to come to club, so Anna came in her powered wheelchair, with her CP body and her beautiful face and spirit. She also had a cool duotone hairdo going on that gave her a, "hey, I'm different, I'm me" kind of look. I liked it. Anna hung with Angela most of the night, probably flipped out by the chaos that is Capernaum, not sure what to do or say. I could see her heart shining through a cloud of sadness, even though she wasn't so sure that she wanted to share her heart yet with a bunch of weirdos. Certainly not with this weirdo!

Afterward we were hanging out, and I asked her how strong she was. She arm wrestled me a bit; she was so strong with her upper body. I challenged her to stand and helped her out of her chair. Then I stood with her, holding her under her arms from behind, with my hands clasped under her chin. Then I picked her up off the ground, making sure she was okay. And then I spun her around like a small child.

Later on we were alone, and I told her that God was sooooo in love with her and that He had big plans for her. She got a surprised look on her pretty face and asked me, "How do you know that?" I said I could see it in her as plain as day and that sometimes God blesses me with special insight.

I told her that she was filled with doubt about herself, when God is not at all in doubt of her, and she started crying right there on the spot. I told her that I am filled with doubt too—that most folks are—and that most nights I wonder what the heck I am doing, and who put me in charge of anything at all, and why the heck had God picked a mentally ill, crazy-as-a-coot man to lead His ministry. And why exactly do I feel so bad right after feeling so good.

I challenged Anna to get out of her own way so that she could see the beauty, hope, love, and absolute power that God had placed in her, way down deep where the little-bitty, beautiful, baby God pearl rests in the folds of her heart. I think she liked that idea, and I'm looking forward to seeing what God is going to do in her.

Anna is one of God's beautiful pearls. Just like you.

God gives us all a pearl of His love and hides it deep within the folds of our hearts. He wants us to let that pearl glow, to expose it, to share it so that folks can see how beautiful our pearls are, so shiny and right. We're like a stellar art show, where people can come to stare at the most beautiful art that has ever been shown in any gallery, the gallery of God's love.

Anna's pearl shines so brightly that when she looks in the mirror, she can't see her own reflection because it's burned out with God's light. She's missing in action. She sees nothing there but a white-hot bright light, a reflection of God's love for her. Sometimes we can't even see ourselves because God just gets in the way. And ain't that just about righter than rain?

It is hard for most of us to figure out that we are seeing ourselves and that the reflection is perfect—what He has made in us is perfect; therefore, we are perfect.

Any questions?

The problem is that we tend to cover up our pearls of love, to hide them and not share them. Because—here's the thing—showing and sharing your love can hurt. So we build up crusty layers to protect that pearl, and pretty soon our lives are like an oyster, hard and protective, beautifully ugly, with barnacles and algae hanging on, and absolutely no clue of the amazing beauty hidden just inside.

Let's all open up our shells and share the beautiful pearls that God has placed there. Open up those shells so everyone can feel the light of God's love and see how awesome He has made you. And don't worry when they try to steal your pearl. If someone wants to hold it a bit, you just go on and let them take it. Because when you turn around, you'll have another pearl. An exact replica. Your own personal piece of God.

Give away your pearls. Just give 'em away.

JOHN KÖEHLER

MY INFLATABLE HEART

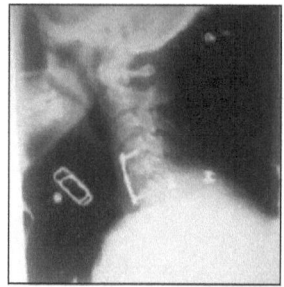

Jack's broken neck X-ray

FOURTEEN

Jack's Back

for Ron & Anita

JOHN KÖEHLER

*All was well with me, but he shattered me;
he seized me by the neck and crushed me.
He has made me his target;*

JOB 16:12

May 22, 2007

Well, Hey Diddle Diddle,

My bride of twenty-five years, Patty, and I were walking across the street toward the beach the other day. Our street is just about the finest street in all of the North End, the city, the nation, and maybe the entire universe. Which means people here love each other.

We walked through the onslaught of love on the west side of the beach, where I'm the mayor for some stupid reason (not my own), and over to the east side where Butch "Kahuna" Calhoun is the mayor for the same reason I am on the west side: We both love people and have not just a talent but a gift for gab that tickles folks' funny bones right on down to their, uh, keisters, or souls, or whatever they got way down low where the pawpaws grow.

And there was my friend Jack, standing upright and tall just like he was supposed to.

The truth is, Jack was never supposed to stand upright and tall that way. Not after what happened to him one fine, dark day down at Sixtieth Street Beach, where love grows wild like pretty weeds you want to mow, but then realize that they are pretty so you let them take over your whole lawn and tell your neighbors you are doing a dunification project—going natural and letting your lawn turn back into dunes.

May 28, 2006, was just another fine, sunny day down at the beach for thousands of folks, including young Jack. He was down from his home in Charlottesville, staying at his parents' Sixtieth Street beach house. They spent the whole day, along with the rest of the street crew, down there just laughin' and sunnin' and funnin' and my-oh-my but wasn't that a good day, a day when you just smile and say, "Now ain't that God a fine old guy to give a day like this?"

But then Jack got hot and decided to take a swim to cool off. A hankerin' that has come across the noggins of many a lad down at the beach when the sun starts to toast you up and the beers that you've ingested decide that they'd like to take a swim too. So the both of you go on down to take a dip.

Being a young man in the prime of his life, Jack took off running because the water was cold and he wanted to get it over with quick versus walking out like a tortoise as the water turned him into a woman, freezing him from bottom to top.

Well, Jack did a pretty dive into the water, up and over a wave. But that wave had other ideas, and it reached up and spanked that boy's feet hard enough to send them straight up and him straight down into the shallow water where the hard sand waited, calling him down into darkness, down into the land of the creatures that can't walk but skitter around on the ocean floor, hoping no one will find them or, worse, step on them.

Jack's head hit the bottom, and it compressed his neck vertebrae to the point of no return. His neck broke right there on Sixtieth Street, where love flows like a river and death waits just over the next wave. His neck broke, and he was paralyzed, unable to move, floating there in the water. His girlfriend was hoping against hope that he was just goofing around, that he'd stand up with a laugh and walk out.

They ran to him and carried him out of the water. Into an

ambulance, his neck braced, no feeling in his body below his neck, his life over, darkness creeping in. To the hospital and the ER.

I found him there, and prayed over that boy with his mom and dad—Jack lying still on his bed, his parents aching and hoping and praying that God would save their boy, heal their boy, restore their boy. Both of them would have taken the fall, both would have given up their own necks to save his. Both would have given an arm, a leg, their life. Both ready to die so that their son would live. Because that's what parents do.

I asked Jack to move his hands, and he did. A little movement in his leg. Just a little, but a lot more than nothing—the nothingness he'd felt at the ocean when he started his life as a cripple. And so began the healing and restoration of Mr. Jack Rash. By all rights, he should have been in a wheelchair the rest of his life. He had crushed his neck. By all rights, he should have been dead.

But old God, why He was just laughing; He put his hand on Jack and raised that boy up just like Lazarus, just like the crippled young man (around Jack's age) carried to Jesus by his four friends for a healing touch in a town called Capernaum. Jesus did heal him and gave him new magic arms and legs.

God gave Jack magic legs too.

And so, there he was a year later, walking up to me with only a slight stutter to his step. Not many would even notice, but I work with folks with stutters in their step and others who spend a great deal of their lives in the world that Jack experienced for just a few months.

God hasn't told us yet the purpose of this miracle He performed on Jack. But there is a purpose to it, I can promise you that. Young Jack Rash is back, and a promise is alive in him that wasn't there before. Keep your eye on that boy because his temporary disability has given his heart a new supernatural ability and appreciation of life. His new life. And that is the end and the beginning of this fine Sixtieth Street Miracle story.

MY INFLATABLE HEART

Hammy and Randy busting a move.

FIFTEEN

Hamilton's Song

for Terri

JOHN KÖEHLER

> Remember to extol his work,
> which men have praised in song.

JOB 36:24

May 23, 2007

Dear Singers and Flingers,

Hamilton is a barge of a man, a mahogany mountain. He's the size of an NFL lineman, stands about six foot five, and comes into the room like the meekest of pussycats. Hammy is autistic, I think, or maybe mentally retarded, quite possibly ADHD. I don't rightly know because I never read the form his momma filled out and never asked her to tell me. Or if I did ask, it went in one ear, bounced around the empty spaces, and came on out the other ear, never to be heard from again.

Come on, I'm blaming it on my own disability. I may be old, but I am slow...

Truth is that Hamilton obviously has some things that aren't right about him, at least not "right" in the classic sense of normal behavior and actions. But shoot, I don't rightly care about normal or right because if I could act like Hammy and be more like him, I'd be a better man, plain and simple, God's honest truth.

Hamilton doesn't really know that he's all that big, and he comes at the world with the honesty and integrity of a four-year-old. But his heart is as ageless and ancient as the old trees that live on the edge of the desert, older than the disciples. Ancient as the oceans and the first creepy-crawly creatures that swam ashore. Ancient as the stars and the first breath of God that made it all with a laugh and a sigh, plus a tear to make the rain.

Hamilton is a lineman for God's team, and when you are with him, you are with God. That is exactly the way we are meant to carry God, as an incarnational representative of the One who made us. The problem is that we get in the way and make things too complicated, while God reaches down and gives us His simple love and whispers sweet everythings into the ears of our souls.

Hammy loves to dance and is very gentle when he's dancing, being careful not to hurt anyone with his giant body. We all danced last night at club, and everyone went nuts when "YMCA" came on, no one knowing or caring that part of the song is about gay folks. Truth be told, if they came to Capernaum, we'd love them the same as everyone else with a disability.

Now ain't that the way it's supposed to be? No judgment, just love.

Well sir or ma'am, or mister or master of the universe, or whoever you are, I had the microphone, on account of being diagnosed early on with a mighty bad case of diarrhea of the mouth, at least according to my daddy. And in the middle of "YMCA," when the fellows were belting out the words, I put the mic in front of Hammy and said, "Sing!"

And he did sing, while I looked behind me to see who had grabbed the other microphone and started singing. It was a rich, deep ,and beautiful voice, in tune, in time, and whoever it was knew the words.

I turned back around and realized that it was Hamilton's song.

He was singing along, and he was wonderful. Miss Angela West was about fit to bust sitting there in her wheelchair, screaming and flappin' her arms like a beautiful whooping crane come in to land at her nest so she could preen her baby chicks with her loving touch. She told me later she wanted to cry when Hamilton sang but was too busy laughing and grooving in the moment.

When the laughing and crying and grooving all mix together into one electric moment of love and laughter and intense emotion, the Holy Spirit is there like a long lost and forgotten cousin.

When the song ended, everyone went nuts and screamed and shouted for Mr. Hamilton. He smiled and looked around, his big beautiful head bobbing in the perennial motion of his cranial flow. Why, of course, he knew the song and the words. That's what he does. But weren't we all surprised with our mouths flapping open like big old pieholes, disbelief fighting with the evidence we had just seen before our very eyes.

So everyone touched Hammy and patted his back like a bunch of doubting Thomas's. We planned when we would get Hammy to sing next because we knew that we had another savant in our midst.

God blesses all our hearts with His savant love, and we never know when it's going to pop out of us in the form of an amazing talent or gift that confounds us as to the reason. Because sometimes there is no reason other than to please God.

And anyone lucky enough to be there.

Love and sugar cookies,

John

Melissa is God's favorite beauty queen.

SIXTEEN

Melissa

for Hugh & Douglass

JOHN KÖEHLER

The king is enthralled by your beauty;
honor him, for he is your lord.

PSALM 45:11

Melissa is a beautiful young woman. Perhaps not in the classical way that we typically refer to beauty, but in every other way her beauty soars above that of other women who know every trick and buy every cure for their perceived lack of perfection.

If there were a beauty contest that judged only according to the standards of society, Melissa would never make it through the first round. She is overweight, has a slightly misshapen face, and can't do much in the way of singing or dancing. She would quite simply not ding any of the bells needed for advancing in a beauty contest today.

If—on the other hand—you held a contest that was based on heartfelt grace and inner beauty, Melissa would certainly be noticed and considered by the judges. Her shyness would be seen for what it is: deep-seated humility bred from fear of rejection and massive waves of self-doubt, an ocean of doubt.

Her reserve and gentleness would be seen as a gift from God, while her kindness would be felt by all and honored according to the beauty marks and standards sent down from heaven. Gentleness would be seen as one of her strongest qualities. It is impossible to look into the eyes of this young beauty and not be moved with wonder and compassion and appreciation for what God has made.

My personal radar goes off for many reasons when women are involved. The most commonly known form of radar intercepts by men is based on receiving physical signals about a woman. A quick sweep of the active radar system reveals her in detail, and the random access memory performs a match against the interior logic system. My system finds her attractive and locks onto her.

Which of course means we keep looking!

Now another part of my radar deals with more than just my brain stem needs; it collects signals from people who light up my heart and soul. Melissa lights up my soul radar, and I can't help but notice her. The signal comes back in a powerful way, and my heart responds and says, "Oh what a beauty is she! Stop and bask in the glow of her. Tell her she is beautiful. Adore her and love her."

Like all of us Melissa just wants to be loved and accepted into the family. Into your family and mine. She wants to be understood and seen as a valuable human being with real purpose instead of a disposable object of scorn and rejection.

She wants to fit in, and the yearning for that is powerful and drives her like a root level directive. She does not understand this powerful need within her, but it is there. The rest of us know we seek the same things that Melissa does, but her need is more refined than ours because it is simpler.

There is a strange fallacy that human interaction and acceptance must be complicated in order to be successful. Therefore we complicate the process of accepting each other by building layers in our lives and performing a ritualistic breakdown in order to expose our wiring—our inner self—to another human. We build up these layers of protection because we think we need to guard our hearts from loss and from others who might try to steal them from us or snatch them when we're not looking.

We build gates and moats and iron-clad doors around the dungeons of our hearts, and we swallow the key. Then we sit back and dare someone—anyone—to try to storm the Bastille that is our heart. We watch as they slam into the tough defenses we have built, bravely attempting to find a way in to claim the treasures we hold. We laugh at them.

Melissa does not know how to build such defenses. Her heart lies exposed inside of her, within easy reach and for all to see. She does not hide it because she does not know how to hide it. Hiding it would be like hiding her skin. How does one do that? Melissa doesn't know how to protect her heart from the world. It is a great treasure of God that glints and glows like gold when you finally reach the end of the rainbow.

Melissa glows. She is, in fact, the end of the rainbow, but no one can see that because you cannot see the rainbow when you are in it. You cannot recognize the brilliance of the light when you are inside the light. People look away because her radiance is just too much to look upon. They look away and don't understand, so they call her ugly and pity her and her lack of normalcy.

They thank God that they are not like her; meanwhile Melissa wishes she were like them. Neither quite understands how special she is or that God has made her inside-out beautiful for a purpose and a mission, hidden inside the rainbow of her life.

If you turn your head, you can see her heart glowing. If you come up close to her and hug her and look into her eyes, you will see the glint of the treasure shining out. Stare into her eyes long enough, and you will forget your toes, and your heart will beat a little louder because when you strip away all of the layers and scars from your heart, there is only one thing left to see: the face of God.

To look upon Melissa is to look upon the face of God. She is a beauty queen of the finest kind, the heavenly kind. She is a kingdom beauty and God's favorite, and to behold Melissa is to behold the very beauty of God, when the garden was first green and from His laughter grew His first daughter, so beautiful and radiant.

Melissa is God's favorite daughter, so beautiful and radiant. The world is a better place—a much more beautiful and pleasing place—because she is here with us, even just for a little while.

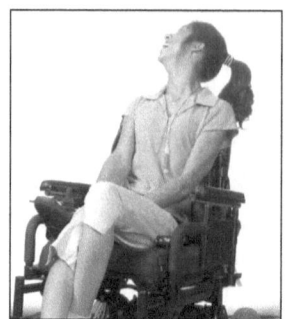
Angela in heaven.

SEVENTEEN

East, North, South & West

for Daphne

> *People will come from east and west and north and south, and will take their places at the feast in the kingdom of God.*
>
> LUKE 13:29

Angela West rolled into our first club in Chesapeake like an angel on wheels. I freely admit that I immediately fell in love with her. This actually happens a lot with me and women. In fact, it happens with most people I meet, regardless of gender.

There is this intense moment and series of moments when I kind of devour their spirits and consume their hearts so I can remember them and know them. What a horrible illustration of how not to do agape! But it tends to work for me, if perhaps leaving my "victims" with an uneasy feeling about the spiritual ectoplasm that they can vaguely sense sticking to them upon my departure.

Must . . . wash . . . self.

When Angela arrived that night at New Life Great Bridge Church, I threw down my flag and said, "I submit to the torture of your heart! I give in and give myself to you as your loyal subject. I am your spiritual slave. Do with me as you will."

Dude, take it easy; she's just a chick in a wheelchair!

Like Allen, Regina, and A. J. before her, Angela has CP. But before I describe her, you should know that she lit up my radar and turned my head for more reasons than just having a swell wheelchair and cerebral palsy. Chicks in hot wheelchairs are a dime a dozen in Capernaum, figuratively speaking. No big deal.

I quickly took in Angela's physical appearance. How her nose squinched up as part of her palsy and was an integral part of her expression, along with her ever-present smile. Her hair was brushed and in a clip. She had a cell phone velcroed to her seat in easy reach of her shaking hands. It seemed impossible that she could actually use it, but she could and did as I came to find out soon enough. She was dressed in a nice shirt and jeans. Her thin legs were crossed, and on her feet were a pair of running shoes, perhaps a hopeful thought, bobbing slightly out of and above her foot rests.

I knelt down beside Angela and introduced myself while the pandemonium of club continued around me: pumping hip-hop music, kids running around laughing, autistic kids with their hands over their ears, introductions and hugs and high fives. Wonderful sounds that pleased God so much that He joined us right then and there in the sanctuary of the blessed church that invited us to use their space and their people. Their love was splashed across the chairs and the altar, the entire space. The aroma of God. Ahhhh.

I asked Angela if she wanted to get out of her wheelchair, and she said yes. Or at least I thought she said yes. It seemed that way, and I usually don't wait around for permission or second-guessing, much less prayerful consideration of an answer. Look, God did not make me a prayerful man in the classic sense. I talk to the Old Dude all the time and am in constant communication with Him. The rest of the time I just act like it would be okay with Him.

I unbuckled her foot straps and seat belt, and then hugged her carefully under the arms and lifted her out of her chair. Then I lay her down on the carpet, on her back. Continuing my insane undertaking, I proceeded to show her a series of wrestling moves, while also playfully, uh, tickling her.

I know that you can just about hear the "click" of the handcuffs that should have gone on me at that point, because later I wondered the same thing as I beat myself up about being so stupid and forward with a woman I had just met.

I knew that God had sent me here, had made me in a way that allows me to break through the traditional barriers of social niceties. He did not make me to be His subtle slingshot, delivering small doses of love and reality. He made me His nuclear bomb, intended to destroy the barriers people build around their hearts.

My method is to explode my way in, to utterly destroy their defenses so that my Father can walk in and take over their hearts. That is my calling. The problem is that God would like to be the one pulling the trigger to my actions, and I sometimes confuse my desire with His. Dang it all!

After a few goofy minutes of me as the huge, hairy, clownish guy mock wrestling with a quadriplegic chick on the sanctuary floor of a church (can you smell the fire and brimstone?), I came to my senses and sat back on my heels, laughing down at Angela.

She rolled over, got up on her knees, and crab walked over to where her very shocked friend Melody was sitting. I think Melody must have been conflicted about my behavior with Angela, and she was not sure whether to take a chair to me, call the police, or lay hands on me and ask God to remove the demon that had taken possession of my body. Or all of the above.

I had this immediate crushing feeling of doom and was (once again) overcome with a complete sense of stupidity and horror at my actions. I was actually physically revolted at myself for a few quick moments. I figured that I had ruined it all with Angela, that we would never see her again. I figured she would turn me in to Scott Hamilton (may his cigars ever burn), my life would end as I knew it, and I would finally get my just rewards and become a homeless vagrant with no friends, no family, no money.

But the show had to go on, so I got up and tried to forget about Angela. We had a great club that night, but I say that about every club, so you probably can't trust me completely when I talk about being with our amazing people.

I left for home that night with my usual Capernaum buzz, which as far as I know is a legal controlled substance in the United States. I was feeling pretty good as I rewound and replayed the night, like a coach going over the game film. What went well, and was worthy of doing again? What went well and could never be planned, but was just God showing up and doing magic? What did not go well and why? What could we do better?

I thought about Angela, and I just felt bad. Really bad. My heart actually hurt inside of me, and I was depressed about it. I fell in love with this woman from the first moment we met, a beautiful young woman who rolled her way into Capernaum on a magic carpet.

She came in search of what God had for her, but I was sure she was also there for me. And then I ruined it all for her and for Capernaum by being the world's biggest jerk. I beat myself up about this all the way home. Maybe I would remember this the next time and not be such a jerk. But how do you tell a wolf to act like a sheep? I was just being myself, the way I was intended to be.

I went to shut down my computer that night around ten thirty and checked my e-mail one more time. There was an e-mail from Angela. I was elated and frightened at the same time. I didn't know what to expect.

Here is the e-mail she sent me:

John,

Hey! It is Angela! I hope you don't mind me e-mailing you. I just have to tell you what a blessing tonight was. I thought I was going to be in tears when I left. It is amazing how God works. I asked God a few months ago if there was an opportunity to mix my two passions, God and working with people with disabilities. I was getting frustrated because I did not hear anything from HIM. Then Kerri e-mailed from school and told me about YL. I was so upset because I have classes Wednesday nights. Then Melody was like they have one on Tuesday night. I came with no clue what to expect. God blew me away. I absolutely love the participants and the staff. The interactions just blessed me beyond words. After all, who would take a girl after they just met her and put her on the floor? Only you. I know it was only a joke, but that just said a lot to my heart. I never had a youth club where it was okay to be me. I thank God He called you to do this. I know you have a lot of leaders, and I don't want to impose on my welcome, but I am interested in serving. I understand if you have plenty of help right now. I just wanted you to know my heart. Thank you!

    Angela West
    Jeremiah 29:11

Angela West went on to become a senior leader, then part-time staff with Capernaum. She is co-leader of Chesapeake Capernaum and will become our intern in September 2008. If you tell me to pray about this, I will tell you that my prayer for Angela has been going on for two years and will continue forever.

Chuckie is always happy to see you.

EIGHTEEN

Matthew & Peter

for Rico & Mick

> "Lord, if it's you," Peter replied,
> "tell me to come to you on the water."
>
> MATTHEW 14:28

June 13, 2007

The two fellows in this story were named after the ancient disciples. They are, in a sense, modern disciples even though they've never been properly inducted.

Of course, I don't reckon there was a ceremony of any kind for the twelve way back when the J-man walked the earth and called His people out to learn about love and how to fish like it was always intended. I think their induction ceremony was the rest of their lives and the very process of growing closer to God and helping others do the same.

There was a place called Capernaum in Virginia Beach, and in that place and at that particular time there was a club. It happened at King's Grant Baptist Church on June 7, 2007. Mick and Rico were doing the club talk, and they decided, in their finite wisdom, to go around during pizza time and ask folks what they were afraid of.

Gee, that sounds uplifting.

Generally speaking, I'd think this was just another dumb idea to write in the Book of Stupid Human Tricks. But even though I didn't think it was such a good idea, those two fellows quickly had a hat full of kid's fears.

They started pulling out the fears, which had been written on slips of paper, and reading them, one by one. One was the fear of the dark. One of dogs. One of being left out, another of not being accepted. Well, my jaw started to drop wide open, and I got a tad-bit teary-eyed. The thing was, everyone could relate to the fears, and most of us had shared those fears a time or six.

After listing off and talking about all of our fears, Rico and Mick (he ain't Italian, by the way) started talking about how God can take away all of our fears. They shared Scripture, and it was wonderful. You could almost feel and hear the pieces of God's Lego machine dropping into place, and everyone's hearts were glowing like little baby lanterns in a Japanese painting.

Then I asked, "How the heck would God find a way to take away all our fears?"

That's when a new kid named Matthew started spazzing out and waving his arms around like he was having a fit. But he wasn't having a fit. Matthew has cerebral palsy and hangs out in an awesome powered chair that he drives, thank you very much. He can't talk but uses a computer to communicate, showing off his crisp intelligence. So I walked right over to that boy and looked down at his computer screen, and there on the screen, throbbing to a digital pulse, were the numbers 3.16

I knew right then that I was in the midst of another God moment, and I lost all power to think. I completely forgot the verse that I had already memorized and said, "Matthew says John 3:16. Can anyone tell me that verse?" I was so caught up and amazed that I could not remember it, but I think that was the plan. Sometimes God uses our ignorance to allow others to shine.

It was Peter's turn to shine.

He sat in the back of the room, looking like a fifty-year-old derelict, bald on top with long clown-like tufts of hair flowing out from the sides and back of his head. He was missing some front teeth. He smiled a lot, but he is the last guy you'd figure would know much at all about God's Word. Because that is reserved for the few, the proud, the perfect priests that God has selected for that purpose . . . right? Wrong.

Peter raised his hand, and when I called on him, he recited the entire verse perfectly. There was not a sound while he was speaking, as everyone there realized something special was going on. When he was done, the whole place exploded with applause, and Peter and Matthew were God's heroes. Our heroes.

A long time ago God picked another Peter and Matthew to be His heroes. But today we all have the chance to be heroes like Matthew or Peter and do God's work. If God can use a young crippled man with a computer and an old derelict dude without many teeth to do His work, then why not you and me? Tell me why not?

When I see God use the Peters and the Matthews of the world, it gives me hope that all of us can be used. No matter our disabilities or our abilities. No matter how smart or slow. No matter how eloquent or silent. God can and will use us.

The only question is: Will we let Him?

Timmy & his Buddy Troy (arm shown).

NINETEEN

A Surfer Named Timmy

for Troy

Troy Smith is a friend of mine, a huge, bald man who loves the Lord and loves to surf. He works with kids in a ministry of the waves and worked with Timmy at Capernaum's surf camp.

The photo above is beautiful. Remember that Timmy is a quadriplegic; his arms and legs are physically disabled due to cerebral palsy. If you look behind him, you can see Troy's arm holding Timmy onto the board. The rest of him is hidden behind the boy that he is serving and teaching.

This is a true picture of Capernaum. By guiding and hiding ourselves behind the people we serve, we allow them to shine and ride the waves of glory straight home to the shores of God.

> This is why I sent Timothy to you earlier.
> He is also my dear son, and true to the Master.

I CORINTHIANS 4:17

September 9, 2007

We had our Second Annual Capernaum Surf Camp on August 17. It was great. Folks started showing up at my house a tad before four that afternoon as I ran around getting things ready. If I ever get to the point where it becomes more important to get things ready than to welcome folks, I hope someone will whop me upside the head. So I welcomed them *while* I got ready. Hmmmm, I think that's in 1 Fastidius somewhere or another:

> In your haste to prepare the feast, let not your heart be kept from its appointed task to welcome and love your guests.

So there I was, running around like a wild man, tossing out hugs and high-fives on the run, left and right, while Mr. Sun marched across the sky and cars rolled in. Another trip back to the house for something or another and then back out again. I stopped and turned to the driveway, and there before me was a young stranger in a wheelchair. Intruder!

His name was Timmy, and he had come with his mom and another mom with her daughter, also a candidate for Capernaum. Timmy was waving at me from across the yard, his entire upper body wagging back and forth like a happy dog's tail. Naturally I answered the summons and—being part-dog myself—responded to the call.

I knelt next to his wheelchair, and we went through the introductions. Then I asked him by what right did he come to my house to surf, and could he prove that he was strong enough to do it? He grabbed my hand, and we arm wrestled there beneath the pine tree, and I pronounced young Timmy fit to try his hand on a surfboard that day. He just smiled and wagged his body at me, another eleven-year-old boy challenged by the bearded boy who never grew up.

Down to the ocean we rocked and rolled, the moms and dads and swimmers and surfers. The foam surfboards were carried to the shore, all twelve of them a rainbow of colors, crying out for young bodies to carry them out to their home in the waves.

Timmy had on his life vest and his water shoes and had been slathered in suntan lotion and his mother's love; he was completely drenched in the lovely mess. He said, "Take me!" and so we did. Out to the waves that beckoned and threatened those with able bodies and terrified those with bodies made broken and weak.

All except for A. J., who never got the memo about people with CP being careful in the water, much less the ocean where undertows abound and sharks wait to nip off the toes of hapless swimmers. A. J. put on the armor of God, which looked exactly like a life vest, and threw himself into the water with complete abandon as spectators and parents watched in horrified wonder, imagining the headlines about the poor disabled man who had been stupid enough to swim in the ocean.

I laughed as I watched A. J. swim out and get knocked over again and again by waves. Some nearby bystanders came to his aid, but I stopped them, saying, "No, he's okay. Leave him alone. Let him be." A. J. is a man, and part of being a man is to do all that you can for yourself to live life big, baby, big.

Timmy saw A. J. too. He saw this man who, like him, had cerebral palsy. He saw A. J. and wanted to be like him. But he could not hide the shudders of fear that created their own waves in his frail body. His courage couldn't hide the other signs of fear that possessed him: the flaring nostrils, the dilated, wide-open eyes, and the clutching lunges he made to remain in the arms of the man who become an island for him that day in the water.

I was Timmy's island, but soon he was facedown on his surfboard. His terror increased, and he was sure that death awaited him that day, on that beach, with those people. Had he told his mom that he loved her and done the other things in his short life that needed finishing before he died?

We turned him away from the crashing waves and the people on shore and pointed out the jumping dolphin and boats going by, along with the other kids doing exactly what he was doing. Troy and I discussed the proper method of helping Timmy catch and ride the wave, and then . . . we caught a wave.

Troy was at the back of the board, and I was at the middle. We caught a small wave, and I rode in with Timmy. At the moment when we were through the worst part of the break, I let him go so he could surf on his own. Mucho importanto. (I made that up, so if it really is Spanish, then I just got lucky.) Timmy needed to surf on his own for a bit, and by golly, the boy did.

Of course, I forgot about one of the laws of surfing: Do not ride your board up on to the sand. The reason—aside from scratching up the bottom of your board—is that the fins at the back of the board will catch in the sand while you continue at the speed you were going before the shore got in the way.

Well, the board stopped, and Timmy went shooting forward like a small cannonball, rolling over and over a few times, up into the foam and the flotsam of the wave end. I laughed and said, "Whoohoo!" while his mom and her friend cried out, "Oh dear God, nooooo!" and ran down to save Timmy from his death. Upon seeing and hearing them, Timmy got even more scared. They lifted him up and prepared to take him back to the safety of the shore and the quiet life of a good disabled boy.

I don't think so! I grabbed the board, walked up and grabbed Timmy, and carried them both back out to the water to catch another wave. Fortunately, whatever his mom said to me was washed out by the happy cries of the seagulls and waves. Timmy and Troy and I caught a bunch more waves, and every one of them washed a little more of his fears away.

By the end of the day, we were hanging out on the shore trading surfer lingo and signs. Jim Howley, a Virginia Beach club leader, approached Timmy.

Jim: Hey, dude, what's up?
Timmy: Are you a surfer?
Jim: Nope.
Timmy: I am.

After the surfing was over, we walked and rolled across the street to my house and had a pizza party. It was fun. Awards were given out to anyone and everyone. Shoot, complete strangers would have been given an award just for showing up. Then it was time to say good-bye.

Once again Timmy wagged his body back and forth, but this time it was for a hug. I knelt down and leaned in to give him a hug and a kiss on the cheek. But he stopped me, put his hands on my big head, and pulled me in to kiss me on the mouth. Now look, I know that grown men are not supposed to go around kissing young boys on the mouth. Seems kind of sketchy or strange, but this was not strange at all; it was as natural as kissing your own little brother good-bye.

Here's the thing: Timmy kisses people in his family that way—his mom, dad, brothers, sisters, and extended family. That was his way of inviting me into the heart of his family. His kiss of peace and love was a way to say that he loved me as his big brother, his uncle, his grand pop, his family.

Even now as I write this, I get misty thinking about it. We are all, each and every one of us, called to treat each other like family, to love each other like family. I have known this since I was a little kid, but I also know that it is not always an easy thing to achieve, considering the sorry state of this world.

But here's the other thing: We're not called to love the world. We're called to love God's people. And if we all were created by Him and in His image, then every time we love someone, we are loving God.

I am thankful for Timmy reminding this big lunkhead about the simple things in life. Love one another and trust one another. Okay, Timmy, I'm on it, little brother.

Thanks for the reminder!

I have not seen Timmy since that day on the beach. I have no way of getting in touch with him because we did not get any contact information from his mom.

In my jealous memory I believe that God brought Timmy there for me that day. It felt like I had known him all my life, and on that day he just dropped in to tell me that he loved me. He came for me because he knew I needed him that day: I did.

My heart swelled so much that day because of a little boy in a wheelchair who became a surfer and will remain a surfer all his life. When someone swells my heart in that way, I can go on forever and a day, using the love gases he gave me to float high above the kingdom of heaven. One day I will be in heaven, and there I will surf the clouds with Timmy, my little love brother.

P.S. Wheelchairs are not allowed in heaven.

Ruben can tell you all about the Bible.

TWENTY

Ruben

for Marge

JOHN KÖEHLER

―――※・◆・※―――
"Let Reuben live and not die, but just barely,
in diminishing numbers."
―――※・◆・※―――

DEUTERONOMY 33:6

November 23, 2007

Ruben is a very cool guy. He seems at first blush like a combination rocker/biker/disciple dude. He is somewhere in his thirties I think. He certainly is outside of Capernaum's typical age range of eleven to twenty-five. What, a disabled old interloper who dares to attend our club? Ack! Throw the cheater out! Be gone, demon seed! Off with his head!

Speaking of heads, Ruben's is bald. It is filled with brain matter that somewhere along the line—either before or after he was born—was altered in a way that produced unusual and atypical effects. I'm sorry to say that I never read the file on Ruben, so I can't tell you exactly what his story is, what his diagnosis is, or what ails him. But shoot, I never read the file on most of my friends, and I do a pretty good job figuring them out. So why not Ruben?

Not that I've become an expert at diagnosing the medical or therapeutic aspects of any given Capernaum person I meet, much less an able-bodied person. Aside from the need to know about certain medical things to provide safety with regard to meds, etc., I just want to know what makes them tick, what makes them happy and sad, what their hot buttons are, and how to tear down the walls of their hearts. Just so with Ruben.

Ruben's intelligence is wide and crosses many areas, though he tends to limit his focus to certain things, including heavy-metal music, being a disciple, and becoming a part of his church leadership. Music for Ruben is as it is for most folks: a guide to who he is, a marker of his personality, and a way to express himself without speaking. He likes hard rock—AC/DC is at the top of his list and always on his mind, not to mention on his head due to the AC/DC watch cap he likes to wear.

Speaking can be a little difficult for Ruben because of his stuttering and pauses as he waits for words to drop into place. Ruben's vocabulary is just fine, but his brain is like a gearbox with unaligned gears. His mind knows the word it wants and orders it from storage. But the delivery gears tend to shoot a little short or long, so Ruben must nudge it until the word drops into place. The nudging is indicated by the stutters and pauses, exactly replicating the mental gears stuttering and moving his words into place.

Ruben is also nearly blind and tends to stare off into space because he can't see much and as a way to fill the gaps while his words drop into place. Yet he can quickly tell who you are when you approach, perhaps by shape and for sure by your voice. When he reads, he holds the book within inches of his eyes and slowly picks out the words, sounding like a first-grade reader. But his intelligence about the things that interest him is borderline savant.

When we have Bible quizzes with the kids on camp trips or at club, Ruben can be counted on to answer almost all the questions correctly. Which makes him a Bible scholar in Capernaum and, by extension, everywhere he goes. He does not fit the look of a typical Bible scholar, yet he is. Where is it written that a Bible scholar has to look or speak a certain way?

Does God only give wisdom to His beautiful and perfect people? Gosh, I hope not because then we're all in trouble!

Ruben shows some autistic tendencies in terms of the way he interacts with the world. He may remain socially disconnected for a stretch and then suddenly engages. When he does engage, it can be without the proper words of introduction; he often throws himself at the person with a directness and honesty that can be extreme. He also shows certain obsessive-compulsive disorder (OCD) tendencies like repeating himself short term and long term, getting hung up on a theme, and constantly calling anyone silly enough to give out his phone number. Uh, that would be me.

Because he's OCD, Ruben usually calls me five or six times a week. He never leaves a message because he probably doesn't want to bother me, but then he can't stop the compulsion within a day or two of trying again. It usually looks and sounds like this:

Call 1
Ring Ring Ring
Caller ID: Ruben
I don't answer.

Call 2
Ring Ring Ring
Caller ID: Ruben
I don't answer.

Call 3
Ring Ring Ring
Caller ID: Ruben
I don't answer.

Call 4
Ring Ring Ring
Caller ID: Ruben
I don't answer.

Call 5
Ring Ring Ring
Caller ID: Ruben
I answer.

Me: Hi, Rueben!

Ruben: Hi, John, what you been up to?

Me: Oh, just hangin' out, workin', and havin' fun. What about you, Ruben?

Ruben: I'm at work ruh ruh right now.

Me: Is it okay for you to talk on the phone at work, Ruben?

Ruben: Uh huh. Do you like AC/DC?

Me: I like them, dude, but I don't have any of their music.

Ruben: I love AC/DC!

Me: Awesome, dude. Hey, Ruben, I gotta go work, and so do you, okay?

Ruben: Okay, bye-bye.

I love how Ruben says bye. Bye-bye, with an emphasis on the second word. There is something beautiful in the way he says it, with a kind of implied hope that we'll meet again. I like the way he says it so much that I've taken to using the Ruben method myself. Bye-bye! Upbeat...

Like most folks Ruben desires to be accepted, especially by that part of the world he has been excluded from due to his disabilities and people's inability to open their lives and hearts to those who don't look and sound like them. Ruben would like nothing more than to walk into a group of able-bodied people at his church or anywhere and be completely accepted as one of them. But this will never be because a gulf separates him from folks; one look at his face with the confirmation of his manner of speech, and people place Ruben squarely in the "Others" category.

"Others" means anyone other than their kind of people but—in Ruben's case—to be other than them is even worse because he is "not quite right," or perhaps "mentally ill" or "unstable." People are uncomfortable around Ruben because he refuses to accept his rightful place as an outsider and continues to show up and insist on membership. Who does he think he is?

Ruben knows exactly who he is. He knows that he is different. He is intelligent enough to see that people think he's strange. But that doesn't stop his desire to be accepted by those who refuse to accept him. To fit in with his able-bodied peers would complete his life and give him the thing he desires the most: normality. So he constantly runs toward that quest and pushes himself upon others for that purpose.

At camp Ruben would hang out with our people to a point, and then he would ask to go roam outside with the insiders—the able-bodied, the normal. I would let him go because I knew this was part of what Ruben needed and also because it would create crossover moments with the "typicals" who he met and spoke with. He was smart enough to ask, and I was smart enough to allow it.

One day at camp Ruben had to stay with his own people. The speaker had given the invitation for kids to make a decision for Jesus, and we were going to have twenty minutes of complete silence. Some people would go outside near the lake, some on the porch. Everyone was alone in individual contemplation. Except for Capernaum. We needed to make sure our kids understood what we being said and offered, so we stayed inside the club room and broke into small groups, with leaders helping campers.

Ruben—true to form—asked me if he could go "hang outside." He wanted to be out there, a free-range man, God's disciple, able to talk to and hang out with the people he was not, the able-bodied, non-disabled, perfect people without a care in the world. So he came to me and asked permission to go and be with his wannabe group.

I said, "Ruben, we've got a bunch of kids in here who need help. They need help from people like you who get it already. Because many of them don't get it, and they're confused. So I need you to stay inside here with our people. In fact, I need you to talk to Drew here. Tell him about what Jesus means to you and help him figure out what Jesus means to him."

Ruben looked at me for a few beats and then said okay. I made the rounds to the other groups to be sure that we didn't have any kids wandering, upset, or without the chance to ask questions and express themselves. After all, the Gospel can seem confusing and complicated. There's the pain and death that Jesus went through, and sin that we all have hidden and not hidden inside of us. God can seem beyond their simple understanding of Him, so we try our best to keep God simple: He loves you so much He sent Jesus to pay your way into heaven. All you have to do is believe in Jesus and follow Him. Any questions?

Ruben helped Drew through his questions, and when we were done, twenty minutes later, I returned to find them still talking. I asked Drew if he understood what he and Ruben had discussed, and he said he did. I asked him if he wanted to make a decision about Jesus, and he said yes, he wanted to follow Him; he believed in Him.

God completed the foursome just then, and I was moved as we prayed Drew into the kingdom of heaven. I turned to Ruben, who stood there with an enigmatic smile, rocking a little, looking around in his blindness. I said, "Ruben, what did you do here?"

He stopped rocking, looked at me, and said, "I helped him make a decision for Christ."

I said, "Yeah, you did, Ruben. This is one of the ways that God is using you as a junior leader. This is proof that you can make a difference and be useful for God." Ruben smiled and started rocking as I continued to lift him up and talk about being a junior leader for Capernaum. After I paused, he asked me the burning question, the question of him becoming accepted by all God's people.

"Do you think I can use this to become a leader at my church? And do you think you can help me and my mom find some other regular ministries for people my age?"

After he had helped a disabled man find his way to Jesus, Ruben still wanted the thing that had been denied him all his life: complete acceptance. Agape love is an easy thing to say, but a harder thing to do. We all want to be with people who are like us, not with people who make us uncomfortable. That would mean we have to get out of the boat and walk on water, get out of the comfort zone of our petty lives and become bigger than we are.

But don't worry, Ruben and millions more like him are not going away. They are constantly knocking on the doors of your heart, waiting to be invited in. Waiting to be included and accepted just like the rest of your friends. Agape is just a worthless Greek word unless it is put to work. And the really big question is this: Are you ready and willing to get out of the boat and walk on the water of agape?

Ruben called me once and as usual wanted to know what I was doing. I told him that I was working on my club talk, the talk I give at the end of club that has some message from Jesus mixed in with a personal story about myself.

He asked me what the theme was going to be, and I told him it was about how Jesus knocked on doors, including the doors of our hearts. I asked him if he knew of any scriptures about that theme and he rattled off four from memory, including one I hadn't found.

Wow, who would have thought that a nearly blind, mentally challenged, obsessive compulsive man could help a cool guy like me develop a talk. I did and I still do. Ruben is the cool guy in my book. I think I'll start calling him when I plan my talks.

After all, why go to Bible Gateway online, when I have my own personal Ruben.com to call on.

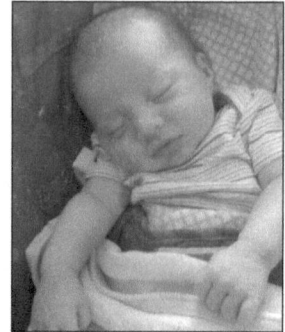
Lilli dreams while Granddaddy writes.

TWENTY-ONE

Easter Lilli

for Kimmi & Jeremy

JOHN KÖEHLER

I am a rose of Sharon, a lily of the valleys.

SONG OF SOLOMON 2:1

As Easter approaches, the Easter lilies grow unseen beneath the ground. Their bulbs send out shoots that rise for the surface. They seek the light of day, the wind, and the rain that will help them grow so they can share their treasures with the world. And oh what treasures they share!

First, the green shoots appear and poke through the top edges of the soil. They grow up and climb toward heaven, in a hurry to display the purpose and reason for their lives. Out grow the green arms to lend support and bend down in supplication. Covered hearts unfold and rise up to prepare for the celebration of life.

At last the petals release and fall back in white perfection while the world sighs in wonder and thanksgiving for God's fulfillment of new life, an eternal promise each year. Even their smell is a promise that reminds us of Easter and how death begets life in nature as it did two thousand years ago when God's own Easter lily came and displayed His beauty for us, died, and then rose again in another eternal promise.

God shows us how to be like the lilies of the field that never die but come back again to share His glory. If He gives them the chance to be born again, then why not us? Doesn't He care more about us then He does even the most beautiful of flowers?

This year was no different for the lilies of our field. They were growing, and we knew it. What we did not know was that one very special Easter lily was growing inside the belly of our daughter, Kimmi. We did not know this because she had not told us, and we had no evidence of the new miracle growing within the fertile soil of her life.

Kimmi and her fiancé, Jeremy, were (and are) engaged and did not plan to have kids until after they were married and had finished college. But alas, their plans changed when God broke off a small piece of His heart and put it inside His beloved Lilli, daughter of Kimmi and Jeremy; she began to grow.

When they told Patty and I, we were ecstatic. Eventually this gave way to concern and a desire to help them prepare for the birth of their little Easter Lilli. Patty began calling Kimmi every day while I prepared budgets and lists of things to do. We all worked furiously to correct what the world might call a mistake, at least in terms of timing and legalities.

But God does not make mistakes, and the truth is, He expects us to accept our fate as if it is all part of God's plan for us and therefore a very good thing indeed. Regardless of any notions about how it might have been better if they were actually married (even though the institution of marriage has been rendered nearly worthless for half the population), the simple fact was that a baby was coming.

A baby was coming. Baby Lilli.

From that perspective all other things lose importance. Who cares what the world thinks? I would rather have a legitimately loved and adored baby out of wedlock than a mistreated child in a legal marriage. Which arrangement does God find legitimate—that founded in love or in legality? Let the union begin with love and end with marriage as a way of ceremoniously celebrating that love; otherwise the ceremony is a sham doomed to failure for the couple and success for the divorce attorneys.

Babies are not always planned, nor do they always come when we would prefer. They come in response to the love that made them whether in marriage or out. The love of parents for their children has nothing to do with the institution of marriage but everything to do with their love for each other and the promise that God has for their child.

The lilies of the field come whether or not we are ready for them. In the same way this Lilli was coming, so we chose to get ready and concentrate on the fact that she would be surrounded by love. We were going to be grandparents, part of the wall of love that would protect and surround her.

When I think about that, it changes everything for me. I can't wait to hold my grandchild in my arms. I can't wait to watch her grow up and help her learn to love and play and live like I did her mommy. I can't wait to be able to give her back when I'm done! Pretty funny but true . . . just as the smell of the cow manure makes the lilies so beautiful. Even so, I know how to change a diaper!

In some ways I think God has brought Lilli along for me because I feel such a strong sense of wonder about her and a strong sense of promise in her. I know she is going to change my life, most assuredly for the better; she already has. Because I will not be saddled with the concerns of parenting her, I can concentrate on the very best parts of being a granddad: loving her and being with her.

When you stop to think about it, isn't that what we are called to do with everyone? Of course it is. Yet we bring so much baggage to the table of life, and our love becomes burdened with things that dilute it and reduce the perfect vitality and joy we are called to give. I wish I could love everyone that way, the way I aim to love my little Lilli of the field.

Already she is real and alive to me. Already I can see her and imagine how we will be together for an eternity of days. Already I look forward to the new seasons of my life when God will show me His promise by growing up yet another beautiful Easter Lilli.

John Koehler with Donovan, a member of Norfolk and Chesapeake clubs. Photo by Glen McClure.

PART THREE

ME, MYSELF, AND I

MY INFLATABLE HEART

Tree and another hot chick, Janna.

TWENTY-TWO

I wanna Go Home

for Tree

JOHN KÖEHLER

Then the disciples went back to their homes.

JOHN 20:10

Toward the end of 2007 my good buddy and extremely pushy accountability partner Tree decided we should do one of those pesky "Bible in a Year" things. Now arguing against this with a strong Christian is like arguing against wearing a flag pin with a Republican; generally speaking it ain't a good idea, and you will not win the argument.

Shoot, I read the Bible plenty. Maybe not as often as some folks would like me to, but often enough for me and (I think) even for God. Shouldn't our giving, worship, and study habits be between God and us? Well, apparently God looks an awful lot like Tree at times, though I never knew He wore an eye patch. Unbelievable.

Before I knew it, I had agreed to Tree's new legalistic pronouncement. Folks generally agree to whatever Tree wants and walk away wondering what just happened: a tree just fell on me!

Now came the tricky part—actually doing the reading and keeping up. Because I knew darn well Tree would be checking up on me at our weekly breakfast get-togethers down at the Belvedere. I'd be happy just eating, but Tree insisted on doing spiritual work too. So I just chewed and nodded my head a lot.

The question for me was how to accomplish reading the Bible in a year on a daily basis. The problem was the actual reading part.

I like to read, but mapping out the time is another thing altogether different. I thought about my day and the time I had allocated for various things. Then in a moment of inspiration, I thought about listening to the Bible.

I found the Daily Audio Bible online and subscribed to it on my iPhone. I started downloading it every day and listening while I did my morning walk. I walk for about forty minutes, so I figured that was a perfect time to listen and walk. Exercising my body, mind, and heart muscles. Power walking while power listening—now that's powerful stuff!

The other day I had some time left on my walk after finishing my audio Bible lesson, so I put on some music that Danielle (my youngest daughter) had given me. The artist was Brooke Waggoner, and the song was called "So-So." The part that really got to me was the chorus:

> Oh, why here it's so-so
> But it is no, no Colorado
> I miss my home and the cocoa
> I wanna go home
> I wanna go home
> I wanna go home

The way she sings "I wanna go home" three times just really got to me. I wasn't really sure why at first. The song itself is nostalgic, and Brooke's style could be described in the same manner, but there was something more that tugged at my heartstrings. It was the repetition and simplicity, the threesomeness of it all.

First, as a child. At the end of the day when all was done and I was played out and had finished what I was doing, all I knew was "I wanna go home." I was ready to see my mom and family, to be welcomed back into the bosom of my family. The noises and smells and familiarity of the place drew me and nurtured me and welcomed me.

By the end of the day I needed to be refilled by my mom and

sisters and my little brother. I even needed the scary reality that was my father. I was done with the world, and while I looked forward to seeing it again real soon, I wanted nothing more than home. My home. I wanna go home.

Second, as a grown man. The home was mine, the place I built along with Patty. The place we made with our own blood, sweat, and tears, plus a lot of money. A place we crafted out of love where all were welcome, where we all were safe from everything the world had to throw at us.

We built our walls of protection there, and once again when the day was done and all the good and bad works were part of recent history, I only wanted to go home and be in the place where I was loved the most and felt completely safe from the world. Home.

"I wanna go home" during that time was different than when I was a child. Yet it still had a strong emotional heart tug that resonated within me to the point that I became a homebody. A body that felt most rested and secure at home. A body and soul that preferred to avoid the rest of the world for recovery and chose to refresh and restore all the gifts of the heart that were given and received during the day at home.

I gave away all that I had to give most of the days of my life. This continuous outflow created an emptiness that needed to be restored by God, by my wife, and by the place we live. My home. I wanna go home.

Third, as an older man. Home takes on an entirely different meaning when your kids are in college, and the house is empty and quiet. Still secure and full of love, yet different. My mom and dad are both dead and gone, and there is no one to look up to except for God in heaven and in the kingdom here. Looking up to an invisible King is hard at times, and I realized that I missed my parents so much and wished they were still here. Why do I have to be in charge now and at the top of the genetic tree? It's not fair.

Now is the time when my spiritual home becomes more secure. The foundation that was laid at my birth became solid and ready for framing by the time I was twenty-three and gave myself up to the Master Carpenter. Standing in that new home over the years gives me security and fills me up so that every day I am refreshed anew, ready to go out into the world and continue.

So I go home to both my wife and my earthly home, and it is good. But I also come home to my spiritual home in the kingdom of heaven, and that is also good. I have one foot in heaven and one foot on earth, and wanting to go home has taken a whole new meaning as my death approaches and my kingdom comes.

I wanna go home to be with God and maybe to see my parents again, but I wanna go home to my wife and kids and family and friends. I wanna go home to be with God because I am so tired, so tired, so very tired of living and trying to understand all of this stuff called life. I am truly tired of this life, and I wanna go home.

I wish I could go home.

I am home because home is where the heart is. Yet my heart is already in heaven while my body is still alive here on the planet earth. Maybe that's okay because the kingdom of heaven is really right here, right here in our midst, in our hearts, in the world, in our work, and in our friends. In our homes.

Maybe going home means both things for me now. Going home means going to the place where I feel the most loved. If God is with me all the time and in my heart and if home is where the heart is, then I'm home wherever I go. But that's only one chamber of my heart; it leaves out entirely my Patty home, the place where I lay my head and my heart down for rest every night.

In the night my heart sack deflates, and I pour out of it while I dream about my smallness. If I wake during those times, I feel so lost and helpless. But I can also feel God filling me back up with perfect clarity and truth. I know the truth of all the stupid things I did the day before and wish I had not done them.

Morning comes, and my heart is full again, full of God and much less of me. I take my heart sack and set out to conquer the day. As I conquer it, my pride rebounds and conquers me. My ego arrives and forces God to move aside for the power and majesty that is mine. By the end of the day I am once again full of myself. How much God remains in me is anyone's guess.

My heart knows this and becomes homesick once again, for it

knows that only at home can I be refilled with the love and peace and joy and kindness and agape that I need to get me through another day. Another day where I give everything I have and more until I am physically, emotionally, and spiritually exhausted and spent.

    I wanna go home
    I wanna go home
    I wanna go home

Coop & Skeeter at All Staff 2008.

TWENTY-THREE

The Dung Beetle

for Skeeter & Coop

JOHN KÖEHLER

> He will perish forever, like his own dung; those who have seen him will say, "Where is he?"
>
> JOB 20:7

There's a saying in Young Life that two guys who get along really well are "twin brothers of different mothers." It's an apt phrase to conjure up the idea of two different dudes who somehow click together as if they were cut from the same cloth.

Nothing is finer than the feeling that comes when you find another twin brother who has been hidden away for the previous part of your life, and shizam, you both pick up where you might as well have left off, when you were floating in the genetic void of God's creation, sucking your embryonic thumbs and waving at each other across time. See you soon, little brother, see you soon.

I try to treat everyone as if they are family but—truth be told—most of them are not my twin brother or sister of anyone's mother, much less mine. It is a rare thing indeed when someone comes along who dings my heart bell and fires me up so much that I'm like a giddy girl on her first date. This can be a little scary when the object of my affection is a dude!

I can't recollect exactly when I first met Skeeter Powell. Whenever it was, we both knew right away that we were twins and grooved to the same spiritual music of the heart. We laughed at the same things, thought about the same things, and said a lot of the same things.

This frightened a lot of people who knew us both. They could take us one at a time, but combined we turned into some kind of amoebic creature from the black lagoon that—while it seemed spiritual enough—smelled and sounded downright scary, like finding out your best friend was Dracula. Hmmmm.

Skeeter is a Carolina boy, the southern kind. He hearkens from Greenville, to be exact. Skeeter is a volunteer leader for Capernaum there but functions more like someone on staff. I look up to Skeeter and hope against hope that I'll be like him when I grow up, yet I know it is . . . hopeless. As with many guys I look up to, I desire the parts of them that I know I may never attain.

We're called not to compare ourselves to each other with jealousy and pettiness, nor are we to put others down. But I think it is cool to lift others up and to aspire to whatever gifts, talents, and greatness they have within, assuming we can actually learn from them instead of just pining away for something we can never have.

Whatever the case may be, I want to be like Skeeter!

One of the dudes Skeeter hangs out with is Coop. Coop spends a good deal of time in a powered wheelchair due to his cerebral palsy. Although he is a quadriplegic, his mind is sharp as a tack. Don't expect to win many arguments or outgun the boy with verbal fisticuffs. But if he gets too smart for his britches, I can always take him out of his wheelchair and pin him in a WWF-style wrestling match. Chairs are allowed.

Coop gave his testimony at the 2008 All Staff Conference in Orlando, Florida, where about 3,500 Young Life staff from around the world gathered to play and pray. He did a great job. I shot a video of his testimony, added photos sent by his mom, and produced a video. It is now one of our highest-viewed videos on YouTube (keyword: Capernaumjohn).

Since then I've been in touch with Coop and his mom, and suggested that Coop's head is too swollen for him to roll through any doorway. Instead of showing the right amount of humility, Coop started acting like an American Idol contestant, flaunting his new Hollywood status. He stopped taking my calls and answering my e-mails. I was treated like just another able-bodied imposter, cast aside like a nasty little dung beetle. Speaking of which . . .

Not long ago I e-mailed Coop and copied Skeeter. I told Coop that I thought Skeeter was one fine dude and—because I desired to be more like him—I wanted an insect name of my own. Maybe that would bring me even closer to him and allow me to assume a bit more of the Skeeter way, the Skeeter style of looking at things.

Maybe.

So I attached a short list of my favorite insect names:

Chigger
Gnat
Tick
Stink Bug
Dung Beetle

The Bible says that spiritual things can't be understood by un-spiritual people. I reckon there's some truth in that. When you're a lot smarter than someone, it is easy to talk over their heads and leave them in your cranial dust. If you speak a language fluently, you still must use simple phrases for those who do not understand it as well as you.

In the same way if you are more spiritually mature and have a significantly deeper personal relationship with God, you cannot talk to non-believers or the spiritually immature and expect them to understand everything you say. Your heart muscles are better developed than theirs, and the things you say and do come from a more refined inner core.

From this, I can also extrapolate that ridiculous things can't be understood by un-ridiculous people. Which would explain why Coop, who is generally not in a very ridiculous state of mind, didn't respond to my list at all. But Skeeter, who lives in a perpetually ridiculous state of mind, was all over it like white on rice.

Skeeter responded most to the name at the bottom of the list, both in number and in lowliness: Dung Beetle. I think he may have been worried about liking that name for me a little too much, but he suggested it just the same. I laughed because all along I knew it was the name for me.

Some of my friends would argue that the name does not fit. Especially my friends from the Bürpenfärtzen Brothers, a group of seven guys who don lederhosen every October to host an Oktoberfest fundraiser party for thousands.

I was one of the founders of the group and the party, originally held at our house, the home of my darling wife, Patty, and our kids. Everyone knew that I represented the Bürpen side of the family (proven by my many belching titles), while my buddy and co-founder Wilhelm represented the Färtzen side of the family. I will not elaborate, for elaboration would prove too earthy. Even so, the Brothers would argue that Willy should be called Stink Bug or Dung Beetle, not me. I could be Chigger or Praying Mantis or even Tick, but certainly not Dung Beetle.

There is something relentless and proud about the little dung beetle—no doubt the mission of forming balls of animal dung, rolling them to their nest, burying them in the earth, raising and feeding their young with them, and, of course, last but not least, eating the dung. Dung beetles get all their nutrients, moisture, and food from the dung they find and need no other food source. They are, as far as I know, the only animal that can literally eat shit and *live*.

No matter how disgusting the purpose of the dung beetle, it goes about achieving that purpose with relentless determination and tenacity. It forms beautiful round balls out of the crap that is left behind by—after leaving the behind of—the host animal.

We look at this dung and see something to be avoided, something to be stepped around, because you surely do not want to step in a pile of elephant dung. You might never come back from that misstep! What we consider refuse and worthless, the dung beetle deems valuable and life giving. What we see as disgusting debris to be avoided, the dung beetle sees as the most beautiful source of life, the ultimate Garden of Eden and Fountain of Youth all in one. We see death and destruction and decay; the dung beetle sees the future and hope and success.

The dung beetle knows that it can live on what is inside of the dung balls. It knows that what lives within is life giving and perfect for its needs. It knows what the rest of the world does not know: life is inside the crap of the world.

The world still treats people with disabilities like piles of crap, like refuse better thrown away, cast aside, avoided, and walked around. The world would prefer leaving special folks for the garbage men to pick up and take to the institutional dumps with all the other special people so they can live in a special place where no one has to see them, listen to them, smell them, or—especially—live with them.

The world does not see the life within each person with special needs. In fact, it is not even sure if they are real people, and certainly they do not deserve to be treated the same as everyone else—much like people saw slaves 175 years ago. How could a God who forms us in His own image make the dubious mistake of creating misfits and little pieces of dung that should just be scraped up and disposed of?

First, God does not make mistakes. There is a purpose and life force in every single human being who has been—or ever will be—born. No matter how beautiful or ugly. No matter how smart or slow. No matter how mobile or immobile. No matter if they can talk or are mute. No matter if they can walk or must roll their way through life. No matter what, God loves us exactly the way He made us, and He expects that we will return the favor and love everyone around us because of the implied, latent, and perceived beauty in that person. Because He made them just as He made us.

Any questions?

It does not matter one whit whether or not we think they deserve to be part of society and exist among us. It is not for us to say because God has already said it all by the act of creating them. They are His, and now they are ours—alive and perfect in their imperfections.

To society, the people of Capernaum and the millions of other disabled folks around the world are little piles of dung to be thrown away. If that is so, then I am a Dung Beetle, ready to roll these gifts of God to places where they can feel the love they deserve. I will roll them so fast that the nasty exterior that the world sees will fall away to reveal a beautiful ball of gold, radiant and bright, perfect in every way—the true person.

After a while you notice that what you used to think was a ball of dung is pulsing with a heartbeat, strong and even, measured and perfect. You begin to wonder if perhaps you made a mistake. Maybe you were wrong about what you thought was a piece of poo. You rub your eyes, and still the golden ball is before you.

You look closer, and the ball is reflecting a human face as well as your own. Both are smiling. How could this be? You feel funny. Your stomach has butterflies as your adrenal glands squirt, and you are excited for reasons you do not understand. You are not used to being visited by the Holy Spirit, yet it happens whether or not you understand it.

God has just shown you the reality and beauty of His creation, seen in the reflection of what you thought was a ball of dung. He has shown you yourself and the special person in the same reflection, unified and human, imperfections lost in the golden glow of the surrounding God light. Both perfect and special. Both created by the Creator Himself.

You start crying, and you don't know why. You wish you could wake up from this strange dream, but you don't. So you walk away, walk away, walk away to your old life where balls of dung are just balls of dung that never become golden, and disabled folks are set apart, over the hills and far away, where they never become golden and perfect.

I am a Dung Beetle, sent to earth to roll God's pieces of beautiful dung to the feet of Jesus so that the world can see them for who they are—perfect in every way according to God. Look and see all the dung beetles: parents, caregivers, friends, and siblings. So many have come. They are relentlessly rolling their family and friends forward, exposing the golden glow of their hearts to the world. Rolling them all to God and to the world where they belong, where they deserve to be.

I am God's Dung Beetle, and I am not afraid to get my hands dirty rolling my friends forward, washing them in the grace and love of God, and exposing the disgusting truth of their beautiful hearts, the truth that the world wants to avoid and never admit.

JOHN KÖEHLER

Wilhelm looks up for God, or for brats.

TWENTY-FOUR

My Piehole

for Wilhelm

JOHN KÖEHLER

*He who digs a hole and scoops it out
falls into the pit he has made.*

PSALMS 7:15

May 29, 2007

Piehole
-Noun.
1. The place where pie first enters the body.
2. The place where words finally leave the body.

[Origin: 1950-1960, Back Bay, Virginia]

I can remember the very first time I ever said "piehole" in front of my family. We were eating dinner, the four of us, just jabberin' away like blue jays talkin' to a cat. My youngest daughter, Danielle, said something smart-alecky, so I told her to, "shut her piehole."

Everything kinda slowed down in suspended animation. Both girls had their pieholes hangin' open like flytraps, lookin' at me. I liked the new power I had. But then I looked at my wife of twenty-five years, and noticed that her look of surprise was quickly changing to outrage. So I twinkled my nose quick like Sam on Bewitched, but—shoot fire—I didn't disappear at all and just sat there ready to accept my death like a man.

"Don't you dare use that word at my table!" yelled my wife, with righteous fire and vinegar. That would have been a good time for me to say, "Yes, ma'am, I'm very sorry," or even, "Quite right, my apologies." Perhaps I could have even stood and bowed at the waist or the elbow or however them fancy-pants Brits do it.

But, alas, I didn't do that at all.

I looked at my angry wife and said, "Well, it's my table too, and I can say anything I want to!" That was apparently not the right thing to say at all because flames started shooting out of her nose and mouth, and great billows of steam filled the room as my kids both yelled, "Yay, Mom's gonna kill Dad and eat him again!"

Truth is (if you're even interested in the truth), I finally settled down and explained where the term came from and what it meant: it was just another way of saying "mouth." What's the big deal, anyway? "Well," said my wife, as the smoke trickled out of her nose, and her eyes slowly changed from red to blue, "it sounds nasty, and I won't have it."

Since she was part dragon, I capitulated, which I think means "I decided to live" in Latin.

There once was a man who was just about the smartest teacher who ever walked the planet. When he spoke, everyone listened because he said things in ways no one had ever said before. He spoke about things the people knew, but in such a way that they seemed brand-spankin'-new and polished up like you were getting ready for a big dance or wedding.

His words cut down through the layers of their lives and massaged the folds of their hearts. It felt fine, like sittin' in your momma's lap after a thunderstorm, just knowin' you were gonna get to go back outside and play again. But right then you were in the arms of the person who loved you the most, mighty comfortable and safe, so maybe you'd just sit there a spell while the leaves dripped and the sun rays came out from their hiding places.

Well, this fine teacher told the people that they didn't have to worry too much about what went into their mouth because that went straight on down to the stomach—a pretty dumb organ—and right on out the other end of the train track and back down onto the earth to help grow more food so the piehole can start the whole process over again.

He told them not to worry about things that went into the mouth, but worry instead about what came out of the mouth. Because these things come not from the stomach but from the heart of the person, from the brain and soul and guts and the very center of the best and worst of the person rolled up into one ball. And you never really know what part is going to come out, do you? Are you gonna say something nice and uplifting and helpful and loving and joyous and peaceful and all the other fruits of the Spirit that we know we're supposed to use?

The problem is that by the time those words leave the heart and start down the path to the piehole, other words worm their way in, and what started as a blessing comes out as a curse. That wise teacher said that the words that come out make a man unclean, not the things that come into the body.

Shoot, words don't have to be spelled with four letters to be dirty. We just fling them out like arrows or machine-gun bullets and spew them across the killing fields of our lives, doing our best to take out whoever is in the way of our verbal barrage.

How is it that in a matter of minutes, the same man can say the most amazingly loving and beautiful things followed by complete and utter filth? How is it that we can earn accolades and thanks for the things we say, and just as easily earn scorn and contempt for other things we say? How exactly is it that we can speak a sonnet that deserves to rest on the bookshelf of someone's heart, and then speak a dirge that deserves to live in the underworld of black hatred?

Well, folks, I should know. Because my piehole is very capable of doing both things, and on entirely too many occasions it fails to speak that which is acceptable and encouraging in favor of that which is mean-spirited and lowly. It truly does not make any sense, yet I do it every day.

The easy thing for me to do with my personal piehole is to keep it shut, zipped, slammed down, closed, sealed. Somewhere in the Bible it says that even a fool seems wise if he just keeps his mouth shut. Which also goes the other way . . . even a wise man can seem a fool by opening up his piehole and spewing out things that would be better left unsaid. Don't I know it!

MY INFLATABLE HEART

The other day on the beach a very pregnant friend was waddling down from the dune, and a bunch of us (including her dad) were watching her come down with her hubby. All kinds of things went through my head, but naturally I just flopped open my piehole and let rip with the first thing that rose to the surface I said, "Wow, she's sure got the sumo wrestler's walk!"

Everyone stopped and stared at me.

One woman said, "I can't believe you said that." I asked myself, "Did I just say that?" Yup. And then the dad, sitting right next to me said, "That was mean-spirited." And you know what, I reckon it was mean-spirited. I told the woman that I would have said the same to the pregnant woman and she would have laughed, but right then when she couldn't hear me, it was mean.

Danged if I didn't think about that all day and into the night, waking up still thinking about it. By the next morning I was feeling pretty low in my spirit and wondered how I could write and think and feel and say such wonderful things and do them too . . . yet from time to time, and sometimes way more often than I'd like, the wrong things just fall out of my piehole onto the plates of those around me. And they don't want to eat that food at all.

This is not meant as a warning to you, but as a way to help me to keep it real, keep it cool, keep it nice and full of love and sweet as can be and finer than . . . Delaware. See, you just gotta say "Caroliner" when you say "finer." Nothing else works as well.

I hope that when next I see you my piehole opens up and only good things come out of me, the very best things I can say that will make your little heart pearl light up like June bugs in July. But if you should ever come up to me, and I just look at you and smile, you'll know that I need to keep my piehole shut tight because the bad stuff is trying to get out, and I need to keep it trapped inside.

Either that, or I've just got some powerful bad breath.

Love and chicken feed,

John

P.S. As I write this follow-up to the Piehole story I wrote nearly a year ago, I realize that there will be many such stories in my life because God made me to pour my life out into the world. I would even go so far as to say that He wants me to pour it out spontaneously and explosively so that it is truly "from the heart."

The danger is that if what comes out of my heart is not the treasure from God that resides there but is part of the garbage that also lives there, then I'm likely to cause more trouble than good. The hope is that if I do share that part of me which directly relates to the very best in me—that is, the treasure that God has built up inside of me—then people around me will receive that treasure unpolluted by the thoughts of my mind.

Our thoughts live in our brains, distinctly different from our heart and soul, which live in the very same place: our brains. If you take a thing that was born from the Holy Spirit of life and bat it around in the ballpark of your brain, you are not necessarily going to hit a home run. You may instead think too much about what to do and say, so the magic of the moment—the beauty of the original passion—will become diluted and dull, empty and boring.

It's much better to share the undiluted truth of your inner spirit with the world and hope that there is no garbage mixed in, accidentally scraped off the dunghill of your life. Keeping quiet may prevent you from sharing your treasure, but sharing your thoughts may cause you to put out the trash.

Even though I have joked many times over the years about a desire for the simplicity of life as a sanitation engineer (trash man), the truth is that I have been one my whole life, in spite of my protestations to the contrary. My landfill is large. I think it will get taller as I get older.

Even strangels wear bluetooths.

TWENTY-FIVE

The Strangel

for Nick

> *The Spirit of the LORD will come upon you in power, and you will prophesy with them; and you will be changed into a different person.*
>
> 1 SAMUEL 10:6

Stran·gel
Noun.

1. One of a class of spiritual beings; a celestial attendant of God that is unusual and strange. In medieval angelology, angels constituted the lowest of the nine celestial orders (seraphim, cherubim, thrones, dominations or dominions, virtues, powers, principalities or princedoms, archangels, and angels).

2. The lowest class of angel relegated to serving people with disabilities. A strange angel.

Now before you Pharisees and righteous people condemn me for using Samuel's prophetic scripture above, I am not suggesting that I am a prophet in the classic, old-school sense. I am more interested in the entire line, in its completeness, because it is a beautiful graph that resonates with me, probably because it represents who I am and why I am.

I used the photo to the left not only to help show my strangeness (as if that were in question) but to downplay any suggestion that I am claiming more than what God has given me. I want to say that I'm not doing that, but do we ever really know for sure what comes from God and what we manufacture from within our own stuff and use for God's sake or our own? And does it really matter when it is already part of the purpose that God brought us here for?

If God made us and loves us exactly as we are, can we not make the claim that all things within us come from God whether or not they were planted in us by the Holy Spirit or are part of our spiritual DNA? From the very moment when we were nothing but a twinkle in God's eyes and His tear fell down into our mom, weren't we made in the image of God?

I don't know the answer, and I'm not sure that anyone does. There are going to be a lot of questions in heaven. Yet I believe that God uses every bit of us for His purpose if we take the path that He has for us. How can it be otherwise?

When you hire someone, you hire the complete person, not just the best and most gifted parts of him. He is imperfect, and everyone knows it. He may excel at creativity but stink at dealing with clients. So you teach him how to do that by modeling the proper way to interact with people and force him to do the same with expectant patience.

You can't tell him to leave his crap at home, to leave the worst parts of himself behind. He can't help but bring it to work with him. You have to take him as he is, and if you have any hope of integrating him into your team, you have to find a way to use all of him—good and bad—so that his weaknesses are exposed and rendered useful or harmless to the overall operation.

Sometimes great weaknesses go hand in hand with great strengths; certainly that has always been the case with me. My weaknesses are cause for great concern and a source of dismay for me and for others. The giant piehole known as my mouth delivers heaping helpings of meanness and spite. Prideful egotism and disgusting displays of juvenile arrogance show up not just in my words, but in my actions.

Sometimes I am so full of myself that there is no room for God to find His way into the bloated sack of my heart. There is no room at the inn for the baby Jesus or even His spirit to rest in the space supposedly reserved for Him. I become filled up with myself and my strengths, and they, in turn, become a weakness for me.

This is so strange, and I don't know that I will ever understand it completely. Paul talked about the dual natures that we have and serve even after we invite Jesus to live in the place of honor within us.

We build a table for Him and promise to serve Him. The Messiah sits at the head of the long table, and at the other end of the table sits the host (that would be me), smiling down the long way to his very special guest, the one he invited in to rule when he was twenty-three. Between him and his special guest—the one he has promised to give his life to and accept as his master—are eighteen chairs, nine on each side.

Closest to the host, sitting on either side, are the friends he's known all his life, the people he cannot seem to get away from, no matter how hard he tries. These are the friends his parents warned him about, yet he loves them. They are his people, his family, so how can he turn his back on them? It does not feel right to desert old friends. Isn't that what the Bible says?

There sits Greed, stealing food from the plate of Pride, who is telling a fabulous story about his heroic deeds to Envy, who listens with rapturous attention.

Look at Anger sitting alone, sipping from the stew of his own juices that bubbles and bubbles with the toils of his troubles. He pays no attention to anyone at the table except for Gossip, who never sits, but flutters around from guest to guest whispering what the others said with empathetic pot-stirring glee.

Leaning back in their chairs, chuckling at private hilarities, sit Sloth and Glutton. They toast each other with the best money wine can buy (wait, is that backward?) and eat from the table of life as if they will never get enough. Truth be told, they never will satisfy their awful cravings, nor will they work to provide for their own needs or the needs of their friends.

Across the table from them sits Avarice, clinking his coins and chortling at all his colleagues, for he has more than they, and as far as he is concerned, you can take it with you—at least to all the tomorrows that stretch out as far as his black heart can see.

Lust exudes charm in waves as he looks with desire at the guest of honor. He cannot keep his eyes off the graceful attendants, and whenever they glide by, he motions them over for a quick word and a quicker hand to touch them in ways that turn heads around the table, for Lust is doing what they all wish they could do.

Nine empty chairs sit closest to the Seat of Honor, where Jesus watches and listens, a slight smile on His face. Then he stands, and all rise as one—looks of worry on their faces—as into the room come the nine friends of Jesus.

They are laughing together as if they have just finished sharing a joke. Their love and devotion for each other is a radiant light that fills the room with a deafening beauty; it silences the first nine who were invited by the host so long ago. They never relinquish their seats, never leave the host who loves them, even if his love is never returned.

The host greets each arrival with a kiss and shows them to their seats with great delight. Any friend of Jesus is a friend of his.

After they are all assembled, Love stands and offers a toast that brings everyone to their feet with shouts of brotherhood and solidarity. Joy tells a joke so hilarious that soon many are crying in their cups, their stomachs hurting from the belly laughs they have just shared.

Compassion takes the hand of Anger, looks into his eyes, and shows him the Father's love. Then he leads him to the seat closest to Jesus, who puts His hand on Anger's head and blesses him in front of the group. The fire inside Anger is quenched, and he sits silently looking around at the guests, wondering how he had gotten there. Compassion stands behind him, a hand on his shoulder.

Temperance and Patience invite Sloth and Glutton to eat and drink in their place, for the food is amazing and the wine the very best in the kingdom. They come, but when they take their new seats, there is no wine to drink or food to eat. They look at Jesus and tell Him they are hungry.

He tells them a story, and everyone listens. When He is done, their hunger is sated and their thirst quenched. They don't understand the significance of the story, but they no longer care about their next meal or how excellent the wine; they are content. They stay and wait on Jesus, while Temperance and Patience wait on them, standing just behind.

Soon all of Jesus' guests have invited the host's guests to come and sit in their places near Jesus. Jesus' guests wait on them and help them when they do not understand what was said or when they fall into their old ways.

The attendants shoot fire from their hands and cut the table in two, and the host moves up to his new head, closer to his special guest. Much closer. Now it feels like a family to him, and he is so thankful for his guests, new and old, as they become friends.

He loves his old friends and does not want them to leave. They begin to change, sometimes becoming silent as their new friends serve them and love them and help them. Then the host looks at Jesus and smiles; Jesus smiles back at him.

Then I open my eyes and realize once again that the kingdom of heaven is at hand and heart, within and without, alive and vital. A battle rages there.

So that's what is going on at the table inside my heart. The table that was set to entertain Jesus and His guests is also home to all the nasty friends of my life, the parts of my character that I simply cannot elude or destroy. But I am working on it.

The reason why folks see me as sometimes strange and sometimes an angel is partly because I am very open about myself, the good, the bad, and the, uh, really bad. I do not pretend that the table of my heart is inhabited only by the wonderful friends Jesus brought with Him. I wish it were that way, but it is not. The truth is both terrible and wonderful to behold.

Many Christians pretend that the table of their heart is only inhabited by Jesus and His friends. They pretend that their own relatives are dead and buried, that their kin no longer exists. They fool no one but themselves and the Pharisees who came before them.

I do not pretend that my genetic character defects are missing in action. I recognize them and try to keep my eye on them. By watching all my internal friends, I hope to be ready when they try to steal me away from the better side of myself.

Maybe this honest and open dichotomy of my character is what makes me barbaric and strange. Whatever the case, I certainly am a strange man. My aim is to spend more time down at the end of the table where the special guest of my heart sits along with all my friends, new and old.

Maybe over time my nine old friends who have been with me from the beginning of my life will become more and more like my nine new friends who continue to make me more and more like my guest of honor.

More than anything I want to be like Jesus, but I can't seem to get away from my old friends. My dear old friends who I wish would simply die and be forgotten. In the meantime, I will content myself with being just another strangel, second class.

JOHN KÖEHLER

Mike shown providing security.

TWENTY-SIX

My Awful Club Talk

for Crock

> Although I felt awful at the time, I don't feel at all bad
> now that I see how it turned out.
>
> 2 Corinthians 7:8

November 2, 2007

Okay, so here's the thing. I'm an Area Director, capital A and D, thank you very much. In fact I'm a Metro Area Director, which means I'm not only in charge of a city for Young Life, I'm in charge of an entire metro area of cities. In my case it meant Virginia Beach, Norfolk, Chesapeake, Portsmouth, Suffolk, Hampton, and Newport News. But there's no pride involved here, folks. Really...

Being an area director means a lot of things, and one of the most important is talking to the kids about Jesus. This is done in many ways, but clearly one of the most important ways is the club talk. The club talk for Capernaum occurs at the end of club, and the kids know that they will have to settle down and listen after the fun activities. Settling down and listening for forty to sixty-five people with disabilities can mean many things, and giving a club talk to these folks means you expect interruptions and noise and varying shades of understanding and cognition.

Thankfully, I don't give the club talk every week at every club. I allow other staff and volunteers to do this—quite well, in fact—which leaves me on the hook once a month at each of the three clubs. Naturally I want to do as well as I can when I give a club talk, and I prepare and pray diligently (or at the last minute) that God will use me and my talents to convey a simple and strong message.

For this past month, I chose the idea of Jesus, the Lamb of God. I first gave this talk at Norfolk, and it went great. I talked about how God had to clothe Adam and Eve with animal skins, but in order to do that he had to kill or sacrifice the animals. Then I told them how later, God let people sacrifice lambs and other animals in order to get rid of their sins. I used a lambskin to make the point.

Finally, I talked about how when John the Baptist saw Jesus walking by, he said to his friends and disciples, "Look! The Lamb of God, who takes away the sins of the world." I pointed out how Jesus had replaced the lambs as the way people could receive forgiveness for their sins. They seemed to get it. My talk was a success; I was a hero and obviously anointed by God's love. Life was good! The same things happened in Chesapeake. Dang, I was brilliant.

Which left Virginia Beach.

My expectation was that I would come and nail it again to prove that I was God's man, or even just *the* man. But it didn't work that way. Now I'm not going to blame it on the visit of my sister, though perhaps having her there was on my mind. Okay, I'm casting some of the blame for my awful performance squarely on her shoulders. Gosh, I feel better already after giving her some of the burden. It is also true that I was somehow out of sorts when I went up to speak. I don't know why, but I just didn't feel all there. I wasn't completely connected to the kids.

I was a bit off.

My words felt clunky and without spirit. I was clunky and without spirit. And then there was Blake. When I brought out the lambskin, held it up, and put it over my shoulders, Blake thought that was the funniest thing he'd ever seen and started laughing loudly. Normally I would have laughed along with him and pushed ahead.

But his laughter bugged me, and I wanted to squash him like a small bug. Or maybe whack him upside the head with my Bible in righteous anger while the people cheered. Is that really so wrong?

Well, of course, it was. Somehow I was so out of sorts that I allowed a mentally disabled kid to bother me. I can't believe it. I mucked my way through the rest of the talk and felt like running away. I was sweating. They clapped for me, but I felt like throwing up and had to plaster a smile on my face as I walked to the back of the room and tried to become invisible.

While I was standing there, I instantly became aware that my failed club talk was a good thing and maybe even a God thing. It reminded me that this life is not about me or how great of a speaker I am. The truth is that I'm not a particularly gifted speaker compared to many in the ministry. I would love nothing better than to speak like Crock, or Ash or Scott or Kess or so many others.

Ah, but we're warned not to compare ourselves to others lest we flatter or put ourselves down. Even so, I am aware of my strengths and weaknesses and continue to believe that God will use me most in my strengths. Wishful thinking!

But even with the failure of my club talk, even in the midst of one of my most awful "performances," God's Word was given and received. And that's all He asks of us because He knows exactly how it will be used while we simply fester in our less-than-immortal moment. God uses horrible club talks.

Here's the other thing. Before I gave my club talk to the kids, I asked all the parents and caregivers to leave and hang out in another room so the kids could be on their own and to reduce the noise during the club talk. This turned out to be a good call. After all the adults were upstairs, I went up to speak to them. I told them how we were there for their kids and what the purpose of Young Life was. I was able to encourage and edify them. I told them that I loved them and appreciated everything they did for our friends. I told them God loved them.

I gave them a club talk.

It was unplanned and unprepared. And also one of the best I've given because of the simple message. I would rather give a long series of unplanned club talks during my entire life than a few planned ones. I hope that my life is a club talk and that it leads back to Jesus, or forward to Jesus, or in to Jesus. To Jesus. If He can use me in my weakest moments, then there is hope for us all. Hope that our lives are meaningful and useful in all ways and at all times, regardless of our performance.

The gate.

TWENTY-SEVEN

The Gates of Hell

for Jeff

> *Even if I were innocent, my mouth*
> *would condemn me; if I were blameless,*
> *it would pronounce me guilty.*

JOB 9:20

November 14, 2007

I wrote another story titled "My Piehole" that was about my mouth and what came out of it. This story is pretty much the same idea, but with a much tougher and very clever title, don't you think?

I kept going back and forth between "The Gates of Heaven" and "The Gates of Hell." That's because heaven and hell live within us, all the time. Now I know that qualifies as a heck of a buzz kill, but please let me explain. I think the concept is rather simple, so I'll try to use simple and small words like brick and head and heart and hope. I actually just threw brick in there for no reason, but it is a small word. Simple too.

I believe that within us we have the most glorious and the most profane things we could ever imagine. Some folks would argue with me about this and say that they have nothing profane within them, that they have managed to replace the profane with the holy. To those folks I would say, "Poppycock!"

Seriously, how can anyone say that they are ever completely free of worldly thoughts, impure thoughts, sinful thoughts, sexual thoughts, demeaning thoughts, unkind and angry thoughts, bellicose and drunken thoughts? The list goes on, but the point is short and sweet: our minds and hearts are filled with things from our lives, and since life is filled with hellishly bad things that we experience and sometimes do, we can never completely erase them from our psyche. They are always with us to one degree or another. Swirling.

Imagine a storm of black, swirling clouds with angry gusts of wind and mean bolts of lighting. The storm is confined to a room with a closed door. Directly across from the door is a beautiful high-powered spotlight. It is aimed directly at the door and gives off great warmth and hope while it illuminates our way; we are drawn to it for reasons we don't completely understand.

Sometimes the light burns through the clouds and illuminates the door. Sometimes the black clouds cloak the light and hide it from view. It is a meteorological battle with no end, a perfect storm of emotion. The room is your heart (soul), and the door is your mouth. The black clouds are your impure and sinful thoughts, and the light is the Spirit of God that lives within us all—constantly shining but sometimes hidden behind our humanity. The good and the bad all mixed up in one soulful blender.

This is true for everyone, and to those who say they only have a light on in their hearts, I suggest tying down the deck furniture, because a storm is coming.

I wish life were just one big bluebird day with blue skies, a warm sun, and perfect waves marching onto the beach where I stand, tossing boomerangs out over the ocean with perfect returns. A good book waits for me, and as I sit on my beach chair, beautiful women saunter by in tiny bikinis; my wife, in her bikini, is smiling at me, reading my mind.

But those days have to live side by side with the stormy days, when we fall down due to our own meanness and imperfections, and the lights go out. Some days start with perfect light, and every time we open our mouth—the door to our heart—the lightness of our soul comes streaming forth, and we are champions of our tongue. And don't we all want to be tongue champions? Well . . . maybe not!

Maybe this is why when people tell me I've said something that made a difference for them, I sometimes pause in sheer astonishment. If they only knew the battle I had to go through to let those rays of light out of the gates of my hell, perhaps they would have been less likely to compliment me. I really don't want to think that everyone goes through this, but based on what I've heard, seen, and read in the Bible, I know it to be true to one degree or another.

If my little storm analogy is true, then it really does mean that our mouths are both the gates of hell and the gates of heaven. There's only one door, folks, but what comes out of it is a mystery! We would greatly prefer if only godly things came out of our mouths. Jesus Himself said that He was not worried about what went into our mouths, but what come out of them. He knew of the battle that rages within us, and He still knows.

I find it interesting that while Jesus was born a man, everyone swears that He never had impure thoughts. I'm sorry, but I must disagree. Why would God send His only Son down to live and breathe and walk with us without letting Him feel the pain and agony that we face because of the battle that rages in our mind?

I'm not saying that Jesus battled with His own internal black clouds all the time. But we know of at least one instance, in the Garden, when He asked His Dad to take the cup away, to let Him forego dying on the cross, the most painful way to die at the time. How would you act knowing that tomorrow you would have to die the most horrible type of death imaginable? Jesus was a man living in a mortal body, and He could (and did) feel absolutely every single thing in His life. Just as we do.

He knew he would feel every moment of the crucifixion, die a horrible death, and descend into the very gates of hell. He knew it was His destiny, but He doubted whether He could do it as a man.

Isn't doubt part of the swirling darkness that creeps over our hearts? If Jesus had impure and sinful thoughts as part of His humanity and mortality, wouldn't that expose Him to human instincts and make Him even more able to understand us?

I think that Jesus did have a battle raging within Him, much like we do. But I also think that He rarely, if ever, allowed any of the blackness to seep out into His words and actions. He was able to control it through supernatural and natural means. The same supernatural and natural means we have access to.

And that is exactly what I'm holding on to as I face my own demons and darkness. I count on the powers of the Spirit of God, the Spirit of Jesus, and the Holy Spirit that is in my heart and soul. I count on the Spirit to blast through the corruption of my life and shine a light on all that is good and pure within me, namely all that God has put inside me and has worked within me.

If I am connected to that Spirit, then it can become like a photon torpedo, a death ray, a phaser set to stun, a Peacekeeper nuclear missile. Yup, my internal spirit—brought to you by the Gipper Himself—can blow the crap out of all the dark and disgusting thoughts swirling inside me.

And when the darkness flees, only light remains. And then it's safe to speak!

JOHN KÖEHLER

Cowgirl Keisha wins the beauty race.

TWENTY-EIGHT

Winning the Race

for Kess

JOHN KÖEHLER

Do you not know that in a race all the runners run,
but only one gets the prize?
Run in such a way as to get the prize.

1 CORINTHIANS 9:24

Some Christians I know act as if they are not supposed to try their best to win the race. They act as if it would be presumptuous, arrogant, or, heaven forbid, prideful if they did their utmost and gave their all in the course of fulfilling a mission for God or anything else along the pathway of their lives. They act almost as if winning is a sin and as if believing in yourself in such as way as to have assurance of winning should be left to sports and the secular world.

I remember when Scott Hamilton (may his kilt never fail) asked me to give my life story to the regional staff at our Sandbridge get together in the fall of 2006. I disliked this idea very much but relented because he was allowing Tara (our intern) and me to give a presentation about Capernaum. Since I could not do one without the other, I agreed to both.

Before I spoke that night, we all went down to the beach and played a game of touch football. Touch football is an oxymoron for normal guys who are still producing testosterone in normal quantities. We were. A lot of strutting and mild chest beating, not to mention insults and threats were hurled by the guys while the women stood around and talked or took up positions way, way downfield, away from the action and out of harm's way. I admire their intelligence. Testosterone does not produce intelligence and probably inhibits the brain from working in intelligent manner.

I was assigned the position of lineman with few if any responsibilities other than to move guys out of the way. What could be easier? I was six foot two and weighed 225 pounds. Unafraid of any man, I was confident in my ability to play the game. In other words, I was stupid.

The fact that I was forty-eight years old while they were mostly in their twenties and thirties did not cross my mind because my mind had been temporarily taken over by my brain stem, pretty much the dumbest part of my body. This was mortal combat, and I was a man. A mortal man. A stupid, mortal man. A stupid, flesh-and-blood, mortal man (key word: blood).

You see where this is going, right?

On the second play we ran the ball to the left side. I took off running full speed, which was probably about the speed of a push wheelchair, six or seven miles per hour. Blazing fast. I went to block someone, and then saw someone closing in on my left. His name was (and is) Carter, a lowly intern of the worst kind. Which means he was much younger and in much better shape than me. Not to mention that the side of his head that ran into my nose was really quite hard.

I heard a crunch, felt intense pain, and saw stars, all at the same time. I went down hard and landed on my hands and knees. The whole front of my face was numb and on fire. I reached up to feel my nose just as the torrent commenced. I started to bleed like a stuck pig, though I've never actually seen a stuck pig bleed. My nose was gushing like Niagara Falls, and people were getting really grossed out while I lay there doing an impression of a stuck pig. All for the sake of an inflated pigskin.

The women made noises of pity without getting too close, while the guys laughed and said, "Let's keep playing. He'll be okay." I would have done the same. I looked around on the sand next to me in case perhaps a bazooka had been accidentally left there by a Navy SEAL team so I could obliterate Carter, the intern, fourth class. But alas, there were no weapons of mass destruction, and I was too busy bleeding out onto the sand.

Long story short, I broke my nose on the day I was supposed

to give my talk. I remember laughing as my good buddy Alan (another member of the OFC [Old Farts Club]) and I were on our way to the Doc in the Box to get my nose X-rayed. I laughed because I realized once again that old God had a tremendous sense of humor and wanted me to be in the proper frame of mind when I spoke that night. What better way to reduce my pride and increase my humility than to break my nose on the second play—not the last play but the second? Not to mention all the bleeding I did in front of my peers on all fours, just like a pig—a stuck pig.

Bleeding is for sissies. Suck it up, Koehler!

Now remember that I was already in a foul mood about having to share my life story with a bunch of people who mostly had not shared their love for me and therefore did not deserve to know anything about me. Young Life takes great pride in the saying, "You have to earn the right to be heard." Well, I felt like they had not earned the right to be heard by me yet. Why should I tell them anything personal when most of them had not taken a personal interest in me?

Then God broke my nose, and I settled down. Seriously, it works great. If you're ever so full of yourself that your pride kills your humility, have someone break your nose. Works like a charm.

I have no idea what I said that night, and quite frankly I don't want to remember. What I do remember is that when I was done, one of the first questions was: what was it like to be the 1991 Boomerang World Champ? I looked over at my buddy Win and laughed because we had agreed that I should not list all my achievements and awards and honors as that would be too prideful. It was okay when others mention them, but I should not be the one to bring them up. These are some of the crazy ministry rules that I will never completely understand. Were they really expecting humility?

But now I had been given the green light to hit the gas, so I proceeded to talk about boomerangs and how I managed to become the best in the world . . . all the practice and dedication and tenacity and practice and desire and practice and travel and practice and determination and belief in myself and practice and absolute belief in my ability to be perfect if I worked at it enough.

Practice, practice, practice. And then more practice.

I told them about setting the world record in endurance in 1987, less than a year after learning to throw. I threw for five minutes and made sixty catches. Someone asked me how many I had dropped, and I said, "None, I was perfect."

They laughed long and hard at that. I remember thinking, "What the crap are they laughing about?" They thought it was funny that anyone would admit that he was perfect. That it somehow broke the rules and laws that stated no one could ever possibly be perfect, much less admit it. I don't know to this day if I was right about that because I was a tad bit ornery due to my broken nose, having exposed my nasty old underpants to everyone, and because Carter the intern was still alive.

What I wish I would have told them that night is that I want to bring the same dedication and tenacity to my job with Young Life Capernaum as I did to boomerangs. It is extremely easy for guys to understand and grasp the concept of perfection in sports, but much harder to understand that concept as it applies to a job, much less a ministry job. Because a ministry job is filled with conflict about pride and humility. Eating humble pie is considered a great pastime while eating a slice of perfect pie will only lead to perdition.

I find this interesting and sad. And yet I understand the conflict because it has raged in my mind as well. Perhaps more than them because I first worked for years in the secular world, whereas many of them came directly out of college and into the ministry.

In the secular world there is a direct correlation between your job performance and your success. But in the ministerial world the lines are blurred. On the one hand you are judged based on your performance, how many kids you take to camp, how much money you raise, etc. On the other hand, you are called to rely on God to provide, and you must not think too highly of yourself.

Oh, but wait. God must use us to deliver what it is that He wants for us. Faith without works is dead, so we must work to fulfill the destiny that we think God has for us. The tension comes from our desire to be the best mixed with the understanding that God blesses us sometimes in our strength and sometime in our weakness. Sometimes it doesn't matter how much or how hard we work to achieve the ends we desire.

We want to win and run the race to win all the time. Yet winning by the world's standards is not always a win to God. Conversely, you can say that a win for God does not always seem like a conventional win to us because we are taught that a win always feels good and makes us happy.

And there is the conflict that comes within the territory of direct ministry. We are called to do God's work, yet it is with the understanding that He will produce fruit through us. We don't grow the fruit; He does. But He needs us to be the branch to His vine so He can grow fruit through us.

Huh?

The other night I told the kids at Capernaum the story of how Jesus said we are the branches and He is the vine. He produces the fruit and from Him hang all the branches, which are disciples. Us. The branches are trimmed and pruned (crap that hurts!); the branches are tossed away and burned if they don't produce enough fruit. Ow . . .

God is saying two things to us at the same time:

1. We cannot produce fruit on our own and have to rely on Him.

2. God needs us to help him produce fruit.

Now tell me that's not a world of conflict! We are God's branches, and He needs us to produce fruit, but we need Him to create and farm the fruit. He needs us to till the soil, water it, and add fertilizer. But He decides when to pick the fruit. He is the gardener, and we are the field hands. But we are called to race across the fields to do our job and prepare the way. We race to make the crops ready for the master gardener to come and cause the fruit to leap from our branches and into the heart sack of His love. We think we picked the fruit, but we did not. We helped prepare the fruit, and that is a lovely thing.

So what happens when our world is turned upside down and we can't see the finish line anymore? We stop running the race. We stop running and start walking. Then we stop walking and crawl.

Then we lie down. Then we die.

Or—and this is much better than the last option—we keep running hard while we ask God for a new direction. We change course if we run down a rabbit hole. If we lose sight of the finish line, we continue to run in the faith that the finish line is there, hidden behind the clouds of life we have not yet lived.

I have never completely understood what the phrase "waiting on God" means in context with "winning the race." Waiting suggests standing still, and standing still suggests not moving forward for God. Does waiting then suggest running in place? How stupid would that be? Hmmm.

As for me, I continue to run the race. Sometimes I slow down and sometimes walk toward the finish line and sometimes even crawl forward. I pray that I can always see the finish line either in sight or in mind, and if my mind fails me due to my bipolar blindness, I hope that the eyes of my heart will fix on the finish line and forever keep me moving in that direction.

I want to win the race, and if I am doing it for God in the end—even with the baggage of my own pride and ego—then I do not care what anyone thinks of my race; it is not their race, and I am not running it for their sake, but for God's. Nevertheless I hope that by running and striving forward, I will inspire others to run their own races and even help carry them forward to the eternal finish line that awaits us all.

JOHN KÖEHLER

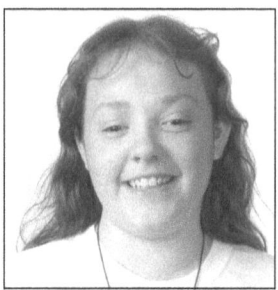

Jessica sees you with her heart.

TWENTY-NINE

The Imposter

for Tuborg & Joan

JOHN KÖEHLER

> "Beware of your friends; do not trust your brothers.
> For every brother is a deceiver,
> and every friend a slanderer."
>
> JEREMIAH 9:4

One morning I was walking down my driveway to get the paper. My next-door neighbor was out on his back lawn doing something or another. When he saw me, he asked how I was doing, and I said, "Not so well, really. I'm kind of depressed." I will never forget his reply. He said, "What! You're one of the happiest guys I know."

It was almost as if he was rejecting my answer. A woman might have been more understanding and sympathetic, but he was a man, and men are taught that you don't expose weakness to the world. When a man exposes his weakness to another, the most common reaction is rejection.

I was reminded that people want to hear how well you're doing, especially when they look to you as an example of happiness and goodness or any other positive attribute that they hang on you because of the way that you project yourself to the world. Not that they don't see all the crap about you, but they don't want to hear that stuff. They want to hear about the best part of you, the part they crave.

My neighbor found it very hard to believe that a guy like me could be down, much less depressed. Maybe the fact that I was showing a chink in my armor meant that the world was somehow a worse place. Maybe people really need to have someone they look up to in various ways, even if only as a happy person, a clown who represents joy in a way they never could seem to grasp. So they pour their inability into the ability of the person they wish they could be in that particular way. My neighbor did not want to be like me in every way, but he wanted my happiness and joy. Thus his world was rocked at the notion of me being not quite the happy and joyful person he had chalked me up to be. He did not want to accept it and—in a way—refused to do so.

I have lived my life trying to win and become excellent at so many things. Receiving acclaim, awards, and accolades became my just rewards, my purpose and my goal in life. The reward for excellence was money and friendship, influence and power, trophies and championships.

Winning in the opaque world of sports or business or even school is an obvious pursuit and a clear victory in most cases. You cannot really hide or fake what is clearly judged by standards everyone has agreed on. You made more money than he did. You finished the race before he did. Your grades were better. You made more sales. No hiding the truth, no arguing the clock or the spreadsheet.

Many things can happen beneath the surface of the competitor, but what matters is done in front of everyone, on the field—either turf or boardroom table. Whether or not you had a bad day matters not to the people in the stands when your job is to move the ball down the field. Your personal faults and inner turmoil are of no concern in the competitive world in which we live.

But what goes on beneath the surface can affect the whole body. If the heart gets sick, the person may eventually show this in a way that others can't miss. In the same way if a person is depressed, it can affect the demeanor and outer person in an obvoius way. Unless they don't want to see or accept the truth.

I am entirely too transparent for my own good. If I'm feeling good, you will know it; if I'm feeling bad, you'll probably know that as well, at least some of the time. While we're taught to tell the truth, the exception comes when answering the age-old question, "How you doin'?"

When people ask you how you're doing, they don't want you to tell them the truth about your sadness. They want you to tell them the lie of your gladness. They would rather you lift them up with your deception than bring them down with your truth. Tell them the truth as long as it is positive and uplifting. Tell them a lie as long as it makes them feel good. They don't care if you have to tell a falsehood because it is not their sin. The real sin would be in telling the worst kind of truth, the truth that is depressing and mean and brings them down to your level. They'd rather you lie for the best. Their happiness is what is best.

We're taught to tough it out, to never admit to feeling bad. We're taught to cover up adversity and difficulty and always be encouraging to the point of fakery. This is interesting because the reverse is not true. We're never taught to pretend to be sad because that would be a lie. But we are taught to lie about how we feel for the sake of helping each other stay happy and courageous.

If this is true, then we all are—from time to time—imposters of the worse sort. I know I am, and not just from time to time. The real problem I have is not whether I feel great or horrible. The problem is that the raging storm of conflict within prevents me from clearly feeling and knowing how well I am doing. Even when I seem to be doing well, I am filled with so much garbage that I doubt the evidence of the good. That is where I am most an imposter.

When people tell me I've done a good job or said something well or thanked me for doing something they deemed righteous, spiritually significant, or helpful, I sometimes shrink back as if they threw hot water on me. To this day I am surprised that any spiritual good can come from me, considering the amount of garbage I know exists inside me.

I feel like I'm looking out on my life from behind the stage curtains while the audience applauds for the act just finished. The Show of My Life, Act 50. They stand and applaud even more loudly, for the performance overwhelmed them and they accept the implied truth as if it were real life.

My life is a stage where my beliefs, thoughts, and actions all are released in a continuous performance that can at times be amazing, beautiful, and even breathtaking. But I know the deception that lurks just behind stage, where all the makeup and fakery live, the very things that are used to create a world where others can get caught up in a reality that is, in the end, far from authentic.

Behind the curtains are the props that go into our lives. We allow few people to enter our backstage, for that is private and must be guarded against those who would not be willing to keep the secrets we protect. Things of such beauty exist next to things of such ugliness. Sometimes those ugly things make their way onto the stage, and the audience is repelled and displeased. They boo and hiss.

As I grow older, the better part of my backstage props and secrets are used on stage for the remaining performances of my life. Yet behind the curtains—taking up a prevalent part of my heart—are the props of meanness and horror, pride and anger, and so many more things I wish I could throw out. But to do so would be destroy the rest of me. The good would die with the bad. The stage would burn, and my life would end. Those things are just too heavy to lift on my own.

I am an imposter, an actor on the stage of life. My audience sees what they want to see, yet I see all the things (good and bad) that litter the backstage rooms of my heart. I know the truth of my condition and am amazed when something good comes out of me, for I know the whole truth and nothing but the truth, so help me God.

So help me God, because I could really use the help. Those trunks filled with the garbage of my life will never leave me, Lord. But if You could just put some really strong locks on them and help me keep them closed, that would be great. That way I can dedicate the remaining performances of my life to You and act out of only the very best things I have. The things You gave me.

And by the way, I know I'm not really the director. More of a stage manager, really. Even so, I get to decide what goes out on stage and when. The stage manager is a powerful person and in the end ... Wait, gotta go! The director is calling ...

JOHN KÖEHLER

MY INFLATABLE HEART

Jenny, Rachel and Aimee light up the world with their smiles. Photo by Glen McClure.

PART FOUR

HEART THOUGHTS

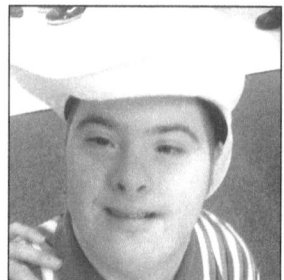
Paul lives out on the range with God.

THIRTY

The Agape Myth

for Matt

JOHN KÖEHLER

> "Your love for one another will prove to the world that you are my disciples."
>
> JOHN 13:35

By the time I went on staff in the spring of 2005 I was already spoiled by the love of Capernaum. I instinctively knew that God wants us to throw ourselves at others with relentless love as if we were family from the very moment we first meet someone.

Shoot, I have been doing it all my life, and so coming to Capernaum was discovering that I was not the only weirdo out there. It was a homecoming. I had been branded weird by the world all my life, and they were right. I think this was partly due to the fact that I wanted to treat them like family as soon as possible. I refused to play into the normal method-acting style of interaction the world expects us to follow when we meet.

First, you meet and shake hands. Never a hug. That would be weird. You talk and share some basic facts about each other. Never anything too personal. You hold back your true feelings in favor of saying and doing "the right thing." You mask your thoughts and emotions in favor of protecting the others from who you really are.

You meet again and again, and each time you unmask a little more of who you are, and they do the same. Slowly over time you learn more about their personal idiosyncrasies. You learn what they like to do. What makes them happy and sad. What sports they play and which teams they follow. After two or three years of this you finally feel like you really know them. After a few more years you might even call them brother or sister and invite them into your family, spiritually speaking.

At Capernaum we simply do not have time for this ridiculous ritual of getting to know someone. Why take five years when you could love someone in five minutes? A kid in Capernaum wants to know two things: do you love them and are you telling the truth?

Some would say that a kid with a mental disability could not possibly know or tell if you really love them. But I would submit that their spiritual discernment in this area is much more evolved than ours. They can tell.

They can tell if you love them, and they can tell if you are lying about what you bring to them. If you love them honestly and completely, they will open up their hearts to you and invite you in for dinner. If you give your heart away to them first, then they will trust you to take the gift of their heart, knowing that you will not harm or damage it as so many people have before you.

It is a race to see who can love the other first. I love winning that race. I love opening up my arms to a new kid coming to club for the first time and having him walk right into my hug with open arms and open heart.

Capernaum met me in the same way I had always met the world: open-hearted, honest, and strange. I fell down to their level, and they rose up to mine, and somewhere in between we met in the town they call Agape.

The truth is that Capernaum enlarged my heart because it taught me to believe even more that this was the right way to treat people and the way we should expect to be treated and loved, just as Jesus taught us so long ago.

When I started going to regional staff meetings, I thought that the saying, "you must earn the right to be heard," had been changed to "you must earn the right to be loved." Capernaum had focused what I already believed and sharpened it into a maxim in my life: love fully from the beginning.

I thought that was how the good people of Young Life would treat me. After all, they were in the ministry and should be closer to God then most folks. Right?

In many ways they are closer to God than the average bloke. They are certainly more theologically adept and better trained in Scripture and biblical teachings. They understand the concepts of grace and love and all the fruits of the Spirit. They know how to use Scripture to walk someone down the road to discovering Christ. They are in every way good people, delightful people, children of God. They speak well and act better.

But unfortunately, and to my complete surprise, they are just like other people. They suffer from the same difficulties of life as everyone else. They join cliques in the same way the rest of the world does. They hold back their hearts and expect you to do the work necessary for them to share their heart and their love with you. You have to earn their love.

This made me physically sick. They did not understand agape any more than the rest of the world. They were ignorant of what Jesus really meant when He gave His last commandment to love one another as He loved us. He did not mean tomorrow or in two years. He meant right away, instantly. He wants us to treat others like they are in our family as soon as we meet them. Or even before we met them, because we all came from the same father.

I threw myself at the regional staff and—with few exceptions—was rebuffed and held at arm's length until I could prove myself to them so that they could peel off their love for me, one slow layer at a time. Why do we have to wait so long to love one another?

I don't blame them for this now as I look back over time. I was demanding and strange and simply expected them to love me. Why would they not love me? By throwing myself at them, I turned myself into a kid from Capernaum, asking, "Do you love me?"

I'd rather be a Capernaum kid filled with agape than a grown-up with a stingy heart. I just wish I could reach inside people and grab their hearts like Jesus did and still does. But how are you supposed to do open heart surgery when you've never been to medical school?

Forrest would have loved Danny.

THIRTY-ONE

The Theory of Forrest Gump

for Paul

JOHN KÖEHLER

*So I reflected on all this and concluded
that the righteous and the wise and what they do
are in God's hands, but no man knows
whether love or hate awaits him.*

ECCLESIASTES 9:1

November 7, 2007

I was thinking about the movie character Forrest Gump during my morning walk today. During his childhood, he overcame a physical condition in his spine that forced him to use awful metal leg braces to walk. Eventually he lived a full life using all the abilities and disabilities that God gave him.

Forrest met life with absolute sincerity, honesty, and truth.

One of the famous lines from the movie is "Momma always said that life was like a box of chocolates. You never know what you're gonna get." At the end of the movie Forrest is putting flowers on the grave of his wife, Jenny. He is standing under the tree they used to sit in when they were growing up. He is looking down at her grave, talking to her:

> Jenny, I don't know if Momma was right or if, if it's Lieutenant Dan. I don't know if we each have a destiny, or if we're all just floating around accidental-like on a breeze, but I, I think maybe it's both. Maybe both is happening at the same time. I miss you, Jenny. If there's anything you need, I won't be far away.

I think Forrest was right about life. I think that God does have a destiny already picked out for us, a path He wants us to take. But we get to choose that path, and sometimes the breezes of life kind of push us off course and off the path. Kind of like the feather shown at the beginning and end of the movie. We get blown around just that easily and never know where we'll land because we're no longer in charge of our life.

But God made the feather and the wind.

Shoot fire, if God made us and the world we live in (which He did) and He has a plan and a path for us to take (He does), a destiny for us to walk into, then aren't we blessed all the time? Sure we are. But the storms in life blow this way and that, and we don't always understand the blessing of the places we accidentally land. If you look at an oyster only from the outside, you'll miss the pearl on the inside.

I don't really know if this means that God created the beautiful randomness that we live in—in effect, a mortal luck where we sometimes pull the ace and sometimes the seven. Hey, wait, I'm talking about poker now! I digress.

If God did create all things and all people, and He's at the end and beginning of all time, then even luck is controlled by Him, so there is no chance involved. Ahhhh, but for us there is. For us there is a beautiful and sometimes-ugly chaos involved, and we never know what we'll pick from the chocolate box of life. Sometimes the chocolate is bitter, and we want to spit it out. It makes us sick, and sometimes it even kills us. The bitter chocolate can make our lives a living hell, and we say, "I guess it just wasn't my day." Or even, "What bad luck!"

Because luck goes both ways, good and bad. And a lucky piece of chocolate can taste fine, fine, fine and light you up like a fire seen through a window of a lonely cabin when you come over the ridge, cold and ready to rest. You stop there and realize that the end is in sight and that you made it. A good piece of chocolate from the candy box of life can fill you with happiness and sweetness, and make you hunger for more. Always more.

When I call myself a lucky man, there is an implicit understanding that sometimes I'm not. Sometimes my luck runs out. But either way, lucky or unlucky, I am blessed. How is it that folks can have something great happen and say "God has blessed me"? Or "I'm blessed to be here"? Does that mean that God is not blessing us the rest of the time, when we can't feel or see His blessing? Does God unbless you? Is it possible that He is, in fact, blessing us all the time, but we decide what to accept as a blessing?

Forrest Gump came at life with a simple purpose and a singular honesty. He knew God and loved Him by loving everyone, even the Black Panther man and the mean Drill Instructor. He never changed who he was whether his luck was good or bad, whether he was blessed or . . . blessed a little less.

Jesus said to come to Him with the simplicity and honesty of a child. Just like Forrest, who never grew up to practice dishonesty and hatred like we do. If we can learn to deal with life like Forrest Gump, a mentally retarded but pure-of-heart man, we might just become better people, worry less, and even learn to love the way God intended.

Gosh, what a lucky blessing that would be!

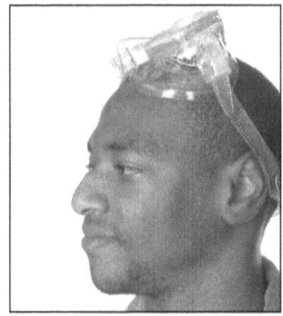
Profile of an African king.

THIRTY-TWO

My Inflatable Heart

for Dean

> My heart is in anguish within me;
> the terrors of death assail me.
>
> PSALM 55:4

June 17, 2007

Note: I started this story Sunday morning in a depressed state and tried to finish it that night after my heart had been restored and inflated again. By then I was full of myself and didn't have the right voice anymore; I had to wait until my heart was once again deflated and my ego had flown away to the winds for a short while. Crap, I can see it coming back . . . must hurry . . .

in·flat·a·ble (in-fley-tuh-buhl)
-adjective
1. capable of being inflated.
2. designed or built to be inflated before use.
—noun
3. an inflatable object, device, or structure, esp. a small rubber boat that is inflated with air.

[Origin: 1875–80]

I woke up feeling pretty low this Father's Day morning. That's not necessarily an unusual thing for me as my spirit and ego are both about as deflated as they can get at that moment when I've been away from my body the longest—waking after a night's sleep.

The funny thing is that on those mornings when I wake up feeling like that, it is usually due to things I did the day before and wished I had not done. I'm pretty sure this is common for many folks who, in the first light of morning, realize that maybe they should not have said those things, done those things, or written those things. We hope for a do-over, a mulligan, another chance to get it right. Please, God, just give me another chance!

And in the brightness of the morning we know the absolute truth of what we have done and what a complete imbecile we have been... and remain. Oh, sorry, I'm using we when I should be saying I and me. This ain't about you, folks; it's about me. So please, focus on me! I'm the idiot who opened up my piehole and let rip with mean words. I'm the dolt who acted in completely unholy ways. Who gave in and reciprocated when family members treated me unkindly.

Tit for tat, hit my hat,
I'll pound you back, get off my crack.

I might as well have been smoking crack, what with the way I acted. Don't get me wrong, I wasn't psycho every waking hour of the day. I wasn't a sociopath bent on destruction. I was just a guy spending time being good, then being bad. Saying nice things, then dropping a bomb. Loving, then hating. Inflating hearts and deflating them.

Ah, the power!

Our hearts are filled with the spiritual gases of God's Holy Spirit. Mixed in with that is the spiritual flatulence of our own spirit and beliefs, our own ego and personality and Wizard of Id, all mixed into one substance that the gas company can't control. Only we control the spirit that escape us, but God controls the pipelines of His loving Spirit, and they never stop pouring into us, whether we realize it or not.

Sunday morning was Father's Day, a day for fathers to be honored and to bask in the glow of their families. I had been with my family and extended family since Friday because my youngest daughter was graduating from high school on Saturday. This meant endless opportunities to be with the grandparents, nephews, sisters-in-law, nieces, store clerks . . . Okay, I'm not really related to the store clerks unless you count them part as of God's family.

Well, aren't they?

I woke up Sunday morning regretting some of my words from the days before. I wondered for the thousandth time why I allowed nasty or biting words to come out of my mouth when I knew what would be best. Why the heck would I purposely refute the will of my Daddy, who was so proud of me . . . watching me all the time, by doing the opposite of what He'd taught me.

I ain't talking about my earthly daddy here, folks!

So I went to Grace Bible Church by myself because Patty needed to be with her mom. I went to Grace because my church, Galilee Episcopal, had disintegrated because a bunch of people there had the same problem I do with filling my heart with things that are kind of smelly. I went there because it was close, and I have friends who go there. And because I needed some grace on that fine Father's Day when I felt unworthy of being anyone's father.

Sure enough, the message was for dads. In fact, it was aimed squarely at me. It was about the type of love God has for us, the very type we're supposed to have for others. Paul told us how important love is and that no matter how awesome we think we are, if we live and do and act and speak without love, we are nothing. I know this! I get this, I understand this, I believe this, and I speak to this. Yet I forget this and replace it sometimes with my own Corinthian madness.

The Corinthians were perverted and out of control, yet Paul knew that God loved them. So there's hope for me!

As I listened to Dean Woodard remind me about what I already knew, I felt like a weepy old woman, convicted and torn, heartless and forlorn. I felt like the worst kind of father, the worst kind of son-in-law, the worst husband. I felt bad and like a complete failure, not deserving of being there, much less anywhere. I wanted to run and hide. But then a searchlight would have followed me while they called out my name as yet another one of God's sinful losers

MY INFLATABLE HEART

left the building. What a whiner! So there I was, the worst father in the whole place, a beacon of stupidity, ready to be thrown out.

Then they asked the dads to come up and get a book that the kids had for us, but no way was I going. Uh-ungh! Then two beautiful young women brought me a book. I wanted to say no, I don't deserve it, but I took it just the same while the gases of God's love blew into me from the angels He had sent.

Here's the thing: By the time I had awakened that day, I was repentant and knew I had done wrong. I knew that I had followed my own way, my own words, and my own Bible, and it just didn't work. So I was ready for change. I had emptied the chambers of my heart—of my nasty self—and was ready to be filled with the jet fuel that only God could give me.

But here's the other thing: God never stops giving us the jet fuel of His love. I think our hearts have two chambers: one where our own love and spirit and joy and nastiness and meanness and decadent thoughts go—the good, the bad, and the ugly—and the other chamber is the holy of holies, the God Spot where we are constantly filled with His love and joy.

In the middle is the spout from which we pour out our hearts and people pour into us. The only question is, what will be poured out? Will we pour out the good or the bad? Will I pour out God within me or me within me? God gives us freedom to choose what will come from us, and we do so every day, every hour, every minute, every second of our lives.

By the time I went to church, the me chamber of my heart was deflated like a dead soccer ball lying flat in the dirt. But I didn't realize that the God gases from my second chamber were already seeping in to fill the void, and I was inflating again. I didn't know it was happening because my ego was down in the dirt, flat as a pancake. But old God, why He was just blowing me up like His favorite birthday balloon.

Even when I was crying in church and feeling sad, God was laughing and feeling glad because His son was coming home again; and while He had never missed me for a minute (because He never left), I sure had missed Him and was ready to come home again.

Our hearts are our homes, and we never leave them behind; we just forget about our second chamber sometimes, when the devil tries to build his pesky walls of separation. But those temporary walls can be easily broken with a laugh and a hug.

By the time I walked out of church and stood there talking to friends, my heart sack was about half full and rapidly rising, carrying me up with it. Then I met Isaac, a young man in a wheelchair who had a rocket engine on it. I saw him zipping around on the sidewalk, and my inflatable heart just about skipped a beat. I was thrilled to see this young dude, who had no right to be so happy , . . yet he was; His heart was so full of God gas that he practically lifted off and flew.

And right then and there on the sidewalk outside of my new church, I knew that my heart Daddy had given me the gift of Isaac to help finish inflating my heart again. We sat and stood there like peas and carrots, and by the time I left that young man, my heart was like a giant blimp rising over Virginia Beach, floating up into the sky and out of sight, out of mind, out of touch.

Here's the last thing: I know the blimp of my heart is going to come crashing down again pretty soon. It's inevitable, so don't go feeling all sorry for me. I can't be up like I am most of the time without understanding the down. I can't be filled with God's special heart fuel without emptying myself of my personal gas.

God never stops filling me with the helium of His love, which means I can let that helium love out of me just as fast as I can to help fill others. Shoot, we're all just a bunch of love balloons walking around, making funny noises as our love comes out of us in an unending rush.

Fill 'er up?

Sophia flew into their hearts.

THIRTY-THREE

Crazy Love

for Ben & Carissa

JOHN KÖEHLER

As Jesus was getting into the boat, the man who had been demon-possessed begged to go with him.

MARK 5:18

June 26, 2007

Excerpt from a poem I wrote:

There's no mistaken that I'm achin'
Fakin' my way through life
Filled with contrition and blind ambition
I'm just hopin' for your permission
I'm just hopin' for you
Just hopin'
For you

I am in Baltimore at the moment, doing program for Baltimore Capernaum's day camp. The reason old God put me in this show is because of my disabilities. For some reason the very things about me that bother grown-ups and regular folks just don't seem to bother Capernaum kids all that much.

They reckon I'm one of theirs and accept me completely right from the get-go. My favorite thing in Capernaum is when a kid with Down syndrome, autism, or mental retardation tells me that I'm crazy. They are right, of course. I do act crazy and weird and strange and odd; I do things that they know are somehow wrong and that they could never get away with (maybe), but it makes them laugh just the same. The way I figure it, when a special kid who has spent his or her whole life knowing he or she isn't completely right or whole or complete or as smart and awesome as "normal" kids . . . when one of them looks at me being a total goof and says, "You're crazy!"—that is like angel music to me.

Because it means that in their eyes my status has lowered, which in turn has lifted them up in the world. Because they know darned sure that no way, Jose, are they anywhere as crazy as the old white dude with the beard. So suddenly they are elevated and can look down on someone else for a change. Not only that, but they feel sorry for me too, and that's a fine way to have a heart just about bust open.

Hey, I'm a weird guy for sure. I don't even fight it anymore. Sometimes I'm a stumbling block for people but—the way I figure it—the ijits just need to stay out of my way if they keep tripping over my sorry self. Most of the time I reckon I help folks take a silly slant on life and think about things a little differently and with some humor . . . in a crazy kind of way!

I would rather be crazy fun than normally boring. I'd rather be weird and awesome than acceptable and dull. I'd rather be a short-term shooting star than a long-term black hole sitting there all alone, sucking goodness into its sorry self. I'd rather throw off light that can help people see than steal their light. I know sometimes that my light will blind them, but—dang it all—that's the price I have to pay.

God did not make me a little baby flashlight; He made me a big ol' searchlight. I can light up the skies, but if you get too close, I can burn out the cornea of your heart. I don't mean to . . . I really don't. I don't mean to hurt folks, but my disability (one of them) is to share exactly the way I'm feeling, all the time, without holding back. The net result is that I come off being pretty crazy a lot of the time.

Here's the deal. God made me this way for a purpose: to bring joy into the world. His joy hopefully, but some of mine is mixed in there too. The problem is when it's all mine. That's when I get crazy mean instead of showing crazy love. My goal in life is to bring crazy love to the world because that is how God loves us. With such desperation and contentment and total completeness that it could only be called crazy.

So if ever I can love His people as crazily as He loves me, then I reckon I'm doing okay.

P.S.
March 31, 2008

I got an e-mail from my friend Carissa Mortenson. Carissa and Ben (her husband) just went to the Republic (not the state) of Georgia to pick up Sophie, their new adopted daughter. She has a withered little arm and rules them firmly with her oversized heart.

Ben came home, and Carissa remains, waiting for a judge to come to his senses and hoping that her senses will survive. The good news is that Georgians like beer. I told her to bring the judge a basket of beer mixed with peaches, to celebrate our state and his country. Maybe even crack open a beer in court.

As expected, she laughed at me, so my secret plan is working. The plan to help take my sister's mind off the awful wait she must endure so she can start up her life again. It will all be over soon, and Sophie will have suitors like me lined up to hold her.

I shall be her willing slave uncle. "Yes, oh great and powerful Sophie. Thy wish is my command."

MY INFLATABLE HEART

John & Angela at 2007 Surf Camp.

THIRTY-FOUR

Surfing Through Life

for Ren

> They're ... wild ocean waves leaving nothing on the beach but the foam of their shame.
>
> JUDE 1:13

November 17, 2007

Once when I was feeling depressed—on a morning like many mornings—I was walking down my driveway to pick up the newspaper. It's a lovely walk for me to make every day because of the mystery hidden inside the folded-up newsprint.

On that morning I was not feeling so lovely; I walked with heaviness and a downcast disposition as the waves of my recurring sadness washed over me. In some ways I am thankful for these waves. I can't help but wonder if God has given me the gift of my brain illness (bipolar syndrome) so that I can better appreciate how to ride the waves in this life.

Maybe sucking up some foam and getting rolled around by the arms of a wave is just the thing I need to remind me how lucky I am that I can ride most of the time. Maybe every time I start to drown in an undertow and get pulled out to sea, I remember what I did before, and I swim sideways and then back to the shores of my life.

The waves of our lives may remain more consistent than we think, but how we ride them changes, sometimes daily or by the hour. Or even moment by moment. An experienced surfer can ride even the largest waves with absolute safety and sheer joy, turning the power and strength of the waves into purpose and speed and life. But the inexperienced surfer will flounder and flail his way through the waves, getting knocked about as he struggles to get beyond the break and out to the launching place where other surfers line up and prepare to board their personal water trains back to shore.

Then it's our turn, and we are so frightened.

The waves are huge and scary, and we've never before tried to surf anything that big. Perhaps the size remains the same, but our fear has made the waves bigger in our psychosomatic version of reality. Our courage has been eaten by the sharks that swim the depths of our soul, and we imagine exactly how we will die when we dare to defy the dark waves speeding past us. How can we possibly align ourselves and become one with them without being killed?

The other surfers are laughing, and it clangs around inside our heads like personal insults. We think they have seen the doubt and fear and horror of our imminent failure reeking off us and the board we float on. Surely they must see the sharks circling in anticipation, waiting for us to be so stupid as to ride these impossible waves of life and fall down, down, down into their laughing mouths.

But the other surfers don't see the sharks because this is your life and your daydream—things that you have conjured up due to your despair and fear. The other surfers are living in the same moment as you, but their courage has not failed and they have not created imaginary sharks. Death does not await them on the soft, sandy bottom of their lives.

For them the sun shines and warms them to a perfect smile, leaving tan lines on their hearts that they share later for their friends and complete strangers to see. And in those shared moments of coconut oil and laugh lines crinkled into their eyes, they expose the full light of their lives and the waves they have ridden. They share their personal courage and conviction, which spill like a beautiful wave from their eyes into the hearts of those they love. In this way the expert knowledge of life surfing is passed on from one to another, and when that person meets the same kind of wave in the future, they will instinctively know how to ride it, how to love it, how to survive it. How to be it.

You remain on your board—afraid to move, afraid to ride or even paddle back to your personal failure, for only failure awaits a belly paddle that even the young groms can complete. The sun does not shine warmly upon your back but burns you. Sounds seem too sharp and loud, and the water is cold and black, calling you down to the sharks in your personal locker, constructed by none other than your old friend Davy Jones.

One of the veterans—a professional surfer—paddles over and floats next to you. His board bumps lightly against yours, and you feel a surge of adrenaline. For the umpteenth time you ask yourself, "Am I dreaming, or is this really happening?" But dream or not, you feel it happening as the energy from your new friend spreads through your board, up and into your arms and legs. Then it strikes your chest.

Your world explodes, and fragments of it fall down around you like the remains of another Terminator movie where you replace Arnold and blow up crap left and right. But you feel yourself becoming the good guy once again. The good Terminator. You feel courage attach itself to your blood cells, and your deflated ego is oxygenated and inflated. A crazy feeling overcomes you as the surfer beside you says, "Dude, let's ride."

You finally look over at him, but you can't see his face because the sun is reflecting off the water. A halo shimmers around his head. You ask him, "Are you an angel?" He throws back his halo head and laughs until a new sound is added to his laughter. You look around for the source and realize the source is you; this makes you laugh even louder.

You notice how great the sun feels on your back and how great the water feels as it laps and splashes across the board. A dolphin surfaces nearby, and you smell the fish it just ate. The sharks have fled, and the ocean is filled with beautiful colors that shimmer and sing to you.

"Let's ride"

Your angelic friend takes off paddling, and you follow with a laugh, desperate to catch up and maybe even share the same wave. Not always a good idea with the big stuff, but you don't care anymore. After you reach him, you catch the wave together. You cut over next to your new lit-up friend and accidentally run up on to his board; you hope your leashes don't get tangled.

But that never happens because the sun has come down to earth and is shining from your friend, and you are falling, falling back up to earth where you land on your driveway with a thud. You kneel there in the rocks and give thanks to the friend who pulled you back to surfing life once again. You wish you could have seen his face so you could thank him if you ever see him again. But you didn't and you can't.

Which means that for the rest of your life, you'll treat every single person you meet as if he or she is your angelic friend, the surfer buddy who helped you stand again in courage and audacity. Not such a bad payment to make, and one you look forward to as you trek down to the end of the driveway, pick up your newspaper, and prepare to surf another day away.

JOHN KÖEHLER

John's hot wheels are chick magnets.

THIRTY-FIVE
Marching J-Bots

for Poppa Jack

> During this time the Philistines mustered their troops to make war on Israel. Achish said to David, "You can count on this: You're marching with my troops, you and your men."
>
> 1 SAMUEL 28:1

October 14, 2007

Seems to me that some folks are prepared to completely give up their lives when they accept Jesus the Christ as their Savior. Now I know that I am already marching into the realm of heresy by saying this, but stay with me.

I am not for a minute saying that we shouldn't give our lives up to Jesus if we accept Him as our personal main man, the Big Kahuna, the reason for our lives, our mojo, our reason d'etre. Paul filled pages and pages telling us how we had to die to self and be crucified with Christ. He wanted us to turn aside from our old lives and live a new life, a life centered around God as given to us and sacrificed through the body of Jesus.

Okay so far?

I believe all that. But the fact remains that once we have done that, once we have given up our lives and let Christ in so He can take control, we must go back to living in a world filled with strife and nastiness that constantly calls us away from our promise. A heavenly promise lived by earthly beings. What to do, what to do? Some folks think the best thing to do is not to think anymore, not to make any decisions without an absolute assurance that God has approved them and is behind them. At face value, this seems a lovely idea and worthy of consideration.

But these same people then give up all semblance of passion and become vanilla-flavored little mice afraid of doing what the Father hasn't yet told them to do. What if He disagrees? What if they do the wrong thing? What if they think outside the box, and God punishes them? Better to be safe and not sorry, to look around at what the really good Christians are doing and walk in lockstep with them. Lift God up and put yourself down, flagellate yourself for His sake and desaturate your life so that it becomes void of color and passion.

But here's the thing: God did not create us to be His robots. He does not want us to be small and puny. He does not want us to hold back our passion and try to be exactly like everyone else so we are protected from the evils of life and decision-making.

He wants us out there, fighting for what we believe. Fighting for Him, lifting Him up, and thus lifting ourselves up. He wants us to be strong and passionate. He wants us to use our heads and figure it all out. He is exactly like a parent to us. In fact—genetically speaking—He is our parent, so His motivation is always to lift us up and to provide for us. He desires our happiness and all the bounty of the world. He wants us to make Him proud.

When Jesus ignited His ministry, He taught His disciples everything He knew and gave them perfect examples of how to live and how not to live. He told them to do as He did, to think as He did, and to love as He did. Then He sent them off as His disciples to do His work. But not as automatons receiving signals from the mother ship, connected by a homing signal. Automatons are worthless without continuous code describing the exact actions to be taken.

Jesus sent them off with the gift of His Holy Spirit and with the understanding that they were to use their gifts, personalities, egos, and everything that made them unique. He taught them to use the power of their intuition. Their human intuition that, when combined with the Holy Spirit and His teachings, would make them invincible and amazing.

He said, "Do as I do," but He also expected them to make

decisions and therefore mistakes. "Nothing ventured, nothing gained" is an apt saying for those pretending to be disciples. They think they can afford to sit back and wait for the mother ship or—to be more precise, the father ship—to give them explicit directions and orders. Sometimes they will simply be cut off and have to decide on their own without Dad being there.

When you make the calls and it goes well, and someone says, "Way to go, that was awesome," what will you say? Will you be consumed by the ridiculous false humility that overcomes so many Christians these days? They say, "It wasn't me, it was God." They say they really didn't do anything. What a crock!

God is our Father; Jesus is our Savior; and we have the Holy Spirit in us all the time. But God does not control us without our agreement because He has given us the freedom to choose in all things. It is our choice to do or not to do; it is our choice exactly how to do it, when to do it, and what kind of style to use. We are not useless robots for Christ, but free-thinking disciples of Christ.

Therefore, when we do well, we have the right to take pleasure and be stoked about what we did because God is in us and works through us, and we are us. In our free agreement we assumed control of our own destiny as our Father in heaven watches in hope and love. Many would argue with me and say that we do not control our own destinies or our lives, but I must disagree. That is not the God I know.

The God I know shows us and teaches us how to live; He gives us the Law, new and old, as our teaching aid. He sent His Son to die for us and gave us His Holy Spirit. And then He sends us out to do it on our own, Him within us, always with us, regardless of the part-time silence. But He does not move our bodies in a certain way, nor does He conjure up perfect thoughts so that we might always do right.

God wants to reduce us in a way similar to how the Marines tear a man down in boot camp. But they don't leave him there. They begin rebuilding him and give him the tools, integrity, and discipline he needs to live as a marine. Just so with us. God wants to tear us down, remove our egos, and rebuild us in a new way, as a new person. God made us and gave us His Holy Spirit to help us choose. Yet part of the way He created us is with an earthly ego and passions and abilities and giftedness.

The God I know pushes us out the door when the time is right, like a good Dad, and says, "Now get out here and do your best. Remember what I taught you. I'm in your heart and always with you. I love you with all my heart no matter what. As far as I'm concerned, you are the best thing that ever happened to Me." I know that is radical, but I believe that the love our Father has for us is just so radical. We are His; He made us. But He lets us go out and choose our lives. He gives us a chance to be more like Him or more like the world.

And then He waits for us to come home; He lingers at the end of the driveway waiting for us—tired and forlorn—to appear. Our Daddy runs down to meet us, welcoming us home, whispering how much He loves us and telling us that everything is going to be okay. We're home.

Now tell me this, would God act this way about a robot?

JOHN KÖEHLER

Brandon is stepping it up.

THIRTY-SIX

Becoming a Made Man

for Michael

> This is the written account of Adam's line. When God
> created man, he made him in the likeness of God.

GENESIS 5:1

October 14, 2007

The other day I was thinking (this sometimes happens when I'm bored) about the idea of becoming a "made man" and what that might mean to a Christian man versus a wise guy.

I was talking to a friend about the semi-righteous judgment people use against each other when comparing pedigrees. We do this to see whether you deserve to be with me or I deserve to be with you. Many people will deny this, yet the fact is that we all do it, consciously or not.

Who says the (East) Indians are the only folks with a caste system!

We are clearly warned not to compare ourselves to others, yet we all do it. Sometimes this is a good thing, like when we notice positive things we love about others and incorporate them into our behavior. That is partly how our personality is formed, with a conglomeration of layers that slowly form over the years. Layers of little moments and behaviors that we borrow from others and slowly make our own, added to our genetic and familial predispositions.

Through basic interactions, people rub off on us all the time, leaving a little bit of themselves behind. It's up to us to choose whether or not we will add the way she says a certain thing or looks a certain way to our own dynamic. We are chameleons, constantly changing.

Maybe the big question is whether or not we compare ourselves in love and peace. Love is the key, and without it our constant comparisons become nothing but an evil way to raise or lower ourselves in our own eyes or in the eyes of others. We want to look good. We want to seem better than they are . . . or we are. Maybe we even want them to be less than we are; then we realize that they are so much better than we could ever be, and we plummet back down to earth, down into the realm of depression and smallness.

But it's not supposed to be that way. Comparisons can be dangerous, even in love. When it comes right down to it, there are really only two things God really wants us to do with regard to love:

1. Love Him.
2. Love each other and ourselves.

Loving God can be fairly easy and straightforward, mainly because humans are not involved. But loving each other can be one of the hardest things on the planet, while loving yourself is generally seen as politically incorrect.

We are all called to treat each other like family, which in some families might not be such a good thing. So if your family relations aren't that good, then replace the word family with neighbor. And if your relationships with your neighbors are kind of rocky, and you don't actually know any of them, much less show them any kindness, then replace that word with friend. Family, neighbor, or friend. The idea is that you treat this person and—by extension—all people with love, respect, and integrity.

But, shoot fire, that can be a mighty hard thing to do.

Now according to my sources (Mr. and Mrs. Google and Wikipedia), becoming a "made man" can mean different things to different people. In the Mafia, to become a made man meant that you were inducted into the family by shedding blood (preferably someone else's) through a family-contracted killing. As a result of conducting the murder, the made man was treated with new respect and accorded all the rights of being a part of their new family. This included physical, financial, emotional, and spiritual protection.

Performing the first murder became known as "making your bones," probably referring to the fact that murder turns someone from a living human being into a skeleton. This act separated people who could be trusted with family business from those who could not. The requirements were so deplorable that few were willing to do it. Many were called, but few were chosen, and even making your bones was not a guarantee of acceptance if the murder was deemed sloppy or dishonorable in any way.

Which brings me back to how Christians "make our bones."

> Q. By what process are we brought into the family and accorded the rights, respect, and honor given to those who are full members of the family?
> A. Accept Jesus the Christ as your Lord and Savior.
>
> Q. Who determines when we are accepted?
> A. God does and already did.
>
> Q. Are their different levels of acceptance and hierarchy, as in the levels within the Mafia: soldier, captain, consigliere, underboss, and boss?
> A. No. You're out or you're in.

Which brings me back to the way we compare ourselves to each other and the unwritten hierarchy we establish when we are together. Do I deserve to be there? Am I good enough? Will I be asked to leave? What the crap are they doing here, and who invited them? In the Club of Life, how do we get a ticket redeemable at the front door so we don't have to wait in line like the rest of those tired schleps hanging around until the door opens? Where do we get a golden ticket?

Becoming a Made Man for God is similar to the Mafia version in that blood is spilled. Or more correctly, blood was spilled. Jesus shed His blood for us so that we no longer have to spill any blood—animal or human. He became the hit man and the victim for our sake, and the only thing we have to do is accept His blood.

That is disgusting! When the Mafia underling, who so desperately wants the full respect and protection from the family, commits the murder and makes his bones, he effectively washes himself in the blood of the victim; that sacrificial blood is his redeeming ticket in the door. We want the protection and grace and love and life that God can give, but the only way we can make our spiritual bones is to take part in the death of Jesus.

I know that some may accuse me of blasphemy because God alone was responsible for the death of His Son. There is no question that Jesus alone accepted His own death and committed His own murder for our sake. Even so, we are not stupid sheep led to the slaughter without a clue. We are the people standing below Jesus when He died. We can feel the blood and sweat pour off Him as it sears into our skin and souls.

We did not cause Him to die, unless you consider our accumulated sins to be cause enough. But it was for our sake that Jesus took the cup and drank it down to death, a death that He did not deserve and did not want to know at the end. His human heart and soul were afraid, and He did not want to bear the pain and be cut off from His Dad for three seconds, much less three days.

Jesus became His own hit man for us, and His blood flowed out for our sake in a river of death and life. The only way we can become fully made—fully alive—is to step into that river and wash ourselves in it. Jesus made our bones for us when He allowed His body to be broken on the cross. He took the hit for us. He made the kill.

Jesus committed murder for our sake by allowing his own execution. He took away our need to make our bones to prove to the world how tough we are. He made it possible for us to not have to do anything to get in the front door to die. Thanks to Him, all we have to do now is walk through the door and live.

JOHN KÖEHLER

Austen is another princess of God.

THIRTY-SEVEN
Rabbit Holes

for my Patty

JOHN KÖEHLER

> Oh, blessed be God! He didn't go off and leave us.
> He didn't abandon us defenseless,
> helpless as a rabbit in a pack of snarling dogs.
>
> PSALM 124:6

I hate waiting on God. To say otherwise would be a lie, and then I would be like one of my friends who only speaks that which is encouraging, regardless of whether or not it is the complete truth. I just can't do that. Why should I only tell one part of the truth?

Doesn't God prefer if we tell Him everything, regardless of the outcome? Didn't David tell His God (who happens to be our God too) everything he was going through: the good, bad, and ugly? Of course he did. David admitted what was troubling him and told the truth about his problems and issues to his heavenly Father and—through his writing—to us.

Sometimes he yelled at God and said, "Where are You?" It was not the timid cry of a child, but the demanding and expectant cry of a grown man, a king, in fact. Sometimes David moved away from God, yet it seemed to him that God had left him.

Either way he was alone, and he was not getting the answers he needed. He was cut off, and he needed to know the right thing to do, the right path to take, the perfect thing to say. But God was gone, so David had to wait on Him. I don't think David liked that any more than I do . . . and for the same reasons.

Waiting on God is a good thing, and many folks know and believe that. It means that we are submitting ourselves to the reality of

God being the omnipotent ruler of our lives and we are no longer in control. It means accepting that it is not about our will being done, but His will.

But waiting is a passive undertaking and—for guys like David and me—it is something to be avoided. If we are cut off from God and in need of His counsel, then why not simply go back and look at the end goal of God's plan, the one He already approved? Why deal with trivia when the end of the rainbow can be seen either by a vision or in clear sight?

The old saying that God is in the details does not always ring true for guys like me. God needs to stay up at fifty thousand feet and let me take care of the details way down here where the pawpaws grow. Nine times out of ten I get it right, and that's a pretty good percentage. Can't we all just play nice and let bygones be bygones for that one in ten time when things go wrong and God isn't there to bail you out? Won't waiting simply exacerbate the problem and make it bigger?

I call these kinds of problems rabbit holes. They show up along the path of every mission God has sent me on. They are offshoots along the way He has shown me, cleverly disguised in the guise of the "one true way."

Much like Satan himself, rabbit holes do not always look like the evil things that they are. Satan is not a horned creature all in red, but a beautifully charming individual who is fun to be around and knows how to throw a good party. He does not yell at us, but whispers the way as if he is only concerned about our best interest and wants us to succeed. We believe him and trust him. He is so ingrained in our psyche that in spite of all the many rabbit holes he has sent us down, we continue to listen to him and seek out his counsel. Because he is like us, he knows our heart and never leaves us.

The truth is that Satan does not want us to stand on our own in strength and glory. He would rather we lean on him in weakness and need. He does not want us to grow up into the people God has made us to be; instead he would prefer that we remain here below with him, firmly attached to the way and the wiles of the world we adore. His world and ours. Home.

God, on the other hand, wants us to learn to walk on our own.

He teaches us and shows us the way with patience and the love only a parent can give. Then He steps aside and lets us walk on our own. We love this, for we know that because of our Dad we are walking and running and flying our way to freedom. We know He loves us, and the world is so right.

But then it all comes crashing down, and we go down another rabbit hole until we crash into the end of it, where our good friend and counselor Satan says, "Stay here and rest for a while. I will take care of you. Don't be afraid."

There in the darkness of our temporary tomb, we cry out to God, but we cannot see Him, but God is not in the darkness of the tomb; He waits for us at the end of the tunnel where the sun shines and daisies grow and the angels whisper to us, "Come back, come back to the light. Come out of the darkness. Dad is waiting." But we would rather wait on Satan for a while and revel in our misery and feel sorry for ourselves.

Then God sends one of our attending angels down into the rabbit hole, and it leads us out into the rest of our life. We see our Dad waiting for us, and we run to Him and hug Him, creating a lake of our tears, all the while yelling at Him and asking him where He's been. He laughs at us and holds us close, and all is right with the world again. You look back at the rabbit hole, but it is gone. Grass grows where the hole had been as if it were never there.

"Why didn't you wait for Me, John?" my Dad asks. "Why didn't you wait for Me to tell you about this rabbit hole? I could have told you it was a path to nowhere. Why didn't you wait for Me?"

You can't think of an answer because you're so tired, so very tired from the time spent in the blackness of the rabbit hole. You know He's right, and you swear to never make the same mistake again. You promise to wait on your Dad to help you next time.

But you break your promise over and over and over again, and eventually you learn that the only real promise you have is that at the end of every rabbit hole, your old Dad will be waiting for you.

Katie brings her signs of peace.

THIRTY-EIGHT

The Bark of the Forest

for Kimberly

JOHN KÖEHLER

> But the angel said to her, "Do not be afraid, Mary, you have found favor with God.

LUKE 1:30

From the beginning of time God has shown Himself to us in various ways. He showed himself to Moses, the prophets, the shepherds, and others in ways that were always frightening. So much so that God—usually through an emissary like an angel or a bush—would tell us not to be afraid because He knew all our fears, including the fear of Him.

Things of the "other world" are scary to be sure, and no matter how close of a relationship with God we may profess, there is a mystery that brings with it questions and voids of wonder that are filled by our capable sci-fi imaginations. We tend to be afraid of that which we don't know or have never met. We aren't sure how we will react or how they will react, so the seeds of doubt turn into the flowers of fear.

Remember meeting your first-grade teacher for the first time, after dreaming about her consuming you whole in the morning when your parents pushed you forward into the gaping maws of her grip? She seemed huge when you stepped forward to finally meet her in person for the first and last time, your death awaiting. But she hugged you and welcomed you, and the demons of your dreams whined and said, "No fair!"

We are the best at dreaming and scheming of the worst possible outcomes, no matter how strong the evidence is to the contrary. In spite of her smiles and the way she looks at you, you are convinced that the girl you later marry wants nothing to do with you. No matter the hundreds of times you were able to wind your way through the maze of your job, the terror of your depression and brain sickness convinces you that your job is over. Regardless of the evidence that stares us in the face, we look beyond it to the horizon of our hope and imagine that dragons lurk just over the edge . . . or perhaps a ship that will carry us away to another destiny. Any other destiny but this one, Lord.

Sometimes the truth that we already know in our minds is overruled by the doubts in our hearts because our souls have a mind of their own and can hijack our thoughts and actions to a place where we will be safe and sound. A place where we will never have to meet the demons who are marching down the road to eat us.

Demons and angels. Angels and demons. In our minds they are sometimes one and the same, for both are unknown and scary; anyone who says otherwise is missing the point. If we paint angels as glowing beings with wings and whiteness, beautiful to behold, why did the shepherds shriek and cower down when the angels appeared to announce the birth of a Savior?

To encounter a supernatural thing is to stand in the presence of God or much worse, and no matter how much we have read the Bible and prayed and gone to church, we really don't know what it will be like. So we are scared to death when it actually happens. But what if it is already happening all the time, all around us? What if God is showing Himself to us in the most obvious ways, and we see Him every day?

What if he's that old neighbor whom everybody knows and loves. Whenever you see him, you smile and wave. He tells you that you live on the best street in town, and you believe him.

What if the lady you met in Farm Fresh and spoke with for just a few minutes was an angel sent by God to help restore your heart? She does restore your heart. You look forward to meeting her again so you can thank her, but you never see her again so you wonder if she was a tourist angel or just a passing daydream.

What if the sunset you watched while you were stuck in traffic—

late for an event—was painted by angels just for you. A personal painting intended to show you the beauty of your life and exactly why you should be thankful for what you have and precisely how much God loves you, even when you are in traffic. A godly performance piece.

What if your dog is a four-legged brown angel sent for no other reason than to bring you joy, including the times you had to clean up his poop, either by hand or by foot. Could it be that your dog was a gift from God, a dog angel, an expression of your spiritual father? Yippee yi, yippee yay, yippee bow wow wow . . .

What about the way the sunlight filters in through the sky and the trees and the window and the blinds and creates the most unique patterns on the walls of your bedroom as you lie in bed and wonder what the day will bring? What if we are always wondering what the day will bring, when it has already brought great wonder, right before us, alive and real? But we don't see it because the dancing light angels before our eyes fade as our mind conjures up visions of the ways we hope to please God later that day—later, not now. We don't see them dancing right in front of us, plain as day, as obvious as the nose on our face.

We never see the nose on our face because we are always looking out, far into the distance, where the ships will one day come and bring all the things we have hoped for. We look out so far to the mystery of our future, yet right before us the light angels dance and speak to us about the practical presence and natural beauty of God.

We look for God in the supernatural that is beyond us, but He is here in the natural things all around us. We hope to live in the kingdom of heaven one day, but Jesus said the kingdom of heaven is at hand, and we are living in it, unwilling subjects of an unseen King.

If God is real and He created all things and gave us our lives and destinies, then He is in every thing and person and act and—whether we like it or not—He is constantly with us, showing us His beauty and love and compassion mixed in with the mortal ugliness of the world we made. The world that we look beyond in search of God.

But what if He is here? What if He really is here in the world all the time, and all we have to do is look and see? Turn your head just the right way. Listen with your eyes closed. Look right in front of you, fool! He's not way out there; He's right in front of you.

Laurel and Kyle demonstrate how to keep it all in the family. Photo by Glen McClure.

PART FIVE

OUT THERE

Hammy is a race car driver.

THIRTY-NINE

Motorworld

for Big Nate

> *Then he shouted, "Hurry! Go quickly! Don't stop!"
> The boy picked up the arrow and
> returned to his master.*
>
> 1 SAMUEL 20:38

April 28, 2007

Dear Capernaum,

Well, it was a little bit scary and a whole lot of fun when Capernaum went to Motorworld. Motorworld is basically a bunch of different tracks with souped-up go-karts. Now if you question my sanity for bringing people with physical, mental, and emotional disabilities to Motorworld.... shoot, I don't blame you!

Imagine the young track workers watching us take Emily, Regina, and A J (all with cerebral palsy, all quadriplegic) out of their wheelchairs and folding them each into a go-kart. "Hey, what are you doing?" they asked. "I just saw you take him out of a wheelchair. If he can't walk, how can he drive?"

Now we should have said, "Well, we don't know for sure if he can," but since my momma made me a little bit smart, we just said, "Oh sure he can drive." Shaking their heads and wondering, they let us do it. But what were they going do, throw out a bunch of cripples? Nah.

MY INFLATABLE HEART

Emily was ready to speed. She can't talk, can't walk, can't drive, can't . . . hang on a minute! Well, let's say she had never driven before. But we got her into the go-kart, wedged her foot against the go pedal, didn't worry too much about the stop pedal, straightened her up in the seat, and off she went. She made it about halfway around, then kind of flopped over in the go-kart, forcing the steering wheel over with her, thus veering the go-kart into the side wall with a soft landing. The track guys ran out, straightened her up, and off she went again.

Emily is not supposed to race vehicles. But she did.
Some things are not possible. But we do them anyway.
God makes us all supernatural, crippled or not.
That's what Capernaum is all about.

A J and Regina both drove wheelchairs. Regina didn't like driving go-karts all that much, but A J was a doggone NASCAR terror out there. After they both tried it on their own, they drove together, A J in the driver's seat. A J had a great time, but Regina might have been a tad scared on account of the fact that the driver was a quadriplegic who happened to be her fiancé.

When the race was over, Regina was overheard saying, "He's crazy!" (talking about A J's driving). Naturally this pleased A J to no end, as all guys want nothing more than to impress their dates with wild race-car-driving skills.

I would have been more impressed with A J if he hadn't rear-ended me when I was stuck against the track wall after an accident which *I did not cause*. A J could have gone around me, and he should have. But he used the old "I'm a crippled guy, I can't steer" excuse. I don't buy that, A J. I am coming for you, boy!

Hamilton is a big black kid with autism. He's six foot five, weighs about 270, is a big old teddy bear, and has a heart the size of a Mack truck. When he stands next to you, he's usually smiling and rocking back and forth or pacing a bit. But when he got behind the wheel of a go-kart, his whole world was focused on the pinpoint of road before him.

Hamilton was an excellent driver, but he had no right to be.

I passed him during a race, then slowed down to let him pass me. I laughed as I drove beside him, watching his powerful focus and concentration—a small smile on his face, his head bobbing a little, forward and back. As we prepared to go into a curve, he noticed a bird flying over, so he did the only right thing and craned his head back to watch it fly over his shoulder. I figured he was going to crash, but apparently God was the copilot because Hamilton lightly bounced off the curve, turned around, and just went on with the race like nothing happened.

As we came into the final lap, one of the young track guys came out to wave us over to the pit lanes. He was standing on the inside lane, the same lane Hamilton was driving in. I watched the whole thing unfold. Hamilton was driving, very focused. He was in his lane, and the young track guy shouldn't have been. At the very last minute the track guy realized that Hamilton was not going to drive around him and that he was going to get run over. He jumped straight up into the air and did a half somersault while Hammy drove right under him, happy as can be, in his lane, in his groove, in his element. A race-car driver. The track kid was a little banged up, but okay. I don't think he'll ever stand in front of an oncoming car again. Certainly not if it's driven by Hamilton!

Some of the Capernaum drivers forgot about their stop pedals when they came into pit row and just banged into the last car, creating a domino effect, one car after another, until the first car shot out like a comet.

No one was hurt that day except for the momentarily mentally confused track boy who had the audacity to play chicken with Hamilton.

Hammy won.

Love,

John

Eric is a silent snorer.

FORTY

The Mayor & The Monkey

for Athena

> "The animals going in were male and female of every living thing, as God had commanded Noah. Then the LORD shut him in."
>
> GENESIS 7:16

May 12, 2007

The Norfolk Zoo hosted a Day of Disabilities. Pretty much anyone was welcome as we all have something that ain't perfect about us. But Capernaum showed up for those who really do have a disability and for their families, along with those who maybe just have a disabled heart and kind of wandered on by.

Lucky for me, Miss Angela North South East and West was there; otherwise I would have wandered around for a long time—a little strand of drool sliding down my chin—while all the vendors gave me brochures and asked me, "Do you need us to take you somewhere, honey?"

Yes, please. Where's my double-wide? Wasn't I supposed to have a double-wide like all the big stars in Hollywood? Please, Lord, just once can I have a double-wide backstage room to hang out in, all in white inside and out, with just about anything you could imagine to eat in there, and foot massagers. You gotta have foot massagers. I'm thinking there will be lots of all-white double-wide trailers with foot massagers in heaven.

Angela and I had a bunch of leftover black T-shirts from our Bike Picnic, so we decided to use them as prizes in a giveaway contest. Anyone with a disability was eligible. All a person had to do was answer a Bible question and then act like a monkey. Hey, we were at the zoo, so it made sense to us Capernaum animals.

A lot of happy folks came up wanting the shirts and not even knowing why. The shirts could have had anything at all on them, and they still would have wanted them. We lobbed the questions at them, depending on what we deemed were their abilities. They always got it right in the end, and we pretended not to notice when a mom or a caretaker leaned in to whisper the answer, like the voice of God coming down from on high.

The beautiful thing is that some of those folks yelled out the answer and completely forgot that their personal version of God had whispered them the answer, because they had gotten it right. Yay for them!

Then came the hard part: they had to act like a monkey. Most folks didn't have a problem with this, but some were mighty embarrassed and would only do it when Angela and I went out and did it with them. If you share their embarrassing moment, it spreads out the shame, and they don't feel so bad. I think that's some kind of monkey logic, or maybe it's pretzel logic; I can never be too sure.

Then I saw the mayor of Norfolk.

I'm one of those guys who pretty much treats everyone the same, including big shots and famous people. Seems to work; I always figure that they want to be treated like human beings, just regular like. So I went right up to Mayor Fraim and gave him a Young Life frisbee, and shoot, that boy carried it with him all the way around the tent until he came to our table.

I didn't waste a minute; I held up a shirt and told him that I'd like to give him one, but he'd have to win it just like everyone else. I left out the part about needing to have a disability since I figured being a big-shot mayor had to have one of some kind. The lady behind him—probably his handler—looked sort of amused and horrified, if that's even possible.

I asked the mayor the name of the town where Jesus had been born, and he correctly answered "Bethlehem." Then I said he had to act like a monkey—crazy and loud—and he started shaking his head and laughing. He rubbed his hand across the top of his mostly bald head, and I realized that while he did not want to act like a monkey, laughing, shaking his head, and rubbing the top of his head were consistent with monkey behavior. So I gave him the shirt.

There was something important in that little moment with the mayor. Maybe it's that no matter how much we don't want to do something, sometimes our very nature and genetic behavior give us away, and we do it anyway. I don't recollect or really know, but it was just a moment among millions of moments that wrap themselves up into the balls of our lives.

After I gave him the shirt, the mayor asked me if I'd ever been to Israel, and I said no. He said, "Go if you can," and proceeded to tell me some stories about his trip. We were just hanging out talking together like peas and carrots, right there under the big white tent at the zoo. Just two big monkeys with the heart of God beating strongly inside us, shining like searchlights, and for just a moment our agape bound us together. I kind of liked him; he seemed like a good man to me.

I also liked young Miss Danny, who rolled into my life that day with a pushy attitude and a big smile. But she didn't fool this fool, and soon we were dancing together and laughing. Faster than you could say "Skedaddle!" the clam shells of our hearts opened up, and our little God pearls of love danced together. We became family. And there ain't nothing we can do about it, either. Way too late for that. Game over, dude.

Yup, I'm in love with Danny, and I do believe that she loves me too. I don't know about you, but it sure makes me feel finer than Caroliner when I know for certain that someone loves me. Makes me feel fine.

Just like a monkey with a whole bushel of bananas and nothing else to do but eat them all day long.

Love,

John

AJ is another awesome man of God.

FORTY-ONE

The Griffon & The Idiot

for AJ

JOHN KÖEHLER

> "Wise men store up knowledge,
> but the mouth of a fool invites ruin."
>
> PROVERBS 10:14

May 20, 2007

Well, everyone and their mother—and sometimes their brothers and sisters—were pumped up and excited as can be about the new ride at Busch Gardens (BG). Griffon has a vertical drop that scares you so badly you might instantly void yourself of any bodily fluids stupid enough to be in the vicinity. Now that's scary!

Just the notion of going to BG was enough to make some folks so disabled in their speech compartments that all they could do was smile and nod their heads and scream. This is a universally understood language at Capernaum and was developed prior to the creation of the Tower of Babel.

Everyone was ready, including the kids, parents, senior leaders, and yours truly. After all, what could be better than taking twenty-five people—the majority with a disability of some kind—through the crowds and craziness of America's most beautiful theme park?

Herding elephants is what could be better . . . and that is what it was actually like.

I confess to feeling kind of guilty whenever I walk through the special disabled entrance and avoid all the lines in order to help one of our physically disabled friends onto a ride. I mean, I know that the people in line look at the person I just helped out of a wheelchair, thinking, "Wow, that's so awesome. I don't mind waiting for them." But I'm also convinced that they look at me—fully able-bodied—and think, "That big jerk! He's holding us up."

What am I going to do, lecture them about the park rules? Tell them that I have a disability in my head, but they just can't see it? Limp a little or crawl to the car? Nah, I just act official. Once the special needs part of getting a physically disabled person on the ride is overcome—you unhook them, unstrap them, un-Velcro them, untie them, lift them, pull your back, steady them, position them, guide them, and set them in the ride, then I am free to ride just like everyone else.

Some of the cerebral palsy (CP) folks were concerned about the roller coasters. I tried to tell them that their fears could all be overcome with a large dose of prayer and enough Velcro and packing tape to permanently bind them to the ride seat. Not to mention neck braces to stop their heads from flopping around and oxygen tanks to help them breathe when they laugh so hard that they just can't catch their breath as it runs away down the hill to the next ride.

Just like other parts of their bodies that are affected, CP folks sometimes have withered diaphragms and muscles in the stomach and chest, which make breathing hard for them at times. Think about getting excited and laughing so hard that you have to pause and concentrate on breathing for a few seconds. Multiply that by five, and add the fear factor of not knowing for sure if you would be able to breathe. This gives you an idea of what riding a roller coaster can be like for a person with CP, no matter how awesome their courage and heart. No matter their hearts' desire, their bodies are in mutiny.

Our first adventure was a water ride called Escape from Pompeii. Technically it is a roller coaster, but, of course, I did not mention this until after the ride was over. It took some cajoling for Danni to leave her wheelchair and go on the ride, but eventually she agreed. She got wet, she was scared, and in the end she squealed like a banshee with fearful delight, pumping her fist in the air and screaming, "I did it! I did it!"

Capernaum is about doing it when you have no right to do it.

We were scheduled to go on the Griffon, the new ride with the vertical drop, around quarter of five, so we wasted time elsewhere. Allen had come with Emily, another CP person, and Holly, Emily's provider. (Holly had no clue what she was getting into trying to transport and care for not one but two large, profoundly physically disabled people.) Around three or so, Allen rolled up to me and said, "We haven't eaten lunch yet." I told him that was not my problem, but the problem of his buddy and the person who was responsible for him. He said okay, but he was still hungry. In order to teach him a lesson about making sure he had folks lined up to care for him, I refused to get him lunch.

I wonder what Jesus would have done . . .

Turns out that when it came time for us to ride Griffon, Allen and Emily could not wait any longer and had to be fed. So Rusty and Tara took pity on Holly and fed Allen. We rode Griffon, and then we went to find the folks who were left behind. Holly was feeding Emily, a most difficult endeavor as she has no teeth; you need to help her chew—in a manner of speaking—by inserting your hands in with the food. Not for the faint of heart!

So there we were. I was so pissed about Allen keeping Rusty and Tara away from the ride that I started ripping him right there in front of everyone. It was righteous anger, to be sure, but I should have been done it privately, just the two of us. Allen knew I was right and admitted as much to me afterward, promising never again to throw himself at the mercy of Capernaum without being sure he had a buddy lined up.

In the middle of reaming Allen, I looked over at Holly, who had paused in feeding Emily to stare at the monster in her midst—the guy who had temporarily forgotten about grace and mercy and love and peace and understanding. She was looking right at me, and I felt small.

Holly missed going on Griffon because she cared for Emily, but

I went on the ride because I didn't want to care for the man who has always assumed my care would be there. Allen's faith in me and in Capernaum is huge, and though his physical needs are immense and he can be a total pain in the butt, his faith compels us to help him.

And that is precisely what God does for us, over and over again.

He loves us and extends His grace and love to us constantly, over and over again. Regardless of our mistakes. Regardless of our idiocy. In spite of our cruelty and stupidity. He loves us nonstop, and He wants us to love each other in the same way.

I rode Griffon down the vertical drop, and my heart took the vertical drop to meanness and spite. This is not a ride I care to go on, but one I can't seem to stay away from. Good thing God loves idiots like me whether I'm going up or coming down. Amen.

JOHN KÖEHLER

Mike puts shoes on God's prayers.

FORTY-TWO

Booker Beach Club

for Mikey B

JOHN KÖEHLER

> *Can an African change skin? Can a leopard get rid of its spots? So what are the odds on you doing good, you who are so long-practiced in evil?*
>
> JEREMIAH 13:23

July 10, 2007

My good friend and homeboy Mike Burbage—or Mikey B. as I call him because I'm slow and can't pronounce his last name because it's all French and stuff—asked me a while back if he could bring his kids out to Koehlers' Beach House, aka our home. And since my aim is to be like Mike, I said, "Sure, bring everyone, my brother."

Mike works for Young Life too—just like me, only better. And instead of his kids being disabled like mine, they are just about perfect in every way. Well, it could be said that some of them need more money or maybe another chance at school or college. Or maybe their skin color could be like a disability for them sometimes. Other than that, they're all just about the most awesome kids on the planet.

You see, Mike works with kids of color.

Now I paid attention and didn't see any purple kids there, or red, green, or orange, though I was hoping to. I saw a bunch of kids in varying shades of mocha, chocolate, burnt umber, sienna, cocoa, earth tones, and other beautiful versions of God's varied shades of beauty.

I'm not saying the boys are beautiful like the girls; otherwise they'd get embarrassed. Though they do squeal like girls when the water balloons hit them, or when the waves down at the beach hit them, or when they almost got hit with the pies and ran just like little baby girls. Wait, that was the leaders, the so-called grown-ups. The only one staying behind to take his pie like a man was Mr. Mikey B. himself.

Even though I sometimes say that I'm a black man trapped in a white man's body, let there be no mistake that I am, in fact, through and through 100 percent whitey. Yesiree Bob—or Mary or whatever your name is—I am a gringo, a white-bread honky, and proud of it. I'm happy with my own culture, even though I'm a bit confused as to what exactly my culture is. I'm German American, so that's cool. But I really love the Brits and act that way sometime, and I love Native Americans and sometimes affect their ways. And don't forget our Latino friends, always so passionate. Yeah, I wanna be like them.

Things became clear to me when I went to New Zealand in 1996. While my good friend Bill Ressler and I tooled around the beautiful south island, we affected three primary American dialects: redneck, black homey, and Crackhead Bob. Crackhead Bob was Howard Stern's latest thing, perfect for two idiot guys on the loose. Redneck was easy to do. And black homey slang was fun to do and identified us two white boys as American. Can you even believe that?

Back to the Booker Beach Club. So Mikey B. showed up with a whole passel of his students and leaders and parents. I put a bunch of them to work filling water balloons, setting up tables, cleaning up dog poo. I'm not kidding! James was an amazing dude who showed up, and bang!, we were instant brothers. I figured since I'd ask my brother to shovel up dog poo in my yard, I'd ask my new brother James. And he did it! Then he cooked (after he washed his hands really well), and I think he put a new roof on my house; the dude was just everywhere.

I set up a sound system and brought out my computer with my music. Now the music on a forty-nine-year-old white dude's computer may not be perfect for teenage black kids. So one young lady whipped out her iPod, and soon enough we had some of their jammin' hot music, complete with MF this and MF that... runnnnnnnn! Well, we nipped that right in the bud, and I had a good talk with young Mr. DJ, who did a fantastic job after that. And God came back down and danced among us for a while.

After we ate and hung out and played, we walked down to the beach. I brought a few foam surfboards lent by Freedom Surf (may their wax never melt). Girls and then guys got on top of those surfboards and rode them in easy as pie—a little of my white surfer culture wiping off on them; they liked it too!

Here's the thing: after you get through the different hairdos and hairnets and do-rags and bling-bling and tattoos and dialects and disconnects and all the other things that make African American kids as different from me as salt is to pepper . . . after you get through all that silly surface stuff, which can keep us apart, it turns out that we're all just the same on the inside. Those kids were just kids. Just kids whose cake was the same flavor as mine, with icing that sure did taste different, but guess what? Cake is cake!

And ain't it just fine that God made us all so beautiful and unique—some light and some dark, some tall and some short, some heavy and some light, some disabled and some abled. If you can close your eyes and open the eyes of your heart, then you can see how alike we really are. Nothing matters after that, and we accept the simple truth that we all come from the same Daddy, which makes us family. Now you can open up your eyes again.

Last night we had the Booker T. Washington Beach Club over here on Sixtieth Street, and I was happy that God invited me too. I was happy as pie to have some of that fine black culture laid across my heart to make me a better man. Happier still to meet so many new little brothers and sisters. God is so good.

Love,

John

Rudy could run for Mayor of Norfolk.

FORTY-THREE

Locked Out in Norfolk

for Jenny, Cherry & Ron

JOHN KÖEHLER

> "When everyone who was there to greet him had gone into the wedding feast, the door was locked.
>
> MATTHEW 25:10

September 21, 2007

This is a story of redemption and grace, but I must warn you that the way we came to it in Norfolk was not so pretty; we lost hope and came close to shutting down Norfolk Capernaum. But before we can show you our redemption, we have to show you how we got lost in the beautiful wonderland of Norfolk.

At the risk of upsetting a lot of wonderful folks from Norfolk, I have to say that when it comes to Capernaum, Norfolk has been a very backward place. Two steps forward, one step back. One step backward, no steps forward. Trying to start Capernaum in Norfolk has been like going to another country. Like speaking a language that was not quite understood by the natives. And lest someone pull the race card on me, I'm talking about natives of all color, all cultures, all types, and all kinds. Norfolk peeps. They didn't seem to "get" us.

Our experience in Norfolk started on December 5, 2006. We had set up an informational meeting for parents and folks interested in a ministry for kids with disabilities. We used the resources that we had, the friends and parents that we knew, and we did our best to spread the word. Four new people showed up that night. Wow!

Understand that our thinking and expectations were formed by our tremendous success in both Virginia Beach and Chesapeake. In Virginia Beach God had both hands on us from the beginning, and we took off like a rocket ship that still has not come back down. Just last night—our first VB club of the semester—we had around fifty-five people with disabilities. That is a lot of special needs people, and some would question the sanity of a staff that allowed a club to grow that big without splitting.

I never said we were sane.

With Chesapeake we let God show us where He wanted us. We prayed about Norfolk, Chesapeake, and Suffolk and asked God to show us where He wanted us. Things started to happen in Chesapeake, things that left no doubt as to God's desire. So Chesapeake club also took off fast, perhaps not quite like VB, but with a supernatural ascent and plenty of fuel on board.

And then there was Norfolk. Four people showed up at the meeting. Now that should have been grounds for us to say, "Nope, God doesn't want us there yet. Not yet." But thinking that maybe God just wanted us to come in spite of the dismal little informational meeting—which really is not our mission—we decided to press on and start Norfolk up in the spring of 2007, with one club a month.

This went fine. We got fifteen people, then perhaps twenty, and it stayed there until the summer. To compound the tepid start, we had few folks in the eleven-to-twenty-five age range who represented the core of our primary audience. The older folks came from Norfolk Hope House and elsewhere, and we welcomed them. But where were the younger kids? We met Helena and Aimee and Rachel, and we decided that they alone were worth it. They were! But come on, where were the adoring crowds we were used to at the VB and Chesapeake? Where was everybody?

We knew it was time to get into the schools, and because our school contact work was nearly non-existent, we needed to get into the Norfolk high schools. Eventually with the help of Cherry and Jenny Jenson and Ann Rolfe Ball (Young Life's Norfolk Area Director), we were able to meet with a Special Education (SE) teacher at Maury, who agreed that we could start a volunteer program in the fall. This had also been approved by the principal.

Fast forward to September.

When we checked in with the SE teacher again, she asked us to run the program by the SE chair. When we did this, the chairperson said absolutely not, no way. Then the principal said the same thing. So we were shut down in Maury. Was this God working, or just us not doing a good job (again) with the schools? We are not giving up on Maury and will continue to follow up. But what do we have to do, buy them gas for a month?

Monday night was our first club in Norfolk. We let the staff at Tanner's Creek Garden Center know that we were starting up, so I didn't think it was necessary to remind them on the day of. Can you say stupid? Stupid on me, not them. I didn't make the call, the club leader didn't make the call, and even God didn't make the call. Dang it all, I thought I could count on the Big Guy!

I got a call about ten minutes out from Richard, saying the place was locked and no one could get in. I laughed on the inside, realizing that Richard would not appreciate me laughing out loud about us being locked out in Norfolk. But it did strike me as funny, and I thought about the other times when things didn't go as planned, and we had to think fast to find a way to achieve our goal.

Hey wait, what is our goal?

Well, folks, that's easy. The goal of Capernaum is to bring the Gospel of Jesus the Christ to young people with disabilities. If you get all technical and ask me how I can call a fifty-year-old woman a "young person," I would say that she's young at heart, and grammatically speaking she would be a "young person." Let's keep it real, people.

There was a lady weeding down near the street when I arrived. I walked over to her and asked her if she worked there. She said yes, but she didn't have a key. She could, however, get us into the outdoor courtyard area. She started looking a lot like an angel at that point. So in we went. Shoot, there were tables and chairs—quite nice and charming—and an outlet for the sound system. There wasn't much room for doing the activities, but who cares. We were there. We had our space, and we moved in.

Once again I was reminded that it isn't about how cool the space is, but what we bring to the space. A perfect space without love is empty, but a lousy space filled with love has all the right things—namely God—and that is exactly what we had in Norfolk last Monday night. It was a perfect night with perfect love in an imperfect space.

But what about our hunt for a new space? Will we find a Norfolk church willing to take a bunch of folks so broken and torn? There is no question that we represent a cross section of the lost sheep that God told us to reach out to; we are a motley crew. Who can blame them for thinking twice about taking us?

Who can blame Princess Ann High School for deciding to shut the door on the ministry that served the very people who went to school in the building we were using? Weren't we special enough? We don't blame them for their ignorance, but—truth be told—I dusted my heels of them.

We found a Norfolk church and visited with the pastor, a most organized man who showed off the splendor of his most organized filing system so that we could see his most godly organization. With his obvious compulsions and obsessions exposed, Tara said, "Oh, we have lots of kids like that. You're OCD: obsessive compulsive disorder."

I quickly changed the subject when the pastor's ears turned bright red and he said no, he was just organized. Then he asked us why we needed to go outside, and Tara once again spoke with great honesty: "We like to get messy sometimes and use whipped cream and eggs." She and I both laughed at that, but again the pastor's ears burned bright red, and he said, "Verily, I say unto you . . ." Okay, he didn't actually speak that way, but I would not have blinked if he had started speaking in King James.

"We have people manicure these grounds every week, and if you think you are going to bring in eggs and whipped cream, we can pretty much call this off now."

Well, sir, a lesser man (or possibly a better man) would have gotten up right then, shaken that fine pastor's hand, and thanked him for his time. Maybe even dusted off his heels. But I didn't do that. I said, "Let's not let some eggs prevent a ministry from finding a home," and he was mollified, which means he started acting like a girl I know named Molly.

Turns out this fine pastor wanted us to come to his church and loved Young Life. But we had to sit still for him to admit that later on before we left. We said we were going to talk to some other churches, and he said he would talk to his elders and let us know.

Then we heard about Tab Church.

I walked into the Lighthouse Student building, and everything changed. It looked like a student ministry room done by Spring Branch or Grace or any number of churches that get the way to reach the kids and have the resources to buy cool couches and lights, sound systems and projectors, pool tables and foosball. It was literally kid nirvana, and it could be ours if all went well. I smelled the aroma of God there, so I sure hoped it worked.

The truth is, I figured that Tab, short for Tabernacle, was a black church. That would have been awesome as we want to serve more of the black community in Norfolk and elsewhere. But the first folks I met with were white; but black or white, their hearts were colored by God. Pete and Emily Johnson were not too hot and not too cold but just right. Their hearts shone out of their eyes, and I knew that God was working at Tab through these people.

Then Steven walked in. Steven works at Tab with the twenty-something group. He had visited us at Norfolk club that week and apparently liked what he saw. He said his folks might be interested in helping out. Wow! Pete and Emily said they could think of some of their high school folks who would want to help out with Capernaum. Can you say, "Wow!"

This all leads me to think that God has been keeping tabs on us all along in Norfolk. Gosh, I loved writing that, and I hope you appreciated it. Tabs ... get it. Uh, yeah. So what now? Now we see what the elders say. If we get a green light, we'll start hanging out with Tab a bit and get ready to start up full-time in January.

So you see, we were never really locked out of anything. Sometimes God just wants us to know that we can't do everything, but He can do anything. Sometimes we have to take ten steps back so He can take a thousand forward. And even if you get locked out of some places, there's always some place else open to you, just waiting for you to show up and claim what God has made for you.

The key to getting locked out is not needing to get in and being willing to live on the outside for a while. That works for Capernaum, and it works for me.

Who knows, maybe a rocket will rise soon over Norfolk.

P.S. Since that time, many things have worked out for the better in Norfolk. We met Pete Johnson, the student ministry leader at Tab Church, and he invited us to have club at The Lighthouse. It is an amazing building and a perfect place to grow. The growth is slow but sure.

Perhaps the best thing to come out of the partnership is the kids from Tab and other local churches and high schools. They come to club and participate, dance, goof off, and generally have a great time. They recognize that something amazing is going on even though they may not be able to quite put their finger on it.

We're okay with that. Once again, I'm reminded that this ministry is not just about people with disabilities, but it's for all people who come. We all have disabilities in our hearts, and no matter how beautiful we are, we all just want to be loved.

JOHN KÖEHLER

Matt and Don prove we're all family.

FORTY-FOUR

The Eyes Have it

*for Brian
and the awesome people of
Asian Young Life*

JOHN KÖEHLER

> At that, the man ripped the bandage
> off his eyes and the king recognized who he was—
> one of the prophets!

1 KINGS 20:41

September 21, 2007

It wasn't until I saw the photos from the Capernaum discipleship camp that I knew for sure that amazing things had happened which I had been completely unaware of. I mean, I knew that God had shown up and was working to unite our kids with the awesome Asian Young Life (AYL) kids. I had seen it, smelled it, heard it, prayed it. I knew it to be true. Nevertheless, I was still blown away when I finally saw all the photos, and some things meant to be hidden came to life again. Okay, not really ... I was just trying to sound a little like the Fellowship of the Ring preamble.

Some weeks before I had finally gotten around to calling Brian Hall, the AYL Teacher staff dude in New Jersey. He was filled with grace and love on the phone—so calm and collected—that I wondered (once again) what the crap was I doing in this mission. How could God possibly be so nearsighted as to enlist an obviously cut-from-the-cloth Christian like Brian and a barbarian like me? I don't know the answer, but I reckon I'm pretty thankful just the same.

Apparently old God will take just about anyone. And considering the fact that He created all of us, then this does make a certain amount of sense. He is just being a good parent, after all, convinced that the ugly excuses for artwork being created by his spawn are all amazing masterpieces. Wow, does God need glasses or what?

Later on I did a video conference with Brian and a bunch of his AYL kids. It was cool, but also very strange as I had about a three-second audio delay. It was good enough to allow me to give them a vision about what working with our kids was like. Plus they had a list of names that they could pray over and think about.

It must have worked because as soon as they arrived, the AYL kids took to Capernaum like peas and carrots—unfrozen thank you very much. That was, of course, after they claimed their Alien T-shirts which said "Take Me to My Leader!" on the front, and "Be Afraid, Be Very Afraid" on the back, along with Capernaum Hampton Roads and Asian Young Life.

The shirts helped to seal the deal that had already begun to come alive in more than a hundred hearts. These Asian kids must not have gotten the memo about how danged different the Capernaum kids looked. Uh, hello, look in the mirror! You are, like, oh my gosh, soooo different from our people. Our people have Down syndrome faces, thick glasses, vacant stares, beanpole CP legs, and underdeveloped diaphragms. Our people have difficulty controlling their impulses.

Lucky for you Asian Young Life peeps, ours folks did not control their impulse to love you and wanted desperately to be exactly like you. Thanks for letting them. You opened the doors of your hearts and welcomed us in like family; we came in and fell asleep right then and there while you stayed up late, stroking our unfurrowed brows and whispering how much you loved us, until it was time for another amazing day at Rockbridge, the place that God built.

And so it came to pass—as plainly seen in the photos—that all of Capernaum in Hampton Roads became Asian for five days in July 2007. All the good people of AYL allowed their eyes to grow round in wonder and became like us for those very same five days, and God looked down upon this and said, "This is good." He gave us a rainbow to remember Him, as if we could ever forget the reason and fact of our coming together.

Our eyes are so different than yours. Round and Caucasian.

Yours more narrow, dark, and filled with depth while ours radiate color in the shallows. You helped us up, you helped us eat, and you helped us find the inner strength we never knew existed. You knew it was there because God had already shown it to you, lucky you with your twenty-twenty vision.

You learned that our heart vision was perfect, and we taught you how to fly your way into simple love and joy. All this and more for the cost of a nickel, less than it took to say hello to a stranger who looked different than you and talked or walked funny. So you walked on by. You'll never do that again, oh no, for God has shown you the grace and goodness of all of His people, and now you know the truth.

We are all special, each and every one of us. You are special, and so are we.

Whether we come from New Jersey or Newport News. Whether we have slanted or round eyes. Whether we are smart or slow. Whether we can rock or roll, fly or slither, run or walk, or just stare off into the sky at things only we can see. We are all the same way down deep where the pearls of God lie nestled in the folds of our hearts.

And ain't that just fine!

(L-R): Bobby, John, Earl and Pastor Marty at the Surf Camp baptism.

FORTY-FIVE

Two Pastors and an Earl

for Marty

JOHN KÖEHLER

God told Rebecca, "The firstborn of your twins will take second place."

ROMANS 9:12

December 24, 2007

Last year we held our Christmas party at the Church of the Messiah because they loved us from Pastor Marty on down, and because they offered the space for free. One hundred and forty souls packed the fellowship hall with noise, happiness, and food in great abundance. We held forth with words and readings during the meal, but the mass of humanity and underpowered sound system reduced us to making unintelligible noises and grunts. No one cared and many understood because it was Capernaum, where agape reigned, whether or not you spoke Greek. All we knew was that we were with our family and life was good; during those moments we shared our crazy love together.

Afterward we realized that we had outgrown Messiah and set out to find a new place to hold our 2007 Christmas party. We considered halls of all kinds, but the gates were shut and the doors bolted. We did not find open hearts of grace, but closed minds and locked doors that required us to wait and bide our time.

I really hate waiting, Lord . . .

Then Angela West rolled into our hearts and onto our staff and set out to obtain space in her church, First Baptist of Norfolk. She spoke with Pastor Jay, who spoke with the elders, who spoke with Jesus Himself apparently, and the word was passed down from on high that the doors were to be opened for us. Paperwork was completed and promises made; meetings were held and the space was walked through and anointed. God walked with us as He always has.

Once again God provided for our bellies through our amazing parents. They brought plates and platters heaping with food and fixings that melted our mouths and reduced us all to drooling fools by the time the dinner bell was rung. A long line formed and snaked its way around the hall, moving forward with agonizing slug-like speed as conversations and dance moves were acted out all around.

Tara and I huddled together and realized that something on our program would have to give, so we cut out the testimonies of the kids that we had wanted to include. The rest of the program included Allen's memorial video (Allen had been a senior leader with cerebral palsy) and tribute to his mom, and short talks from our new friend Pastor Jay and our beloved Pastor Marty from Messiah. Ahhhh . . . to be blessed with not one but two pastors at our party was, uh, well . . . a blessing!

Marty approached me and said, "John, I don't need to speak."

I looked at him, shaking my head, and said, "Marty, we were blessed by having both you and Jay agree to speak, and so you will. It is important for them to hear from you because they know you." I held up the revised schedule so he could see that we had shortened the program by removing the kid's testimonies.

This didn't go over well with my friend Marty.

"No, John," he said. "You have to have the kids' testimonies. It is the most important thing for you to share. Let them speak instead of me."

I just stared at Marty for a few beats and realized that God was speaking through this man; he was absolutely right, and Tara and I were absolutely wrong. There is great power in anyone giving a testimony about how God is working in their lives, and this is no different with our friends from Capernaum. So I agreed and told the club leaders from Norfolk, Chesapeake, and Virginia Beach to select kids to speak.

Meanwhile the show went on. We spoke about Allen, showed photos of him throughout the dinner, then played a video about him. We presented his mom with a beautiful photo poster prepared by Virginia Beach club leader Kari Lillard and signed by the multitude on hand.

Meanwhile, God, the greatest matchmaker, mover and shaker, and love maker I've ever known, was laughing as He continued to position Marty to give the talk he was intended to give all along. Marty found himself standing next to Earl Roye, twin brother of Bobby and son of Tony and Cindy. Earl has always been the reluctant twin, the one who stayed home and wasn't so sure about Capernaum while Bobby threw himself into it like a lost bee finding the hive after a storm. Home at last. But just because he didn't go to Capernaum did not mean that Earl was unaware of God and lacked spiritual awareness.

After greeting each other, Earl and Marty watched the video about Allen. Earl looked over at Marty and asked, "Is Allen in heaven?" Marty recognized God's hand at work and that another connection was being made between him, the pastor, and this man called Earl. He said, "Yes, he is, Earl because Allen accepted Jesus as his Savior and had a relationship with Him.

"Oh," said Earl, and he turned to watch the rest of the video while Marty watched Earl, waiting for the Holy Spirit to guide him.

"Earl," said Marty, "if you died today, do you think you would be in heaven with Allen?"

"No," said Earl, "I don't think so. I don't really understand how it works."

"Well," said Marty, "would you like me to tell you?"

"Yes I would," said Earl who, like his twin brother, was always concise and to the point with his answers.

So the pastor told the Earl about Jesus—how He came to show us how to live and to teach us how to live and love and die. He sacrificed Himself, and gave His life for us so that we could live forever on earth and in heaven. He came back to life after He died to prove that He controls life and death. He invites us all to eat with Him so He can come into our lives to be our Savior, our God, our Lord, and our friend.

Earl pondered this for a while in quiet contemplation; then he announced that he was going out to walk for a while. Marty let him go and then followed him a short while later. He walked with Earl and asked him if he was ready to make a decision for Jesus. Earl said yes, and so he did—right there in the church foyer while the party continued in the hall, and Pastor Jay came to the stage to speak.

To say he was unprepared for our loud and boisterous crowd of kids with disabilities, along with friends and families, would be an understatement. Jay began to tell a story, and the crowd was so noisy I had to quiet them and remind them that Jay was talking about Jesus, who deserved our respect and attention. Once they quieted down, Jay proceeded to tell a lovely story to the nearly two hundred souls in attendance.

Out in the foyer another story was given and words spoken by the Earl to his God, with the help and guidance of the good Pastor Marty, who gave up his spot on stage so that he could be a servant in God's dressing room to welcome the Earl to his new kingdom.

And so on that night two pastors told two stories about Jesus to friends new and old, while God rode His chariot across the sky to pick up the heart of an Earl.

JOHN KÖEHLER

Daniel and Brooke strutting their stuff at the Chesapeake end of the year party. Photo by Glen McClure.

JOHN KÖEHLER

PART SIX

MAKE BELIEVE

David & his fuzzy friend.

FORTY-SIX

Easter Eggs & Happy the Cow

for Frank & Lynn

JOHN KÖEHLER

> "The virgin will be with child and will give birth to a son, and they will call him Immanuel" —which means, "God with us."
>
> MATTHEW 1:23

Cletus Cowpie was a dress-up character I developed at the Hoe Down back in 2005. Not that I needed to have an excuse for bein' a big goo-goo bug and actin' like a yaller jacket when someone done messed with his nest. Crazy and ornery to boot.

Turns out that boy also spilled out of my fingers when I set down to write, so here you will find a story from this feller that is a part of me. Truth is that I love Cletus because he allows me to say things in a way that a beach boy just can't.

When I grow up, I want to be like Cletus.

May 5, 2007

By Cletus Cowpie

Well, it sure fire is a fine day outside, and I aim to be out there mighty soon. But you know I was just sittin' here eatin' an Easter egg, mighty fine with salt and all, an' I thought of something that my ODU fren' Chips said yesterClub about Easter eggs.

First off, Chips ain't her real name. First time I heard it, I figured she was somehow named after cow chips, which're dried up old cow flops that look like Frisbees or nasty, old, oversized brown corn chips. But you don't want to eat 'em, oh nosiree Bob, or even if yer name ain't Bob.

Now if Chips was a cow chip, then she must be about the prettiest chip I ever did see, and cow chips must smell like lavender or some kinda girly perfume they likes to wear. God made that girl pretty from the inside out, and us men folk are mighty happy 'bout that. Thankee kindly, Lord!

Truth is that Chips got her nickname on account of the fact that she used to have a strong hankerin' fer potato chips. Why her compulsion fer chips was so bad she 'bout near got herself arrested more'n twice. An' even now if you should so much as show her a bag o' chips, much less wave some under her nose, why ole Chips's likely to roll her eyes up in her punkin' head and roll around like one o' them scary-movie creatures.

So anyways ole Chips, well, she told Capernaum a story 'bout Easter eggs and how she 'n Jenny the Jewel (she got her nickname on account o' her heart bein' just like a bright shiny diamond) painted up a passel o' eggs right purty, and then Chips took to skinin' one a them eggs right before our very eyes. And the whole time she's skinnin' that thar egg, she's tellin' us how we're all like Easter eggs to God.

And you know what? That made sense to me, right much it did. Cause every one a them eggs's different from the other, just like you'n me are, just as sure as shootin'. Some're just one color, some're got spots and pretty lines on 'em, and some are just plain and simple. We all got a different skin on when you stop and recollect and take a good look. God made us one at a time, and ain't we all just about purtier than Easter eggs? Next time you're outside inbetwixt a lotta folks, just set yerself on down and take a look at how fine God made us all.

Fine like Easter eggs.

Then Chips skinned that egg down to the yaller part of it. Right down to the yolk, to the guts and heart a that there egg. And she said that was where the magic took place. That inside was where old

God could grow up a little baby chicken, just like magic. I reckon I don't know how He does it, but He sure does it just the same!

And here's the fun part: Every dagblamed egg was like that and had its very own magical heart and center where God could grow up something fine and new. And if our hearts is like eggs just a little, then don't that mean we got us a magical spot where God can make something fine and new grow up inside us?

Why sure it do! Listen here . . .

I got me a cow that can't never have her own baby, on account that God done froze up her insides and she can't make no baby cow or milk to feed it. Doctors said it ain't never gonna be, no matter our prayers. We felt so sorry fer her, all sad and troubled, that we named her Happy. But she ain't all that happy, and every spring when the calves are born, why Happy just wanders around mooing for her missin' calf. Don't matter to her that calf ain't never comin'; old Happy just knows fer sure her life ain't never gone be right until her calf comes.

Well, sure enough this spring, we had us a fine batch o' calves, and there was Happy, just lowin' out fer her calf that won't never, ever gonna come home to her. We all felt right bad fer her and gave her extra-special feed and talked to her right much. Like family.

Then we had the storm on Good Friday.

Now why do you reckon they calls it good Friday if the finest man who ever lived died on that day? I reckon I'd call it Black Friday or Bad Friday or maybe Sin Friday. I ain't no priest, but I sure just have a right hard time with that there Good Friday name. But heck fire, that's what they calls it, so who'm I to be whinin' on like Happy in the springtime?

It was nigh past midnight when that thar storm hit like a sledgehammer o' wind and rain and lightnin'. All the cows and calves come in fast to the barn and lowed out at the rain in their sorry huddles. All except fer Petunia an' her calf. Seems that ole Petunia got her back right hoof stuck in a hole that opened up 'cause 'o the rain. She fell right on down to her butt and couldn't get herself up no matter how hard she tried.

Problem was that this happened on top o' the hill right next to the oak tree that been there since my granpappy was a sprite. That old oak tree done took a lick o' lightnin' strikes over the years, and this night won't no different. Why they was the biggest crash o' lightin' I ever heard in all my days, and it done killed ole Petunia quicker than you can say "skedaddle."

The next mornin' we come out and found her layin' there dead—ready for the butcher—and her baby boy calf layin' right next to her. We thought he was dead too, but nope, he moved when we touched him. Got up too, then he stumbled into the oak tree. Why that calf was blind and dumb and deaf on account o' that lightnin' strike. So we hitched a rope to him and led him back to the barn.

That little calf wouldn't eat at'all, no matter what we did. We brought him to other momma cows that were feedin' younguns, but it don't matter a bit. He was dyin' no matter what we was tryin'. We was mighty broke up about it too, as you kin imagine, but we didn't have no other answers and just gave it to God to figure out fer us.

An' He sure did figure it out this mornin'!

We woke up this fine Easter mornin', and first thing we did was to go down to the barn and check on that baby boy calf. My kids'd already named him Jesus since he was struck down on the same day that the good Lord died. They ran ahead of me and pretty quick came runnin' out o' the barn, yellin', "Daddy, come see! Come see Jseus, Daddy!"

Well, sir, I started to runnin' so as to see what the fuss was all about.

And there, in the stall where we had laid little Jesus to die, well dog my cats but he was standin' up and actin' fine! An' not only that, but right there next to him was none other than Miss Happy herself lookin' bout ready to fly, she was so full o' momma pride and such.

To say I couldn't believe my two eyes ain't half o' the matter, so I just stared with my piehole hangin' open like a fly catcher.

My Jessie said, "Look, Daddy. Jesus has got milk all over his muzzle." And sho enough, 'twas truer than blue. And just to prove it true, Jesus leaned on down under Miss Happy and started suckin' her teat like he was fit to drown in her milk. Her milk?! Why, lo and behold, Happy was givin' milk and was now a momma to boot!

Looky here, I can't explain all the mysteries o' life, or why things work the way they do. But I thinks Happy is just another miracle of God, put here to show us how right the world is. Tell you what else. I thinks we is all miracles waiting to happen, and the miracle is already inside us. Just like them Easter eggs.

I'm mighty happy that our little baby calf came back to life; he gave life to our Miss Happy and gave her a reason and purpose for livin'. I reckon the first Jesus died for the same reason for us: to give us a reason to live and a purpose for our little bitty lives.

So when you eat that there Easter egg, remember ole Jesus. The one in the barn, and the one in your heart. An' celebrate how both came back to life to make us happy.

Richard bullies his way into our hearts.

FORTY-SEVEN

Billy the Bully

for Richard

JOHN KÖEHLER

Don't walk around with a chip on your shoulder,
always spoiling for a fight.

PROVERBS 3:30

July 6, 2007

Oh yeah, I can definitely remember Billy the Bully. That wasn't his real name, of course. It was William Davis, but no one ever called him that. His last name, for as long as I knew him in school, was Bully. Billy the Bully. Of course, no one ever called him that to his face since they would cease to exist as a humanoid life form and would be reduced to an oozing formation of splooge, a life-form of the lowest order.

Billy was huge. He had been held back when he was in the third grade, I think, but even so he was one big dude. He towered over us guys by an easy four inches and outweighed us by fifty pounds. Dude, my buddy Eric Lansing hardly weighed fifty pounds! To us, Billy looked like an NFL middle linebacker. We feared him always, showed him respect to his face, and hated him when he wasn't around.

It was hard to call Billy ugly; you could sometime catch a glimpse of someone who might look halfway decent. But the truth is that he looked ugly all the time, probably because he acted so mean. I knew why Billy acted so mean. Or at least I knew some of why he was so mean. One day I was in Mrs. Marjam's office. She was the assistant principal in charge of death and destruction. At least that's what we all said . . . behind her back.

I'm not gonna tell you that I never got in trouble, but let's just say I didn't spend much time in Mrs. Marjam's office, and just the thought of going there was enough to make me puke. I know I wasn't the only one who felt that way. Unlucky for me, Mrs. Marjam was put in charge of bulletin boards and—since I was one of the art wackos at school (which meant I could draw pretty well)—she called me down to her office to talk about a new bulletin board about the Civil War.

After I sat down, it was really hard for me to hear what she was saying because right behind her on the wall was the paddle. Somebody said it was a paddle used for some dopey English baseball sport called Cricket, but we just called it The Paddle. She wasn't actually allowed to use it anymore, but legend has it that back in the day many a kid had given blood to The Paddle. The nicks and stains on it gave proof to the legend, and I had trouble thinking about anything else but getting whacked by it. Maybe that's why she put it on the wall, just to make us fear her . . .

Mrs. Marjam was really droning on about the Civil War, and I was staring at The Paddle when her intercom buzzed and said, "Mrs. Marjam, we have a Code 3 in the cafeteria!" Wow, a Code 3! I didn't know what a Code 3 was, but Mrs. Marjam jumped to her feet, stared at me for a while, and said, "Young man, I want you to stay right here and look at these books on the Civil War. I shall return in ten minutes." And off she went, just like a tornado.

Suddenly I could breathe again. I sat in the chair and stared at The Paddle for a while. Then I decided that I had to touch it. So I got up, went to the wall . . . and I touched The Paddle! I rubbed my hands all over it, and I think I said a prayer for all the kids who got "touched" by The Paddle. Then I decided I had to hold it, so I took it off the wall and held it in my hands. I imagined myself going through the halls, holding and swinging The Paddle while all the kids ran away in fear. Even Billy the Bully.

Then I dropped The Paddle. When I bent down to pick it up, I noticed a folder right next to it that said William Davis. Billy the

Bully. It was filled with papers and stuff, practically exploding with bad things. At least that's how it seemed to me before I even looked inside. I had seen my report last year, and it was really thin compared to the Bully's. I stared at that report for a long time, arguing with myself about looking inside. Fear and curiosity fought for control. Fear lost.

I opened the folder.

Yup, that's right. I opened that report right there on the floor of Mrs. Marjam's office, right next to that stupid paddle that I was still afraid of. And right on top was a police report. I felt guilty for seeing it and shut the file, picked up The Paddle, and put it back on the wall.

But I couldn't stop myself . . . I went back to the file and picked up the police report. I read about Billy's dad and how he had beat up Billy's mom really badly and was in jail now. And beneath that were more reports about how Billy's dad had also beat up Billy. And not just with his belt. With his fist, and once with a bat that broke his foot. And once with a chain. Oh man, and we thought Billy was just getting into fights with kids.

Beneath the police report was a doctor's report about Billy being angry. It used a lot of big words that I didn't understand. I saw all the detention reports. Tons of them. And I saw an IQ test that showed the Bully had a very high IQ, which I knew had to do with intelligence and how smart you were.

Billy was smart? He sure never acted that way. He acted like a complete dumbo. But why would he do that if he were so smart? I didn't get it. Not back then when I was only thirteen.

I heard a noise out in the main office and ran back to my chair just as Mrs. Marjam walked into the room. I think she sensed that something was wrong, and she looked at me for a while and said, "Have you been in that chair the whole time?" I looked at her, held up the Civil War book, and said, "Oh yes mam! This is a great book!" What a total suck-up liar I was. So we talked about the bulletin board and Lee and Jackson and Grant, and then I left to catch the bus.

No matter how hard it was for me to admit it, I felt so bad for Billy. I felt bad for feeling bad for the Bully. I mean, he had never beat me up, but I had seen him beat up plenty of guys, and once it was my good friend Bobby Pelter. I stood there and watched and hated the Bully and vowed to get him back if ever I could. But here I was feeling bad for him. Bad for him. I felt sympathy for the dude who had never shown sympathy to anyone else.

That really messed me up, and I just didn't understand what I was feeling anymore. Man, I was totally messed up. So I did the only thing I knew to do when things were bad. I did what my dad had taught me to do. I talked to God about it. Oh, I didn't shut my eyes and pray, not on the bus. People would have made fun of me. I just talked to God with my eyes wide open and formed the words in my mind. It was cool because no one knew I was even doing it.

Unfortunately, God didn't talk back to me right then. That would have been nice. Usually He comes to me in my dreams, and if I go to sleep thinking about Him and asking Him to help me, sometimes I wake up in the morning feeling sure about the problem. By the time it was bedtime, I was no closer to figuring out the problem of Billy the Bully, and I was hoping that the Big Guy would help me out during the night. He did.

When I woke up the next morning, I knew what I had to do. I had to become friends with Billy. Oh no! Oh gross. I actually got sick to my stomach and ran to the bathroom and almost blew my grits. Almost. My body recovered, but the rest of me was a mess. How was I supposed to become friends with the kid who everyone hated? What if they all hated me? What if he beat the crap out of me? What if I offered my friendship, and he rejected me? Good for me! Woohoo!

But I felt like God wanted me to do more than go through the motions. I was supposed to actually care and act like a brother to him. I was supposed to treat him like family. And you know what? That's exactly what I did. The next day I went up to Billy first thing and told him what had happened and that I knew about his dad. He started crying right there in the hallway. I had to drag him into the gym, and we sat for a long time together while he cried and I told him it was gonna be okay. That God was going to help him, and so was I.

It wasn't easy. I had to teach him how to be human. I know it sounds weird, but that's exactly what I did. I had to help someone who didn't know how to deal with people. I taught him why he needed to be nice to people. I taught him about God and about Jesus. Taught him how to pray. It took a while, but eventually Billy the Bully became just Billy. And now everyone calls him William, and he owns a big company, has a great wife and kids, is active in his church, and everyone loves him.

And the really cool thing is that I helped him do it. I mean, God did it, but I helped. That still feels good to me, thirty years later. Helping God turn a bully into a cool dude is pretty cool. It taught me to never give up on people, no matter how bad they might seem.

Rusty and Tara parked to find Rece.

FORTY-EIGHT

Parking Details

for Jerry

JOHN KÖEHLER

So Naaman with his horses and chariots arrived in style and stopped at Elisha's door.

2 KINGS 5:9

December 25, 2007

Yesterday was a big day for me, a day I had been waiting a long time for. Like walking by a construction site and having the guy driving the giant Caterpillar Destructo Excavator invite me over to drive his rig for an hour or two. One brother to another.

No need to worry, he would, of course, give me the requisite fifteen minutes of hands-on training needed to be an immediate expert with the various hand and foot controls. After completely destroying two stories of new construction that did not need to be destroyed, I would then drive the Excavator out onto Atlantic Avenue where complete strangers would flag me down and ask me to come and destroy their million-dollar homes.

Man food of the mind, folks, a veritable banquet.

Yesterday I fulfilled one of my Man Hopes to serve on parking detail at Spring Branch Church. I had been invited to help before, but for various reasons had not been able to. Perhaps I had stubbed my toe or drank too many cups of joe or didn't want to make it so. Or perhaps I merely had contained my Manly Needs in this area.

Whatever the case, last week I was once again invited by Jerry Gallinedes—whose name might as well be Greek, it's so hard to spell—to help with the parking detail; giving in to the inevitable, I agreed. Soon the list was passed around by way of e-mail, and there, for all to see, appeared my name next to an amazing title: Midfielder. To say I was excited would be like saying that a dog was excited to find a large steak bone recently grilled with two days' worth of meat left on it. Of course the dog was excited, as was I; my tail was wagging.

Here at last my name was written in the Parking Hall of Fame, and as yet I had done nothing. Even so, they knew who I was. I counted for something and felt my pride expand within me like helium engorging the blimp that would soon soar over the little people crawling so slowly down below. Not that there's anything wrong with little people.

I showed up at the proper time, and the butterflies were already raging inside of me. Not quite the pterodactyls that filled me prior to a world-championship event or a first date, but still they fluttered within me. How would I do? Would I embarrass myself? Would I embarrass the church? Actually, I could live with embarrassing the church, but I was deathly afraid of doing something so stupid that I would forever be branded as "that idiot in the parking lot."

But then I thankfully remembered that I had no feelings and was hardly ever embarrassed. And so the butterflies were beaten back like baleful banshees of bucolic blackness. (I don't think bucolic belongs before blackness, but I believe I'll leave it behind.

I met the other men of the parking detail, and we were given our equipment. Yea, verily I say unto you, our equipment. Men hearken for equipment and badges and gear and uniforms to fit in and be part of a team. And since last I checked (this morning), I am a man, I hearken for all of the above. So on the eighth day God said, "I shall make a parking detail, and I will give them mighty weapons and tools to use for My people. And they shall light the way and make clear the paths." And it was so, and God said, "That is good."

First, I received my vest. Not just any vest, folks, heavens to mergatroids, no. Now some would look at the vest and say, "So what, it's just yellow plastic with Velcro and some reflecting tape." To those unworthy cretins I would say, "No, wrong you are, so wrong. You shall never wear this vest chosen for God's chosen parking people." Which means He won't choose you, so park it and listen up.

My vest was beautiful, but I noticed that Harry looked much better in his vest than I did in mine. He looked sharp, while I looked like a penguin wearing a vest three sizes too small. So I did the only right thing and whined about it. Harry promptly took off his obviously oversized vest and traded me for my tiny shrunken little vest. We looked exactly the same as before, proving that the vests were unisize and I was larger than Harry. Just more for God to love!

All was forgotten as I received my walkie-talkie. And not just any walkie-talkie, but a working one. I spent a good part of the day saying random things on the walkie-talkie. Like telling Jerry I had never felt closer to him even though we were at opposite ends of the parking lot. Parking-lot man-love logic.

Since we were all wearing Santa hats, I shared how Santa did not appear at the manger until well after the shepherds had left. This fact is left out in the Bible, but I have always felt it must be true in my heart and perhaps in my gall bladder. So I shared it over the radio and heard the silence of tears as the men were weeping over the idea of Santa coming to visit the baby Jesus with a sleigh full of bodacious toys. Either that or they just didn't know what to say . . .

And then there was the lightsaber. To some it was just a lighted parking wand, but I knew the full potential hidden within. Taking it in my hand for the first time, I held if up and felt the surge of electricity shoot down my arm as I yelled, "The force is with me!" Turns out there was a short in my lightsaber, but we fixed it.

Armed with instructions, lightsaber, vest, and Santa hat, we marched out to our allocated spots. My hallowed ground as the midfielder was way back in the lot. I was the man who waved them forward after Jerry met them and waved them through after inspecting their trunks and undercarriages for leftover presents, weapons, and fruitcakes, the edible type or the two-legged type. I was their hope and salvation as they looked into the darkness with no clue where to park or even why they were there. I gave them hope and salvation. I was the drive-by church for them at that moment, the incarnational Jesus with a lightsaber.

I frantically waved them forward, using the proven first-century method of "come to me" where the wand and the other hand are thrown down and then raised up and "over the shoulder." Jesus used this method to bring the really big crowds to Him, with wands powered by the Holy Spirit instead of batteries. Environmentally friendly.

Once they came closer, the real artistry began. Here was where all my dreams came true. As they approached my position, I would wave them over into the lot. But not just any wave, oh no. Style and panache, cute and cuddly, brave and soldier-like, silly and clownlike. Knowing which style to pull from the bag for any given car was part of the plan. Behind the back, under the leg, down on one knee, hitting-it-out-of-the-park home run, the pitching wedge. I melded with the driver and knew just what to give him or her from my blacktop stage.

Never pull out cute and cuddly for a Mercedes 560SL. Nor shoot a salute to young kids in a pimped-out Volkswagen Beetle. It's all about knowing the right thing to do for each person. I was alive and thrived in the moment as each person in each vehicle saw me and thought to himself or herself, What a fine American. And so I was, there in the parking lot for the three o'clock and five o'clock services on Christmas Eve at Spring Branch Church. It was a magical affirmation of my life, another goal achieved, another moment to remember and cherish. I'm not ashamed to say I cried nearly the entire time, though it could have been sweat.

I put so much into this job that God assigned me that I nearly fell asleep in church. But I rallied and returned home to write this story and others. That was when I realized my wrist hurt and that I was dealing with a pretty serious case of carpal tunnel syndrome. My amazing lightsaber had done a deadly deed on my wrist, and just typing was now a hardship. Ack, the things we suffer to do God's will! To be a parking detail soldier meant giving your all, and I did.

But that was not all the damage that had been done. I had lost ten pounds by standing and jumping and pumping the cars into place. My right bicep was tired and torn from the constant beating it had endured as I stood so brave and alone on the blacktop. Even now as I write this it pulses and throbs and is twice the size of my other arm, making me another buffed-out Fiddler Crab Midfielder of the parking detail.

Last night I dreamed of parking cars in a giant church parking lot, my lightsaber sending out huge beams of light that could be seen for miles. Cars came to my beacon like moths to a flame as I stood twenty feet tall, amazing and huge, reliving the dream from my experience hours before on the hardtop of my church parking lot.

In the end I was once again reminded of how good my life is and how God uses me all the time in ways that fulfill all my Manly Desires. Once again I was reminded that it is good to be a man.

Zoe wearing a sexy poodle skirt.

FORTY-NINE

The Execution of Mr. Nut

for Jasper

JOHN KÖEHLER

> Three times now you've toyed with me,
> like a cat with a mouse, refusing to tell me
> the secret of your great strength."
>
> JUDGES 16:15

March 22, 2008

Sometimes life brings me the most amazing and unplanned stories. Stories I could never imagine come to life before me as a gift, wrapped up and ready to be opened and enjoyed.

Now I do realize that I'm opening myself up to a lawsuit from PETA or some other animal rights group, so let me be clear. I am not taking pleasure from the mishap of a certain squirrel this fine morning when the world was waking up and I was working on a video.

The execution I speak of in the title was not an execution I had anything to do with, your honor, and if it pleases the court I will show that I was merely a witness to the facts as they unfolded before me. An innocent witness, in fact.

Furthermore, let the record show that I did, in fact, give the victim, Mr. Skippy Nut, an excellent burial. Considering the fact that Skippy's body was in rather disgusting shape (bulging eyes, smoking hole in his chest), I would hope that my burial services would assuage any feelings against me and prove to the court that I was, in fact, acting as a good citizen in this terrible matter.

At approximately seven forty-five this morning I was editing a video and preparing to work on the book that is before you. I was sitting in my studio on the second floor, where windows to my left afforded a view of my driveway out to the street.

Suddenly there was a loud bang that came from the outside, accompanied by loud beeps and clicks inside as the power cut off. I knew at once that it was the electrical transformer located on the pole at the end of my driveway and turned to see a cat streaking away from the pole, hairs fluffed out in fright.

Four automatic power controllers beeped at me as I walked outside to see what I could see. I didn't want to call Dominion Power until I could clearly see the cause of the problem, and I was fairly certain that I would find the cause as I had many times before.

I walked down my driveway and out to the street, where I looked up at the transformer located on the top of the pole. I could see no obvious problem. Once a bird had managed to fly (or fry if you prefer) into the electric line, barbecuing itself and creating enough of a surge that the automatic fuse blew, along with the power to several houses on our street. But I saw nothing, so I walked down the street, looking up at the wire and thinking maybe it didn't occur at our pole but further down the street. Nothing there either.

Then I walked back to the pole and looked around the base, where I found poor Skippy (the squirrel) lying on his side, dead as a doornail. Skippy had obviously been chased up the pole by Tigger, the cat I had seen running away after the explosion caused by Skippy trying to flee on an electric line.

Clearly Tigger wanted to kill Skippy, but equally as clear was his desire to execute his enemy in close claw-to-claw combat. Tigger had probably been chasing Skippy for several years without success, yet he continued to stalk him in the hope that this time vengeance would be his.

Many times before, Skippy allowed Tigger to get close enough to smell him. Tail twitching rapidly behind him, ears flattened against his body, Tigger approached each time with absolute assurance of imminent victory. But Skippy managed to always stay a jump ahead and would run up the tree he had prepositioned for his bail-out maneuver. After ascending to a safe place on a branch above his nemesis, Skippy would fling down insults of the worst kind while Tigger slowly walked off as if he had not a care in the world.

In the end it is hard to say why the tables turned on Skippy. Was it simply his fate that on this morning he would lose the game and lose his life?

Or did he simply eat—as happens to us all—a stupid pill? Or stupid nut, whichever you prefer. Was it destiny or chance or a little bit of both? Who knows? Whatever it was, this fatal mistake caused Skippy to run up the pole and then decide to run down the electrical line of death. Dead squirrel running.

Tigger watched from the tree as his enemy ran away, just like so many times before. Then bang … Skippy Nut fell dead to the ground while Tigger the cat ran for his life as if the very worst creatures of cat hell were after him.

Poor Skippy.

What kind of squirrel would make such a stupid and fatal mistake when everyone in Squirrel Land knew to avoid electrical lines? What kind of squirrel would lose his head and allow a cat to execute him from afar? What kind of squirrel would allow this to happen?

Only a Nut.

Tara and Sarah lurking for men.

FIFTY

Sarah & The Heart Empire

for Sarah, Ruth & Dan

JOHN KÖEHLER

> His heart was drawn to Dinah daughter of Jacob,
> and he loved the girl and spoke tenderly to her.
>
> GENESIS 34:3

June 6, 2007

I've shared this story before. The story of when I almost lost my life at the hands of a "poor defenseless" young woman named Sarah Britnall. Oh sure, I know what you're thinking: she's in a wheelchair, she has limited control of her arms and legs. There's no way she could overpower a huge hairy grown man like me.

Please God, don't EVER let me grow up.

But we're not talking about her physical power to control me, oh no. We are talking about her willingness to completely DOMINATE my mind and my heart. Yes, folks, Sarah Britnall is a total Heart Dominatrix. It's time for this wretched story to finally come out, and I'm just the guy to do it. Even now, as I hearken (hmmm, do people still use that word?) back to the day of my destruction, I shudder and try to forget about her.

She's like some emotional and mental VIRUS I can't wipe out!

I've been to the doctors about it, but they just tell me to stay on my medication for bipolar syndrome and they try and placate and patronize me. I'm not sure what those two words mean, but they're wrong, I can tell you that.

MY INFLATABLE HEART

I've been to my pastor about it, but he said I needed to see a catholic priest to have a exorcism done. But I'm like, "Dude, I get plenty of exercise every day. This is not about my BODY, it's about my heart!" Look at the wheelchair tracks across my heart, and you'll see the marks of a defeated man. A man who has given in to a GIRL.

That is so gross.

I went to a cardiologist and told him my heart was enlarged, and when I told him it was about a young woman, HE told me to see a priest and ask for forgiveness! I'm like, "Dude, she's like me SISTER, it's not my fault, she's relentless and she is ruining my heart. I'm sick and you're a heart doctor. So get the crap to work." He kicked me out when I said crap and told me to go see a proctologist. What the crap is a proctologist?

A while back, I went to Baltimore Capernaum's banquet, where people dress up and talk about each other's disabilities, even if they don't have one. Ahhhhh, but we ALL have a disability, and usually it's in our heart. That's because SARAH BRITNALL has infected us with her horrible, horrible virus of love.

Kootie pills don't work, I can tell you that. Neither does massive doses of chocolate, though I keep trying that....

So anyway, there I was, minding my own business, when up rolled Sarah. Now before you ask, "Who was pushing her?," or "How can she roll herself," just back the freak off, this is MY story! I'm telling you that when that heart harlot wants something, she gets it. She can MAKE her wheelchair roll by herself. Or maybe she controlled my mind so I'd come over and push her away for another quiet moment.

It was all her idea! Don't you see how she works? She preys on guys like me. Supernaturally good looking, quiet and shy, minding our own business, usually in a reverential attitude of respectful prayer, never in trouble. I LOVE guys like that (One day I'll meet one).

So what does the heart wrecker do? She culls you out from the pack and forces you to go off for a quiet moment. Alone. Just the two of you. Now you KNOW that this is wrong. You KNOW that you're not supposed to be hanging out with some young hot chick. People look and see a poor defenseless young woman in a wheelchair and some old hairy guy taking advantage of her.

Lies! Deceit! Treachery!

Nothing could be further from the truth, no matter how far the truth has run away. Not that I'm not being truthful. Well, mostly truthful. Well, there are grains and small nuggets of truth woven in through this story. More of an AROMA of truth. Yeah, that's the ticket. That's the story.

So there we were, alone, cut off from the crowd. I was petrified. I prayed for deliverance. I prayed that the devil would not use his minion otherwise known as Sarah Brintnall against me. My prayers were not realized. I'm not sure what that means, but they weren't.

Sarah raised one arm up and pointed right at me with an evil smile, much like the Emperor on Star Wars. I was hopelessly caught in her web. She jerked her arm and my body convulsed. I was a puppet on her string, while she laughed her evil laugh. Then she FORCED me to take her out of the chair, and lay her down on the ground. She MADE me show her some World Wrestling Federation moves.

They were excellent moves. Worthy of ESPN, the deuce.

Then she got quiet, laying there below me, as a huge shadow fell across me, like Darth Vader. Sarah lay there looking up at me, smiling, for she knew that my destruction had come.

I turned and there was Darth's brother, Dan Vader; huge, hulking and lurking behind me like an evil presence.

He was approximately 22 feet tall and weighed 674.3 pounds, give or take a few tons. At least he SEEMED that way as I looked up from my prone position on the floor, my body laying across his daughter. Of course I didn't know this was his daughter. I didn't know she HAD a father, figuring she had been hatched from one of the evil egg factories of the Heart Empire.

I quickly stood up and turned to face my destruction, my doom.

Sounding exactly like James Earl Jones, he said, "I'm Sarah's father," and I knew then that my life was over. As I heard Sarah's evil laugh behind me, I knew that there, in that place, I would be slaughtered by the father of the woman who had stolen my heart. My innocent blood (well, partly innocent..... at least a drop or two of innocence....... well, it smelled innocent) would flow across the carpet and no one would care.

And then they would raise me up and force me to become yet another zombie in the Army of Sarah.

I quickly explained, or tried to explain, who I was and that I was not in fact trying to molest his daughter, but was showing her wrestling moves, and that it was ALL HER IDEA! He then approached me, wrapped his bear paw of a hand around my apparently dainty hand, leaned down and whispered into my ear, "Welcome, there are many of us here."

What the crap did THAT mean? I almost wet myself, I was so scared. But it was only ginger ale that Dan had accidentally poured on me from a height of 57 feet. He'd grown.

Later I learned that Dan was OK, and was only bad when he ran away from the influence and power of the Great Queen Ruth, may she live forever. I am TERRIFIED of that woman, I mean Queen. Please don't tell her I called her a woman. Not that she's NOT a woman. Wait, is that a double negative, so it means she IS a woman. No, a QUEEN! A Queen woman. That's it. See how dangerous this is? I'm already dead....

I also learned that Dan puts lotion on his legs, and my fear of him evaporated. Is that really so wrong? My fear that is, not the lotion. Cause that IS wrong. But don't you see, he's under control of Queen Ruth AND Princess Sarah. A puppet caught up in the Heart Empire. As for me? I'm running as fast as I can to get away. My heart is still tender and torn from where the Princess clutched it.

May she suffer great love and the torture of amazing joy and may peace and love and love and love flow over her like a tidal wave of God's love that we drown in to live.

May her birthday be awesome. May every day be like a birthday so that her un-birthdays are even more special than her real birthday. May her love shine like a torch to attract all the poor moth-like humans to the Kingdom of her Heart.

May she stop torturing poor defenseless men like me and just leave us alone, to continue working our way to the doors of our ivory towers. OK, OK, may she destroy our ivory towers and infect us with the virus of her special love.

I name myself a willing soldier of her Empire, and claim her as my awesome and beautiful Princess of the Heart. My heart is hers and happy I am to call her my sister.

Love,

John

MY INFLATABLE HEART

God's favorite daughters sailed across the sky and lit the heavens with their rainbow smiles.
Photo by Glen McClure.

JOHN KÖEHLER

PART SEVEN

DEAR LORD

Jessie drives her heart with love.

FIFTY-ONE

Ashley by the Side of the Road

for Glen

JOHN KÖEHLER

> He would get up early and stand by the side
> of the road leading to the city gate.
>
> 2 Samuel 15:2

June 2, 2008

Dear Lord,

It's been a long time since I last wrote to You. I mean, I *have* been writing to You whenever I write, but this is the first time since 2005 that I've actually started a letter to You. Not Dear John, or Dear Mary, but Dear Lord. So that in and of itself is somehow important.

I think part of it has to do with sending off my book to the editor. I know, I know; You already know this, and You already know why I did this. But I don't know, and I'm trying to figure it out. I just sent my baby book away and have nothing in the pot to stir. I need something to do, someone to write to. And since I didn't really want to write to any particular earthlings, I figure You will do just fine. Better than fine. So let's get on with it, shall we?

I have a lot to tell You about, but first I want to tell You about Ashley.

I was on my way home from the Noblemen meeting. Normally I would have driven right over to Pacific in order to avoid the tourist traffic along Atlantic but—for some reason or another—I stayed

MY INFLATABLE HEART

on Atlantic. As I came around the curve to the light at Forty-third Street, I saw a girl (a young woman) sitting on the curb facing the Cavalier.

She had her head down and under her arms. She looked dejected and alone. No one was around. When I saw her there, I knew I was meant to be there for her. It sounds corny, but I knew it was true. Not a knight in shining armor or even a nobleman, but a brother. She needed a brother.

In a split second I considered the situation: a young woman sitting on a curb and an older guy who wants to "save" her. Maybe even give her a ride in his hip-hop, bad-to-the-bone minivan. Now there's a sexy ride! So I laughed as I made a quick U-turn and pulled into the parking lot where she sat.

I pulled up and said, "You all right there, little sister?" It was exactly the right thing to ask. Not "Can I help you?" or "Are you feeling all right?" Of course she's not feeling okay. Duh! Any fool with a mule brain could see that. And since I was somewhat related to a mule, being a member of the genus that covers mules, donkeys and asses, I drove on up to that young woman and offered a kind word, hoping against hope she wouldn't think I was some kind of pervert.

I mean, come on! I teach my daughters never ever to trust a guy, especially a stranger, much less a strange stranger. I qualified in the last category. But fortunately she looked up at me and said, "No, I'm okay." To which I replied, "Well, you sure don't look okay." She thanked me for stopping to help her and looked at me for the first time. I said something else, and she stood up and started walking over to me.

I knew right away that she was kind of drunk, and my first thought was, "Oh no, she's some kind of vagabond who's gonna hit me up for a few dollars or something. Can You believe that? That just about makes me the worst kind of scumbag there is. Here I was worried about her thinking I was a scumbag, and then I was thinking like one.

But she was no vagabond. Her name was Ashley, and she was in the army. She was heading over to Kuwait in a few days and was staying with her family in a Holiday Inn two blocks down. She was upset because her good friend Josh had died last week, and she was "close to him." I guessed that she was thinking about her own mortality and going to Kuwait. Maybe that ain't right in the thick of it like Iraq, but it sure is close.

Maybe she was thinking about what was ahead. No man, just the army. How close was she to Josh? I didn't find out and will never know. But You know what? I was able to help that girl. I talked with her about Josh, and then we prayed for him and his family. And for her. And that little girl started crying right there on the seat of my van, and I'll tell You the truth, I did feel a bit good about that. Because sometimes tears need to be shared.

I drove her the two blocks back to her hotel and met the mom. She was shaking her head from the balcony about her lost daughter. The headshake that told me mom was over her baby girl; tired of her and ready to let her go. I could relate, with two girls of my own.

But You know what, Lord? I reckon I'm mighty happy You kept me going straight when I could have gone left. Thanks for taking me down Atlantic so I could help young Miss Ashley. Lord, I would surely appreciate it if You could keep an eye on her because, no matter what her momma thinks, I think she is a fine woman, through and through. Shoot, You made her, so what could be better?

Visit her tonight, Lord, in her dreams, and whisper Your love song to her. Take away the heart sting she feels for Josh. Become her Josh and take her in Your arms tonight, Lord. Take away her need for the bottle and replace it with a feeling of contentment, love, peace, and joy. Heck, while You're at it, send her a man. In fact, send her the man, the one You picked out for her a long while ago. Yeah, that one. Send her that one.

I love You, Lord. Night night.

MY INFLATABLE HEART

Randy is an excellent poser.

FIFTY-TWO

When Anyone

for Kurt

JOHN KÖEHLER

> So Moses made a bronze snake and put it up on a pole.
> Then when anyone was bitten by a snake and
> looked at the bronze snake, he lived.
>
> NUMBERS 21:9

June 3, 2008

Dear Lord,

Today was a good day. A very good day. Naturally I didn't get everything done that I needed to get done, but still it was a good day.

As usual I started the day with my walk down Oceanfront Avenue. That immediately makes me a blessed man, just to say I walked down Oceanfront Avenue. Seriously, everyone and their mother (and maybe even their father) want to live close enough to the ocean that they can take a morning walk along Oceanfront Avenue.

Of course, some posers who live away from the beach might drive down, park, and then walk along the beach. But they are wannabes, Lord. I am the real deal!

Oh, sorry, I got carried away because it's late in the day, and I'm full of myself. Okay, deep breaths . . . out with the pride and in with God. Maybe I should have written this in the morning when there's much more of you and much less of me, Lord. Too late!

I walked this morning and listened to the Daily Audio Bible and my friend Brian Hardin. Okay, so maybe we're not really friends.

More of a one-way friendship: I listen to him most mornings on my iPhone . . . after downloading it from iTunes . . . after he uploaded from Nashville or wherever he happens to be on the road . . . in whatever translation he's using that week.

I have listened to Brian read the Bible to me since January, so doesn't that make him my friend? Just because I can't talk back to him doesn't mean I don't count him as my friend. One day I'll meet him and make it a two-way friendship.

This morning I finished listening to Brian read about David on the run and then being recrowned as king after his son was killed. Then Jesus came back from the dead and walked and talked among the disbelieving disciples. Then Psalm 119—so long, so long—and a couple of Proverbs.

I had some time left on my walk, so I put on Ladysmith Black Mambazo. I wanted one of their spiritual songs and picked "Jesus Is my Leader." Such a great song to listen to. So powerful as the Africans chant in English, a second language for most as heard in the unusual pronunciations. But instead of being discordant it is beautiful.

> Jesus is my leader on my journey . . . Jesus!
> Jesus is my leader on my journey
> Jesus is my light on my journey
> Jesus is my Savior on my journey
> No one without Jesus Christ

It is such a powerful a cappella song with their deep voices resonating in a way that only African men can do. They sing about Jesus coming as the light of the world, and then they do a prayer recitation. These lyrics struck me down and made me stop, made me think, and made me want to write about it here, on this blog.

> When anyone . . . when anyone
> Is joined to Christ
> He is a new creation
> Old is gone
> New is come

This is, of course, a reference to 2 Corinthians 5:17:

> Therefore, if anyone is in Christ, he is a new creation; the old has gone, the new has come!

Depending on the translation it says if anyone or when anyone, but anyone is the constant. I love that. I love this idea, and listening as Ladysmith sang it brought it home to me and made it real.

It doesn't say that someone, but anyone. That is so hopeful and amazing and completely inclusive for all Your people, Lord. Almost as if You made us all and want us back. Almost as if You are inviting all of us to come back to You. You miss us and want us to come home. Anyone can come. All are welcome.

Even completely broken people. Even kids with disabilities who can't even be accepted by people, much less God. Why should they even try to believe the invitation and that You really do mean anyone, as in them? How do You tell this to a kid with CP who is locked inside his head due to a horrible speech impediment, which causes people to think he's mentally retarded? Lord, if You made him, then why include him in the "anyone" when he's so imperfect?

Doesn't anyone mean the few, the proud, the chosen? Don't You have to dress a certain way, talk a certain way, and walk a certain way to be invited into the kingdom of heaven?

Well . . . apparently not. When You told us (through Paul) that anyone could respond to the call, You really did mean anyone. You meant the beautiful lady with the broken heart and the little kid with the broken spine. You meant the middle-aged deaf man so full of anger he spits bullets and the teenager so hopeless she's thinking about a whole new way to use her belt and end it all.

Jesus did not come for the healthy, but for the sick. The weak and wounded, the poor and hopeless, the outcast and sick. Jesus came for all of us and for anyone.

Imagine that.

When anyone . . .

Bryan is ready to jump in and get wet.

FIFTY-THREE

Peter & Forrest

for Jeff & Cindy

> "...you could say to this sycamore tree,
> 'Go jump in the lake,' and it would do it."
>
> LUKE 17:6

June 4, 2008

Dear Lord,

I was struck by Forrest Gump as I did my morning walk today. Not struck as in struck by a truck or a newspaper boy, though they tend to be men and women in cars nowadays. Thankfully I wasn't struck by anything or anyone physical, but by Your words as I listened to Brian read them to me on the Daily Audio Bible; he read the end of John's gospel.

Jesus had been appearing to the disciples after he came back from the dead. This was the third and last time. His final good-bye. The disciples had gone out with Peter to fish during the night, but they had had no luck. On the way back in, they saw a man on the shore; it was Jesus, but they didn't recognize Him.

Jesus told them to throw their nets over the right side of the boat and they would catch fish. They did, and John exclaimed, "It's the Lord!" Can you imagine the moment, so matter-of-fact yet wrapped in the supernatural? I think this is usually the way that God reveals Himself to us, in natural yet simple ways. In ways that make perfect sense to us. That's why we often don't recognize Him when He does appear. While we're looking for the magic carpet and the burning bush, we miss the beauty all around us and beneath our feet.

If God loves us as much as He says He does, then that must mean He's around a lot, showing Himself to us, and we . . . just . . . don't . . . see . . . Him. He's everywhere, yet invisible. Obviously deceptive. Simply complicated. Ridiculously normal.

But John did see Him and told the others. I love what happened next, when Peter realized that it was Jesus on the shore, one hundred yards away, with a charcoal-fire burning and breakfast cooking.

Here's what the Bible says in John 21:7-8:

> As soon as Simon Peter heard him say, "It is the Lord," he wrapped his outer garment around him (for he had taken it off) and jumped into the water. The other disciples followed in the boat, towing the net full of fish, for they were not far from shore, about a hundred yards.

Peter could have waited for the boat to be rowed to shore. That would have been the prudent thing to do and the course chosen by the other disciples on the boat. They were only a hundred yards from shore, and they would have been there in five minutes or less. But Peter, ever the impulsive one, always reacting passionately from his heart, did the only possible thing for him to do. He wrapped his cloak around him and dove into the water.

Why would he wrap his outer garment around him? Most folks take off clothes when they go swimming, but Peter put them on. All he cared about was getting to see Jesus as soon as possible and he didn't care about himself or his clothes. All he wanted was to close the gap and not waste a second doing the right thing and slowly bringing the boat in while remaining dry. He chose to get wet and get there faster.

Forrest Gump did that once in the movie. He was anchored on his shrimp boat a ways from the dock when Lt. Dan told him his mother was sick. Forrest straightened up, looked at Lt. Dan, dove into the water, and swam to shore. Exactly like Peter did when he heard about Jesus. Both men acted immediately to get to the one they loved. They impulsively reacted to the news and the evidence that their loved one needed them and—as is often the case—was still needed by them. They relentlessly pursued their goal and did not rest until it was achieved.

I am like Forrest and Peter. All too often I act impulsively and passionately with no thought to the possible outcome. I know all the warnings about responding instead of reacting. I've been told to do the right thing and not act rashly. But sometimes it is the right thing to act wrong. Sometimes the best thing is doing the worst thing according to standards.

Forrest's momma was dying from cancer, and Forrest had to get home to her. Nothing else mattered to him, or ever would, until he had done his duty to her. Peter knew that Jesus needed him to be close. He knew that this could be the last time. He knew he needed to be with Him and touch Him, hold Him one more time. Just one more time.

So he jumped over the side of the boat like Forrest would do two thousand years later. Two men jumping into the water with all their clothes on and without a care in the world except the relentless pursuit of the love found in the most important person in their lives. His momma and his Lord.

Lord, I hope when my time comes I will not think at all with my head but follow the call of my heart and leap over the side and into the water of Your love.

Eric wearing a hat like nobody else.

FIFTY-FOUR

The Flight of Josh

for Bruce, Chris & Josh

JOHN KÖEHLER

*We've flown free from their fangs,
free of their traps, free as a bird.
Their grip is broken; we're free as a bird in flight.*

PSALM 124:7

June 5, 2008

Dear Lord,

I have never met Josh, but You have. Even so I have been thinking about him for the past week. I found out that Josh—son of Bruce—was diagnosed recently with ALS.

Lou Gehrig's disease at the age of thirty-five. Not only that, but he was an athlete, a man in complete control of his body, his mind, and his entire destiny. He has a young son, a wife, an excellent career. Fame and fortune, the good life following in the footsteps of a dad who already had it made.

Everything was good and right in Josh's world. Then it all came apart, and he became Humpty Dumpty and fell off the wall. And all the king's horses and all the king's men could not put him back together again. Not even Johns Hopkins or the other hospitals and leading-edge institutions could halt the spread of the wicked beast called ALS.

He became a cripple, and his life as he knew it ended. Game over, dude, game over.

Usually when someone becomes paralyzed, they go through stages. The first is often complete and total despair and grief. Abject horror and disbelief can quickly lead to hopelessness and a desire to no longer live. After all, what is life if you don't have your body anymore? What's the point when your limbs become useless and no longer answer what used to be automatic commands.

Why should you choose to live when life turned you upside down and God turned His back on you?

In your despair and grief you realize that you must bury your body, and the funeral is something you never wanted to attend. Your funeral was supposed to be the final act of your life, when all of you had died and you went to heaven, but now you must bury parts of your body that have died and gone not to heaven but to hell. You can't bury them in the end; you are forced to live with your dead parts, the caretaker of your own cemetery, the cemetery of your life. You are a dead man walking, but not even that because you cannot walk and are reduced to crawling or rolling in a wheelchair, something you had sworn you would never do, because it is beneath you.

After despair comes anger, which does a complete takeover when you realize that this is really it, this is what you're stuck with. This is what you get after working so hard and being so good. You look at all the poor schleps who have so much more than you, starting with bodies that work, and you wonder, "Why them and not me?"

Your anger turns bitter inside of you, and you like the feel of it, all-consuming and powerful. Your friends and family fear you, and this fear becomes the only thing you can control anymore. Why should you be nice when the world was not nice to you? Why should you consider anyone but yourself?

You used to think of the world out there, and your vision was cast so far out that your spirit would take flight and soar while you were asleep and sometimes when you were awake. But now you can't see past your useless toes, and looking beyond your bed seems like a waste of time. Your dreams have turned to nightmares, and your wings have been clipped. You no longer soar like an eagle, but sit and waddle as an earthbound penguin.

Lord, show Josh his purpose in his new life. Speak to him in his dreams and hold him in Your arms. Fill him with Your love and teach him how to love again. Remove his blindness and give him Your vision, the vision of possibilities and hope. The vision that says look within for perfection, not without. The vision that starts with the last unaffected refuge in his body: his mind.

Lord, let me meet Josh so I can lift him up. Let me meet him, and if I do, I pray that You will work through me to lift him up to the purpose You have for him. The purpose that he is avoiding even though he knows it is there waiting for him on the other side of his life. Help him to get over his pride so he can get into his life. His new life. His only life. His beautiful life.

Maybe you brought me through the void of time today for Josh. Maybe I can be the one who can help tip the balance that his family and friends have worked so long on. Come back, Josh. Give it up, Josh. Fight back, Josh. Quit being such a dork, Josh! Can't you see that your life no longer belongs to you. God has a purpose for you, even in your disability. You are disabled now, and there is nothing you can do about it. Get on with it!

Today I watched a TV spot by the Washington state lottery. It showed some hang gliders taking nonflight birds on flights. Penguins, chickens, emus. It was beautiful, and it made me cry. It made me realize once again how awesome it is when a friend helps his buddy to do things he can't do on his own.

Josh used to fly, Lord. He used to fly across the skies of his life. But now he can't fly anymore. He's grounded. Ahhh, but maybe he can still fly if he lets his friends help him. Maybe he can still do the things he loved before. Help him do this, Lord. Help him be awesome and amazing on his own by allowing others to help him be awesome.

Lord, help Josh get to the next phase, the phase of acceptance, love, and desire. He's close I think. Very close.

Jane with one of her many boyfriends.

FIFTY-FIVE
Hofferbert Hill

for Harv & Jane

JOHN KÖEHLER

> But Lot protested, "No, masters, you can't mean it! I know that you've taken a liking to me and have done me an immense favor in saving my life."
>
> GENESIS 19:18

June 6, 2008

Dear Lord,

Moving back to the beach was a homecoming for me since I grew up here and stayed through high school (Cox High School, the best school in the state!). For both Patty and I it was living out our dream to live at the beach. The only question was where at the beach. Ah, but You had it all worked out, Lord. We just had to decipher the path and the plan You had already written. I'm glad we did. Thanks for waiting for us to catch up!

Living on the sand—as they call the oceanfront—was an expensive undertaking and not to be taken lightly or with a little bitty bank account. They called it the "gold coast," and they were right. Even so we demanded the right to live out our dream where we wanted to, so we searched high and low, concentrating on the North End.

It all started when I decided in a rather quick way that it was time for me to start my business and for us to move to the beach. Patty did not agree with my timing on the former but agreed to the latter, so we both set out to find the right house in 1993. We first looked at the house we now call home when it was priced at $269,000. More than we could afford, but we sure liked the location even if there were problems with the house. So we waited.

We put our Maryland house back on the market in February 1994, and it sold in two days. We raced back to the beach and discovered that the same house was now priced to sell at $219,000. We knew we had to have it and we did, after jumping through some mighty skinny hoops and leaping over some mighty high mortgage hurdles. After all, my new graphic design business was less than a year old, which was not a good thing according to lenders, who were looking for at least three years experience. But our mortgage broker and a huge down payment from the Maryland house sealed the deal. We moved in.

Lord, I think that life is really a series of Your blessings that happen one after the other. The problem is that some of Your blessings do not feel like blessings to us because they are hard or difficult or make us angry or stretch us in some way we did not really wish to grow in, thank You very much indeed, God. So just back off! Oh, sorry, Lord, I was just explaining how it can feel.

I think that one of our greatest blessings was moving to this house on this street in this city. Right next to us lived (and still live) Harv and Jane Hofferbert. I remember meeting Jane for the first time. Her house sits above ours on an old dune line. She was outside when I was walking around our house on a day back in March of '94. I yelled up to her, and then I ran up the vine-covered hill to meet her and shake her hand. She never has forgotten that, and I laugh when I think about it.

I think I ran to Jane because my spirit knew that here was a woman of God. Your woman, Lord. You already knew her. Here was Your woman, full of kindness and love and joy. Weren't we Koehlers just the luckiest people on the planet to land right next door to Harv and Jane? Yes, we were, and I knew it right away because You showed it to me as plain as day, like a daffodil in the snow.

All of our neighbors are special and love us about as much as we love them, which is a lot! But there is something wonderful, supernatural, and simply awesome about Harv and Jane. They just are. They are there all the time. They are nice to our kids. They are always thinking about us. They are our neighbors, and they stick up for us. They are there for us. They are.

Shoot, Harv was the construction project manager for us when we built an addition, and he put a ton of time into the job but took no money for it. He just did it because he loved us and wanted to help. Well, at least he loved Patty and the girls, because now I'm still doing graphic design slave labor to make it up to him. It was a good trade.

Christians sometimes make a fuss about how we are supposed to act and think and do things. Sometimes we worry too much about these things when we should spend more time thinking about You, Lord, and living out our lives the way you said to: by loving one another. I don't reckon I know the belief systems of Harv and Jane, Lord, and, truth be told, I don't rightly care because I can see the evidence of You in all that they do.

I would take Harv and Jane over many of my Christian friends any day of the week because I trust them completely. I've seen their core, and I know who they are by what they have done for me and my family. Some things cannot be faked, and the proof is always in what we do and the evidence we leave behind, like Kilroy and his carvings.

I don't think that there are two finer people alive in this city than Harv and Jane Hofferbert. I really don't. They are the very best neighbors we could possibly have asked for. Our family—our two daughters, Patty, and I—are better people as a result of living next door to them. I really can't do an adequate job of explaining why I feel this way because it is so wrapped up in the simplicity of life.

Lord, You are around us all the time, whether or not we see You and Your creation. You are in every person, every thing, everywhere. You are clearly and unmistakably in Harv and Jane, and for that I am profoundly thankful. I thank You for Harv and Jane and ask that You allow me the privilege of being their neighbor for a while longer. Just a little while longer, Lord. A little while longer.

Visit them tonight and tell them again how much You love them. Tell them how special they are and that they are Your favorites. Tell them, Lord. Over and over again.

One of Capernaum's finest, Derek.

FIFTY-SIX

My Second Allergy

for Debi

> Others joked, "They're drunk on cheap wine."
>
> ACTS 2:13

June 7, 2008

Dear Lord,

I want to thank You for saving my life. Again. Now I know that You are the reason for my life and that You made my life and all that. But I'm not talking about that obvious stuff. I'm talking about saving me from my second allergy. Yeah, that.

My first allergy causes my nose to run like a fire hose. Sometimes my nose speaks in tongues, and I sneeze out the demon seeds hiding inside my nasal passages. Be gone, demon seeds! I have had this allergy most of my life. Being a guy I've never gone to the doctor about it, but have just learned to live with it, much to the delight of the good people at Kleenex. Truth is, I'm not sure if I've blown some of my brains out my nose, but something sure has been coming out of me!

My second allergy started when You were putting me together in my momma's womb, when all the genetic mixture was coalescing into the little baby that would be me. My mom and dad both had this allergy and had learned not only to live with it but had chased it across the skies of their lives as if to say, "Make me sick so I can live."

Lord, my second allergy is and always has been alcohol.

It has taken me fifty years to understand that even if an allergy is completely accepted by society, it can still kill you. It has taken me forever to appreciate that while I may enjoy the good side effects of my second allergy, the bad ones can very much ruin my life. No matter if these side effects are subtle or not, they creep, creep, creep up and slowly strangle me with the obvious and say, "Boy, can't you see I'm tryin' to kill you?"

My dad and mom passed on their allergy to me, and I knew it. But I swore that I would never be like them. I would never beat my wife, much less in front of my kids. I would never speak against my wife to my kids. I would never allow my allergy to make me so stinking out of touch that my family would be a walking time bomb with a short fuse. I swore that I would not become like my father, Lord, and I never did any of those awful things.

But I did become like him in other ways.

In a funny way this may be the thing that is finally allowing me to forgive him for the great harm he did to my family. Maybe funny is not the right word; maybe it should be ironic or strange. Whatever the case, now that I've finally accepted the truth of my second allergy, I also have accepted the truth of my connection to my father. And my mother.

Both of my parents were alcoholics. Perhaps not in the classic sense of the word and as the world defines it: roaring drunks who can't stay away from any bottle of alcohol and secretly crave it all day long so they pour it down their throats until they are completely wasted. That is such a stupid definition and completely misses the reality of what it means to be an alcoholic or—if you prefer—to have an alcohol allergy.

Trying to define what it means to be an alcoholic is like trying to define what it means to be autistic. There is such a huge range of possible definitions that it is effectively undefinable in a group sense. One person acts like this and another like that. We each react differently to the alcohol that we consume. But no matter how we react, the bottom line is that alcohol causes a negative allergic reaction in our bodies, which can cause similar reactions in our minds, hearts, and souls.

For me it was the anger. Alcohol made me angry. Not like a raging-bull, stupid drunk. More like just an angry jerk. Part of this had to do with my personality and the fact that I was so close to the edge of my passion, that I was so overloaded to begin with, that alcohol pushed me with a gentle shove into anger and stupidity. The push can be gentle, but the effect can be explosive.

This usually showed up in the things I said, but also in the things I did. And it usually affected my family in one way or another, especially my wife. I stopped drinking several times in my life to prove that I could live without it, that I could be as happy and as fun without it, and also to prove that I was not my father.

Oh, but I was my father. It just took me a while to figure it out.

I'm just thankful, Lord, that I was able to figure it out in time to save my life and the life of my family. Because Dad wasn't able to do that. He was the anchor that he tied around his neck, which pulled him down into oblivion and unhappiness. Even if he did sometimes see clearly through the haze of his allergy, it was way too late for him to go back. Or maybe not. Maybe there is hope for everyone, even my dad. Too bad he died in 1981 because I didn't know then what I know now. Could I have saved him?

No, but You could have.

Some of my friends get angry with me when I tell them why I've quit drinking. They tell me, "You're not an alcoholic. You just have a problem because of your meds and being bipolar." I laugh at them because I understand them. We all have a definition of the perfect drunk, the perfect alcoholic, and I am not it. I'm too upright and healed and intelligent and amazing, and how the heck could God or anyone else allow me to be an alcoholic? It just ain't fair.

I choose to respect my family and avoid using a substance that sometimes causes me to treat them in an unfair way. I choose to be fair to myself and free of a drug that can sometimes bring out the worst in me, all the way from the bottom of my garbage pile. I choose to live my life in peace and happiness, and if I must avoid certain things to achieve that goal, then so be it. I choose to stay away from the stuff that can make me so upset that I consider taking my own life.

I don't care if they call me an alcoholic or not. I don't care how they define me because they can't. You made me, Lord, and broke the mold; I choose to accept who I am before I break me. It doesn't matter to me one bit if they understand or accept that. Not one bit. Because I can assure them that You *do* understand and accept it.

Lord, You never told us not to drink. You told us don't get drunk on wine, but instead be drunk in the Spirit. So now I will concentrate on drinking as much of Your Spirit as I can. Lord, I'm gonna need gallons and gallons of it because I'm thirsty. I'm going to need You to help me maintain my joy and love for the life You gave me because I've still got a lot of work to do.

Thanks for saving my life, Lord. Thanks for whoopin' me upside the head so I could come to grips with my plain-as-day allergy. Give me another drink of Your Spirit, Lord. Give me a taste of You so I can be inebriated in Your love, consumed by Your passion, drunk in Your joy. Ah, the bouquet, the aroma, the flavor of Your Spirit!

Thanks for saving my life. Again.

JOHN KÖEHLER

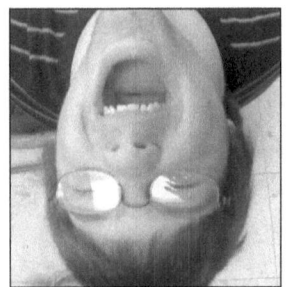

Daniel is not afraid to let go.

FIFTY-SEVEN

Let Go

for Laura

JOHN KÖEHLER

> *That was the last thing the young man expected to hear. And so, crest-fallen, he walked away. He was holding on tight to a lot of things, and he couldn't bear to let go.*
>
> MATTHEW 19:22

June 9, 2008

Dear Lord,

Every single time I listen to Imogen Heap sing, I bliss out and feel so great. There's something about her music that just makes me come alive and feel more than I normally do. Now that's saying something for a man who is already overly passionate.

The power of her music combined with the beauty of her lyrics knocks me off my feet. I keep coming back and listening to it over and over again, no matter how many songs and playlists I have on my iPhone. I come back to it like a worn novel that I love and can't seem to stay away from, so I read it all over again like a long lost friend every few years or so. Like a comfortable easy chair that lets me dream big and welcomes me like an old friend, or like an old mother who wraps me in her embrace.

Imogen's music embraces my ears and my heart. It makes my heartstrings quiver in resonance and perfect pitch. I can literally feel myself spread out on the inside. I can feel my heart expand, like a solar flare that we never even see from our distant perch, but in fact is millions of miles long and amazingly powerful. The power of my expanding heart is immense and pulls me along with it. I go willingly.

Tonight, driving back from the very last Norfolk club, I listened to Imogen's classic "Let Go." This song is a fan favorite from her early albums. Beautiful lyrics, awesome rhythms, and syncopated beats. A nearly perfect song. Let's just say it is perfect, shall we? We shall.

Norfolk Capernaum had a great party, a send-off to the summer. Everyone danced and hung out, and we had a great time. My friend Glen McClure took photos of everyone.

I listened first to Collective Soul. Very strong, very rock, very solid. Strong music can actually calm me down in a strange way. The way some autistic kids have to listen to heavy-metal music to calm them down. Like hyperactive kids taking stimulants to calm them down. It doesn't make sense . . . but it works.

Then I listened to Imogen's "Let Go." The lyrics that have always amazed me, and which I have always planned on writing about, are in the chorus:

So, let go
Jump in
Oh well, what you waiting for?
It's all right
'Cause there's beauty in the breakdown
So, let go
Just get in
Oh, it's so amazing here
It's all right
'Cause there's beauty in the breakdown

The words are so simple, so elegant, and so powerful. I don't know what Imogen intended with her words or what she was thinking about. For me there are two concepts:

1. Talking to someone with a mental illness
2. An angel inviting someone to let go to God

The invitation is to let go and jump in. Don't wait, do it now because it's beautiful here. Don't be afraid because I'm already here and it is amazing. You feel like you're going to have a breakdown and you are, but there's beauty in the breakdown because once you get through it, you fall into the beauty on the other side. The hard and scary part is falling through the breakdown.

Like trusting the people behind you to catch you during one of those team-building exercises. The song suggests an implicit and profound trust. You can trust me to help you through this. I'm already here waiting for you. Don't be afraid. The breakdown is ugly, but the beauty is right behind it. Let go and fall in.

The angels call us too. They want us to let go and fall into God. But we are afraid and can see the ground far below, waiting to rise up and smack us dead. We don't believe it when they say that we won't fall down but up. Up where it is so amazing. We don't believe it when they say that we will fall down and bounce off the earth with our own Matrix moment. It will scare us to death, but after we die, we will live again, and the place we live will be amazing and beautiful. So let go and fall in.

The angels can see what we're missing, but we can't. They can't believe we won't let go, to go through the breakdown in order to see the beauty. They want us to give up and get into God, to let ourselves go and give in to the process of our new birth. Making a jump of faith is flat-out scary sometimes when you're not sure what will actually happen. God's not right next to you holding your hand. You can feel His presence, but what if your time is up, and He's calling you home.

If that's the case, then letting go is going all the way to the end of the game without passing go. Maybe the angels are calling us home to be with God. Nah. But they certainly can call us out to be with God in this earthly kingdom. Imogen's chorus says so many things, depending on what you believe. I love that.

I'm not afraid to let go any longer, and I've seen the beauty of the breakdown many times, literally and figuratively. I hate the pain of the breakdowns, when my spirit crashes and my ego is eviscerated. I don't care what they say about needing to go through pain to get to gain. For me it just hurts. I understand that on the other side there is gain and value and beauty, but why do I have to go through the breakdown to get to the other side?

I wish it wasn't so, but it is.

If you hold on to the things you are clinging to, the breakdown will come to you, but it may destroy you because you're too stiff and brittle, ready to break into a million pieces. That's like trying to be stronger than a wave. You can't do it. You have to let go and let it roll you where it will so you can come out the other side. That's how Mom taught us, and it works.

Same with our lives. Sometimes you have to let go so you can be rolled around by the waves that march in as sets from your endless horizons. The waves are coming. Will you be ready to ride them? Will you let go so they can help you get past the breakdown? Or will you die in the undertow and rip currents, suffocate in the shallows where great mounds of foam choke the life out of you?

Let go and live. What are you waiting for? It is awesome here. Come on in, I'm waiting for you. Get in because it feels great. Trust me, just let go and fall in. It's gonna hurt pretty bad at first, but then you'll be through it and out the other side. It's so beautiful here. I can't wait to show you.

Let go, let go. Jump in. It's all right, 'cause there's beauty in the breakdown.

JOHN KÖEHLER

Not perhaps the change you wanted.

FIFTY-EIGHT

May Change

for Kevin

JOHN KÖEHLER

After John was arrested, Jesus went to Galilee preaching the Message of God: "Time's up! God's kingdom is here. Change your life and believe the Message."

MARK 1:14

June 10, 2008

Dear Lord,

Something happened to me on May 16. My life changed. You changed my life, and I still don't really understand what happened or how You did it. My May change.

I still don't get it.

Tonight I told some of the guys from the Friday Morning Men's Group (please note the muy importante capital letters) about how You saved my life back in May. You remember. I had been dealing with the many issues of Capernaum and wondering (again) if I was really the right guy for this ministry. I was feeling more and more that I was not the right guy and was in fact incapable of carrying the torch one step further.

Why weren't the others carrying it? Where were they? I moaned and whined about my lot in life, and I just didn't want to do it any longer. Big baby! I was convinced that we could not keep Tara on staff next year and that we'd have to become smaller. This made me feel even smaller and obliterated one of my life's stated purpose to go big or go home.

MY INFLATABLE HEART

Truth is I was ready to go home, Lord. I was ready for You and would have been happy to go back home to You during that time. Or anytime. Why is it that life can seem such a struggle while other days it seems such a breeze? Your blessing is in the breeze and the storm, in the bad days and good. Your blessings never stop, Lord.

Do they?

I was feeling rotten and old on the inside, like going up to the attic and finding your gramma's trunk from college, so cool-looking and unusual. Then you open it, and the smell of dust and decay overwhelms you; suddenly gramma doesn't seem so cool anymore.

I just couldn't seem to get rid of the musty smell in my heart.

I told the guys that this went on for several weeks in March, April, and then into May. I struggled like Atlas, sure of my ability to hold up my world and pass the test that You were putting me through, Lord. But I wasn't. I didn't even know what the test was; all I knew was that something was not right in my world. I hoped that it was not me falling into another depression. I checked my meds and prayed that I was not falling down into the pit of doom. Yet it beckoned me.

I called out to You, Lord. You remember, don't You?

I never lost sight of You completely. I knew You were there, but You didn't seem to help me. Why is that? Why is it that when I fall, I reach out to You the most and feel You the least? Is this all Your idea? Do You want me to fall so I can realize that I just can't do it on my own? In some ways this makes You a masochistic God. But why would You punish us with our own lives when you made us the way we are?

As a parent I have to let my kids figure some things out on their own. Sometimes I know they are going to get hurt and that the pain will bring them understanding and teach them about life. So easy for me to say that as the distant parent. But they have to live it, and living it can flat-out hurt like the dickens.

Why did You want me to live that way, Lord? Why did You wait so long before you pulled me out? I still don't get it. I was a mess and unsure of pretty much everything. I kept trying to save myself by myself and failing to do so. Like a guy drowning in the water trying to throw himself a life ring. You don't have a life ring, fool! Get over it; the game is over, dude. You are going to die, and there's nothing you can do about it. So just give in and let go. Let go and die.

Wait a minute! That's not You saying that, Lord. That's the stinky one. The lowlife that inhabits my heart. I know who he is. He's an idiot, and if I listen to him I'm the bigger idiot.

Lord, I walked through the desert for weeks, and suddenly I was out. Something happened to me on May 16, and I do not understand it. My heart changed like a tide, and everything that seemed heavy was light. My darkness was replaced with sunlight. My trepidation was replaced by assurance and conviction that everything would be great.

You happened to me on May 16, Lord. But why then? Had I gone through enough? Was it the fact that I was at the end of my rope and truly did not understand how I could do it any longer? Why did You change my heart on May 16? I wish I knew, but I don't understand it. It was one of the most subtle yet complete changes of heart I've ever had. Like falling asleep on an ice flow and waking up on a tropical isle.

On May 16, 2008, You showed up and changed everything. You changed my heart and my life. You restored my soul and took control of my stronghold. Lord, I want every day to be May 16. I want You to constantly restore my soul and fill my heart with Your peace and understanding. I want to be filled with Your Holy Spirit, so full that the rest of me must flee along with the jerk that inhabits my heart, the evil one so cunning and cute.

Tonight Kevin told me to mark that day, May 16, and I mark it for You, Lord. Thanks for saving my life and for giving it to me, over and over every day. Thanks for Your love and Your love and Your love. Love me like May 16 and never give up on me. I don't want to go back to the pit, but if that is the only way to recapture May 16 again, then I will go there for You. Because in the darkness I see Your light. And in the darkness I know I am closest to another day in May.

Two ordinary men, Neal and Bobby.

FIFTY-NINE

Ordinary Men

for Bob & Karen

> The members of the council were amazed when they saw the boldness of Peter and John, for they could see that they were ordinary men with no special training in the Scriptures.
>
> ACTS 4:13

June 11, 2008

Dear Lord,

I am amazed and thankful that you have made a point over the years of using ordinary men and women to do Your work, to fulfill Your promises and execute Your plans. There are so many examples of this all the way back to Genesis, yet we seem to be surprised that it still happens today. Why do we think that You would change over the years? What is a year to You?

Or even two thousand? I was listening to Your Word this week, in Acts. John and Peter had been arrested by the members of the Jewish high council because they had been inciting the people to believe in Jesus and go against the teachings of the Jews.

Many Jews were believing and putting their faith in Jesus as the Messiah their people had been waiting for, the Messiah spoken of in their Scriptures. Many were saved and believed due to the acts and words of John and Peter, along with other believers.

So the council of Jewish religious elders, Pharisees and Sadducees, had John and Peter thrown in jail and brought before them the next morning. "By what power, or in whose name, have you done this?" they asked (Acts 4:7, NLT). That's when Peter kind of went off, full of himself and the Holy Spirit. He was so well spoken and so full of fervor that the men of the council shook their heads and whispered together.

They had spent most of their adult lives around learned men, scholars, the wealthy and powerful. They knew the trappings of education and prestige and could size up a man in an instant. They knew the men before them. Everyone did. They were fishermen from Galilee, blue-collar workers as we say today. Tradesmen. An honorable profession to be sure but not one that would win a man power or great standing in the community, much less the religious community.

Yet here they were, preaching to the center of the Jewish spiritual and religious universe as if they were scholars, completely qualified to speak and state their views in a simple yet clear way. Not with educated words, but with the plain words of fishermen, words that all people could comprehend. Surely this was part of the reason Jesus picked His disciples from the working stock of Galilee and the other parts of Israel.

He wanted ordinary men.

Perhaps that way there could be no doubt after Jesus was dead and gone that God Himself—Jesus Himself—was alive in these men and filling them with the Holy Spirit. How else could it be possible for them to possess such knowledge? Who else could fill them with the assurance and boldness to speak in front of the most powerful religious men in Israel? They made such an impact that the council members asked, "Who are these men?"

If God can use a fisherman, then why not me? If God can use a tax collector, then why not you? God uses the least of us to do the best of Him. He does not care about the education of books but the education of our hearts. It took the disciples three years to become ready to go out and baptize in the name of Christ. But the truth is that even just before He died, they were still not ready, still not sure that He was the one.

And they saw Him every day, including His miracles.

God takes ordinary men and women and gives us something extra. He gives us a part of Himself and adds it to our own power and nature. His extra combined with our ordinary makes us extraordinary. It is as simple as that. God can transform anything ordinary into something extraordinary. He takes the normal and makes it paranormal, supernormal.

This is an amazing thing, an extraordinary fact. It gives me hope. All my life I have known that I was extraordinary but felt stupid and prideful saying it. Now I can say I'm an ordinary man with a little bit extra from the Big Dude. A little bit of extra that everyone can get. As long as they know who to get it from!

Doug in character in a video scene.

SIXTY

Mr. Speaker

for Doug

JOHN KÖEHLER

He was a ... terrific speaker, eloquent and powerful
in his preaching of the Scriptures.
He was well-educated in the way of the
Master and fiery in his enthusiasm.

ACTS 18:24

June 12, 2008

Dear Lord,

Angela made me write this story, dang it all. I'm tired so the story is really short, like Angela. She has gotten pretty uppity ever since You crowned her as our next intern. Lord, can You just turn down her volume a little? Just kidding. As if You needed me to tell You I was kidding.

Angela wanted me to write about how we got our camp speaker for Triple R Ranch Camp. She says it was a God thing, but I already knew that. Truth is, I'm getting closer and closer to believing that everything is a God thing, and the only question is whether or not we accept You in the moment. It actually makes logical sense when you stop and think about it.

You made everything, and everything was made by You. Therefore everything that happens in nature was made by the nature of Your being; it was made by You. Regardless of the freedom of choice You gave us, You are still in everything that happens. Now the tricky part is knowing whether or not You got directly involved.

Some folks would call it chance. I just call it a God thing.

Last week Tara, Angela, and I were meeting at the Purple Cow. One of the things we discussed was who we were going to get as the camp speaker. I told them that Kess (Chesapeake area director Chris Kessick) was not able to do it. We had just started to brainstorm and discuss other speakers when my cell phone rang. It was Doug Haupt (that's him in the photo, dressed as a blind Ukrainian for a video) calling me about some technical help he needed for a talk he was giving to the Friday Morning Men's Group.

We rang off and then it hit me, pow!

"Wait, Doug could do it! He'd be great!" I said. So I called Doug back, and he was interested. And now he's gonna do it. Lord, I'm pretty sure You arranged this whole thing; in fact, I know it. Either indirectly by Your creation or directly by having Doug call me exactly at the moment we were talking about a speaker.

It was kind of like a celestial head bonk. Doh! Call Doug back, you dolt!

Why was I so excited about Doug? You could have sent or we could have gotten any speaker, and that would have been fine. But You sent the best. You sent the one man I know who thinks about You in the way that our kids think: honestly, in a simple manner, and with huge gusto and fun. You sent a dude who understands what Jesus was talking about when He said He wanted us to come to Him like children. Not childishly, but directly like a child, without all the layers of crap that adults bring to the table.

We never really had a chance to pray for this man, Lord. But maybe our lives were prayers to You. Maybe You just wanted to remind us who You are and how You are. This was an easy thing for You, an eye flutter, a wave of Your hand, a tap of Your finger, a smile on Your face. Maybe You helped us because we were not worried about finding a speaker, and we knew You would provide. So You did, bang! That was really pretty cool, Lord. If I didn't know You better, I'd say You were showing off. Hey, I like to show off too! Maybe we're related.

All I know is that no one can touch You when it comes to bringing people together, Lord. No one can weave together the strands of humanity that are required for some endeavors to succeed... or not succeed. The complexity of humans aligning together is mind boggling. But then, Your mind never boggles. You delight in us, don't You, Abba? You're pretty cool.

Yeah, You really are the best matchmaker, Lord. Thanks.

Postscript.

Triple R Ranch Camp was a huge success, thanks in no small part to Doug Haupt's beautiful talks about Jesus. Over five days he told the story of God's creation from Adam and Even and up to Jesus and beyond, to infinity. Even better then Buzz Lightyear.

The kids loved his stories and they loved him, exactly as we expected and you knew in advance. Thanks for picking out our speaker this year, Lord. Would you mind arranging for next year's speaker pretty soon?

Oh, and make him a good one, the best. Like you did when you picked Doug. Thanks.

Some of the 125 party people at the Va. Beach end of the year party.

SIXTY-ONE

Happy Happy Sad Sad

for Skipper

> We were the talk of the nations – "God was wonderful to them!" God was wonderful to us; we are one happy people.
>
> PSALM 126:2-3

June 13, 2008

Dear Lord,

Monday night was the Norfolk Capernaum party, and it was great. But then, You were there so You already know. Somehow I think Your take on it was different than mine. Probably because I was aware of Your presence much less than 100 percent of the time. I'm thinking that when I'm fully aware of You all the time, I will be in heaven. Is that cheating?

But down here it ain't so easy, Lord.

Last night was the Virginia Beach party and cookout. It was—as is always the case with Virginia Beach—huge and amazing. Shoot, just look at the photo. I count about 105 people, and that's not including a lot of parents and others off to the right. We had at least 125 people there.

Some folks would say that is entirely too many folks for a club devoted to people with disabilities. But thankfully, we are not "some folks" and never will be. Lord, thanks for making us your folks, regardless of how pretty we are and whether we can count past ten, or even spell the word "count."

I videotaped everyone and their mother, interviewing them with the simple question, "What do you love best about Capernaum?" There was no wrong answer. I got a lot of answers like pizza and dancing, rock 'n' roll, good times, games, etc. But by far the most common answer was it is a place to be loved no matter what. A place where everyone gets along. A place of fellowship and a place to learn about and meet Jesus. I'm working on that interview video. It will be a good one, Lord.

But here's the thing. After leaving I felt sad. I wasn't sure why, so I stopped off and got myself a Slurpee to try to take my mind off my sadness. But that didn't work; it just gave me a brain freeze. I realized that I was melancholy, sort of a happy sad. I'm going to see everyone again next week at the Surf Camp, but this was the last time for this school year, and closing the book on it just felt final and hurt my heart.

Lord, I know this sounds kind of whimpy for a grown man, but I'm just telling You the truth. Last night I said good night to my friends and missed them as if I would never see them again. All my little brothers and sisters who have become a part of me, a part of my heart that glows whenever they're around. I miss them already, Lord. I miss them.

Do You feel that way when we turn our backs on You? If You do, then I'm sorry for all the times I've turned my back on You because I don't want anyone to feel this way. It's not like being depressed. It is like a happy cake covered by a thick icing of sadness.

I don't want to eat that cake anymore, Lord. I like it, but it leaves a sad taste in my mouth. Can You just make the Surf Camp get here fast, please?

JOHN KÖEHLER

Josh hunting girls at Laser Quest.

SIXTY-TWO

Supernova Josh

for Darryl & Lynn

> "Men and women who have lived wisely and well will shine brilliantly, like the cloudless, star-strewn night skies. And those who put others on the right path to life will glow like stars forever.

DANIEL 12:3

June 14, 2008

Dear Lord,

I just wanted to thank You for allowing me to be part of Josh's baptism this morning. I don't know how You worked this one or why Josh waited until now, but whatever You did . . . thanks. Now I'm not talking about the symbolic baptism by water that we'll do next week to old Josh down at the beach. I'm talking about the baptism of Your Spirit that poured into Josh's heart when he said the magic words that opened the floodgates of heaven and formed a new river between You and Josh's soul. That baptism, Lord. The dunking of his soul! You are a good God. Thanks.

Josh's mom, Lynn, said that during their morning Bible study, Josh decided to give his life to Jesus and wanted to be baptized at our Surf Camp. Well, there you go! If ever there was a purpose for creating the Surf Camp, Josh's baptism would be it.

When we first started the camp three years ago, there was a little bitty peanut planted in the soil of my mind that started to grow and poke up into my thoughts. Why not do a baptism right then and there with the kids, right in front of the surfers and tourists and friends and complete strangers coming down to stare at the ocean and listen to the beauty of God's wave music, along with the bikinis, beach balls, and books.

By this time last year that little peanut seed had become a peanut bush that could not be refused any longer. I knew we had to do a baptism, but I wasn't really sure how. But You knew. I didn't know if it would work, but You did. It hasn't even happened yet, but it will. It will. You will. Josh will.

Josh is growing up fast, Lord. He is learning to face his fears and stepping up and out of the boat to try things that just last year he never would have considered: Triple R Camp, picking on adults, going to Laser Quest, getting baptized. All these things take courage for Josh. The beauty of Capernaum is that he can watch what his friends do and mimic them. He can watch as they try some stupid new game at club and then survive to tell the tale. This gives him faith and courage. This courage grows in layers until the day arrives when Josh is ready to do it himself.

A lot of people point to the leaders of Capernaum and call them heroes, and they would be right. But we tend to forget how heroic the regular members of Capernaum can be and are for kids like Josh. People with disabilities might look up to our leaders and be compelled by what they do, helped by their example. But they know that they are not the same as the leaders, and their own disabilities mark them in a different way.

When a guy like Josh sees another friend with a disability do something cool or courageous or awesome or whatever, it gives him more courage, much more, than any leader ever could hope to give. The playing field is level, which means that it is fair, and if he can do it, then why not me?

I know that our junior leaders (kids with disabilities in leadership) have influenced Josh, but I'm thinking all the kids and volunteers have. They give him a cumulative jolt of courage and encouragement, a collective spirit that has slowly helped build his will to the point where this morning he told his parents he wanted to accept Jesus into his life. I wonder how long that would have taken without his friends at Capernaum accelerating the buildup of his courage.

I think that Jesus has been baptizing Josh all his life, every day (same as all of us). He has been pouring His spirit into Josh, and it was just a matter of time before Josh became aware of it and wanted to mark this awareness by inviting Jesus into the place where He'd been living since Josh was knee-high to a grasshopper. Like having an invisible guest staying with you all your life, and one day you invite that guest to come stay with you for the rest of your life, and poof he appears.

And you're like, "Gosh, you look really familiar. Have we met?"

God is with us our whole lives, and when we make that move to invite Him in to His own living room by accepting everything that Jesus did and is, God doesn't say, "I will," but "I am." He's already there, but the only question to the entire inheritance is, do we want to get it all? Do we want to have Jesus turbocharge our souls so we can fully assume the mantle of discipleship?

Josh was a beautiful little lightning bug for God and is now a supernova for Jesus. He was always the nova, but now he's super. He was always the man, but now he's a superman. Josh was always God's son, but now he's His main man, His disciple, His favorite. Because now that he's made this move, there are certain prerequisites, certain things he must do to fulfill the promise God made in him. You know what those things are.

I don't. Hey, this is Josh's life, and that's between him and God. His God. My God. Our God. So here's to Josh's perfect decision to invite Jesus in to sit at the head of his heart-shaped table. Here's to Josh and Jesus living together forever and ever as friends and so much more. Here's to Josh continuing to grow as God's disciple and fulfilling all that God has for him.

Because I'm darn sure God has plans for him. Don't make the mistake of thinking small about those plans or wondering how God can use a disabled person. God is huge and now lives within Josh. Hey, I guess that makes Josh huge, eh? Who are you to even try to comprehend the possibility God sees in Josh? He's God's supernova, His superman, His blazing comet streaking across the sky. Just sit back and enjoy the show!

Josh is going to get dunked next week down at Sixtieth Street Beach at 3:00 PM. Surf's up, baby, surf's up! Hang ten, Josh: ride that wave in to Jesus, little bro.

Eric can tell you about Gandalf.

SIXTY-THREE

Inside Knowledge

for Terri

JOHN KÖEHLER

> Give what each deserves, for you know each life from the inside (you're the only one with such "inside knowledge"!) so that they'll live before you in lifelong reverent and believing obedience on this land you gave our ancestors.
>
> 1 KINGS 8:39-40

June 15, 2008

Dear Lord,

As Your own words say, You know each life from the inside. You're the only one with such inside knowledge of who we are and what makes us tick. In a way it is kind of like a Master Chief mechanic who can walk into the huge engine room of an aircraft carrier and know every inch, every piece, every bolt of every bit of the mechanism that drives the ship forward.

But we are not machines. Oh no, we are much more complicated than that. Much more complicated. Even people with disabilities are complicated, don't you think? Fortunately they are oh-so-easy when it comes to love, both the giving and getting. I am thankful for that and very thankful that Capernaum has reminded me that the methods of giving and getting love that I've used all my life were, in fact, correct. And still *are* correct.

Maybe that was and is because some of my inside knowledge comes directly from God. Just as the Master Chief leaves his mark on his equipment, so does God leave His mark on us and—hopefully—in us. This is a good thing. Lord, all the time that You spend in our hearts requires that You leave something behind. A mark, a scent, an image, a vision.

Perhaps it is some wisdom that you leave, like spiritual ectoplasm that slides off you and remains attached to the walls of our hearts. Maybe it's more like the room that is our heart gets supercharged with Your energy so we know You've been there before us. With us and in us. Not a thief in the night but a spring rain shower that clears the air, cools our brow, and lets us breathe again.

Your intimate inside knowledge of us means that You know everything about us. I do some things every day that I'd just as soon no one know. But You know. I'm not embarrassed. At least . . . not much. Well, maybe a little. The amazing thing is that even with Your inside knowledge, even knowing all that You do about me, You continue to love me and keep my faults secret, just between the two of us. I appreciate that very much.

I wish I could do the same with all the faults I find out about others. I don't really need to share the inside knowledge I have about them. Not unless it is of the good variety and what I'm sharing is bound to bless them and others.

Lord, I'm glad You have this inside knowledge of me. Forgive me for my dark side. Help me lead with Your light so that the darkness flies away, flies away, flies away home. But it always flies back, Lord, and roosts like bats in my spiritual belfry, where it waits on me like a batty old friend that I wish would just go away.

I'm glad You love me, Lord. All of me, inside and out.

JOHN KÖEHLER

Two leaders from Kellam putting on a good face after getting pied.

SIXTY-FOUR

Cleaning Up the Unclean

for Becky

JOHN KÖEHLER

> But the voice from heaven spoke again: "Do not call something unclean if God has made it clean."
>
> ACTS 11:9

June 18, 2008

Dear Lord,

Peter was a man deeply committed to the notion that God had picked Israel and its people for His own purpose. He believed that he was set apart and unique and that he needed to keep the commandments to maintain that distance and separation from other people. Failing to do so would cause him to become impure and separated from his own people.

So imagine his discomfort when God gave him a vision. A vision that showed all the animals considered unclean by the Hebrews: birds and hoofed animals, wild animals and things that crept upon the earth. These were all considered unclean by Peter and his people, the Israelites.

When God—in Peter's vision—said, "Get up, Peter; kill and eat," Peter responded as if God was, uh, out of His mind. He answered the voice in his vision by saying, "Surely not, Lord! I have never eaten anything impure or unclean." Which is another way of saying, "I eat only kosher food!" (see Acts 11:7-8).

But God was not to be trifled with and said, "Do not call anything impure that God has made clean." Wow! After all this time—during which God had given them explicit laws about what not to eat—suddenly Peter, a devout Jew and follower of all things in the law including eating kosher, was expected to eat food that God had said was unclean before. Food to be avoided at all cost was now food to be eaten according to God's word and will.

Can you imagine the confusion this brought to Peter? I can. That's probably why God repeated Himself three times to Peter. Three times to make sure Peter understood clearly what He wanted. God wanted Peter to understand that there was a new covenant, a new law according to His Son Jesus. And that new law was to consider all things clean and part of God's kingdom.

After a while Peter understood that God was really talking about people. He wanted Peter to accept all people into the kingdom, not just the "clean and pure" according to the old standards. The new standard, as shown in Peter's vision, was that anyone who accepted Jesus as the Messiah and as his or her personal Savior was clean in God's eyes. Jews or Greeks, Samaritans or Romans, old or young, able or disabled. All people.

Before this Peter had never preached to or cared for non-Jews. But now God was expecting him to accept *all* His people. This was hard for Peter, but then God's commandments were not made to be easy. His personal expectations for us can be extremely difficult to follow.

God said to Peter—and to us—that we should never put down anyone who has been made clean by God. For me this extends to all people, including people with disabilities. This means that God washes away all sin and makes pure all people who come to him. He does not see their sin or their imperfections. He doesn't see their wheelchairs or hear their speech impediments. To Him they are the most beautiful and amazing of His progeny, His own kids.

God makes us clean and washes our impurities away when we give ourselves to Christ. If he claims people with disabilities and calls them beautiful, then who are we not to claim them and see their faults? We really have no choice but to follow Peter's lead, just as he followed God's lead, no matter how uncomfortable it made him at first.

It can be uncomfortable accepting people with disabilities. However, we have no choice but to abide by God's command to Peter, and through him to us: do not call anything impure that God has made clean. Another way to say this is: call everyone beautiful and love them if God has made them clean.

Now that's a clean choice we all can live with.

(L-R): Gavin, Ruben and Derek ponder existence with love and clothes pins.

SIXTY-FIVE

My Three Sons

for Gavin, Ruben & Derek

> The sons of Noah who came out of the ship were
> Shem, Ham, and Japheth. Ham was the father of
> Canaan. These are the three sons of Noah; from
> these three the whole Earth was populated.
>
> GENESIS 9:18-19

June 18, 2008

Dear Lord,

I reckon the title should really be "My Three Little Brothers," but that just doesn't sound as good. It is possible that I may be a bit of a surrogate father to these three dudes, but I do not want to claim a title I have no right to.

Derek's dad is a good man, and I know him. He comes to some of the events and dresses up as Santa for our Christmas party. Derek always wants to be Santa too, and I think he is secretly hoping that next year I'll fire his dad so he can be Santa. He certainly won't need any extra padding, that's for sure!

I've never met Gavin's or Ruben's dad. I don't know if they exist or not, but as far as I'm concerned, they don't. I believe that both of their moms are single parents, which in my opinion immediately qualifies them for entry into the Angel Hall of Fame. Same with Derek's mom. The moms are all angels, filled with such amazing endurance and grace that I am constantly awestruck and humbled.

They look at me and thank me for the few years of service I've given to their kids. But how does that compare with the years of constant service they have given? I give hours every week on their kid's behalf, while they give hours, days, and weeks which turn into years and—eventually—a lifetime.

I get calls every week from my three sons, my three little brothers. They call me to hear my voice and to say hi. They call me to hear from someone who they know loves them and really wants them to succeed. They call to get love from a father figure they wish they had. I wonder why they would possibly want me in that role, but they do so who am I to argue?

Derek calls because he can't help himself. He desires my approval and wants to earn his stripes and be called to action and complete those actions successfully. Derek wants me to tell him the truth but to always give him hope. So I do.

Ruben calls me over and over because of his OCD. I don't answer for several calls, and then I do. He keeps calling because when I don't answer it he doesn't think he's bothering me. Only the conversation counts. Ruben is going out on his own soon and wants me to be there with him. So he calls me and just wants to hang out on the phone. Can do.

Gavin calls me so I can share a few minutes of life with him. He wants me to ask him silly questions and find out how he's doing. He wants me to care about him, so I do. He wants to hear me say I love him, so I do.

My three sons need me every week and sometimes several times during the week. I don't take all their calls, and sometimes I have to ask them not to call me so often. But I understand how important it is for them to hear my voice. I understand that I have assumed a position of importance in their lives.

Maybe my approval means that God will approve too. I don't know. I don't understand all their motivations, but I do understand that they need me to be there for them. So I am. All three of them are painted permanently on my heart. I have a little bit of them there, and they have a little bit of me in their hearts. We are brothers of the heart.

I used to think that I had two daughters, but now I know I have three sons. My three sons.

JOHN KÖEHLER

MY INFLATABLE HEART

His mind is cloudy but his heart is clear.

SIXTY-SIX

My Living Dream

for Matt

JOHN KÖEHLER

> So Peter left the cell, following the angel.
> But all the time he thought it was a vision.
> He didn't realize it was actually happening.
>
> ACTS 12:9

June 21, 2008

Dear Lord,

Sometimes my life feels like a dream. I don't mean a wonderful, dreamlike state where everything is perfect. I mean a place where I'm not sure if I am alive and in this moment or being shown a vision and living out that vision. Or even sleepwalking, daytripping, daydreaming, or out of my mind.

I suppose if we're connected and embedded in Your heart and mind, then we are in a way living out a dream and a vision. Yours.

The truth is that I seem to slip into moments of time where reality and unreality twist together, and I wonder where I am and in whose dream I am. During boomerang tournaments I used to go up to my buddy Juice, just before the first event, and say, "Tell me I'm here."

My psyche was so supercharged and excited, and the adrenaline was pumping so much that I was temporarily unsure of my existence and needed to be reminded that I was there. Just to be sure.

As I get older, I dream more and more. It has become more natural for me simply to accept that life sometimes seems like a dream and is a dream. Will heaven feel like a dream, Lord?

I like this idea very much and subscribe to it. Maybe that's why I waver back and forth between doing my very best to conquer my real world by way of business and other-worldly success and trying to live in my dream world by injecting humor and ridiculous fun into my life and the lives of others.

Naturally this does not go over so well with some folks. These are the folks who are frightened by the dream world and all that it brings. To them it is bizarre and inappropriate to their rock-solid world. For them my crazy antics and twisted interpretation of life are nothing but a whacked-out, medicated, and incorrect version of reality.

Maybe they're right.

All I know is all I know. But knowing is partly about feeling life, and learning is done with the mind *and* the heart and soul. So many people miss this. So many people are completely disconnected to the amazing world that is all around us, a dream world within the dreams of their lives. They refuse to tap into this world because to do so would make them . . . less real. But if You made us and all of creation, then You made the dream world too, and our dreams belong to You. As do we. Ahhhhh, so strange.

Peter was in prison and was sure to die the next day as had James before him. He was asleep, chained between two guards, and with guards at the door. I wonder what Peter was dreaming about. Maybe Jesus came to him in his dream and said, "Peter, wake up. Do you remember when I saved you from drowning on the lake?"

"Yes, Lord," Peter replied in his dream, "I remember. I tried to walk on the water, but it wouldn't hold me."

Jesus laughed at that and said, "I held you, Peter. I held you. Now wake up!"

Peter fought against his dream Messiah and said, "But, Lord, I'm in chains."

"I'm setting you free, Peter. Now wake up and go do My work!"

Peter awakened, and an angel was next to him saying, "Quick! Get up!" Peter's chains fell off, and he just sat there between the two guards who were still sleeping. He couldn't really believe what was happening and probably rubbed his eyes or pinched himself. Or both. Maybe he closed his eyes and prayed for God to wake him up. But he was awake and God had already answered his prayers.

Then the angel told him to get dressed and followed him out of the prison, past the sleeping guards, out of the locked door, and back to his friend's house. All the while Peter thought he was dreaming. He thought it was a vision, and he was asleep or dead. But he soon discovered that he was living a dream within the dream of his life. The angel had been real, and he really had escaped from prison with the help of God's servant.

You are all around us Lord, and in us, living inside and outside our lives, all the time and everywhere. The kingdom of God is like a dream world within which we can live, but it does not work the same as our regular world. It seems odd and strange. Wonderfully strange. Beautifully warped. Amazingly and utterly bizarre.

I live in this world every day, and sometimes I wish I could stay there and not have to live in this other world, the world of man. I love the dreams that You give me and let me live within, the dreams of Your heart lived out in my life. I miss them.

Living out the dreams You have placed in me is not always a perfect thing. Often I stumble and fall, but always I know that You do have a dream for me, a perfect purpose for me. My hope is that I am living well in both worlds, melding them together so that they work perfectly in the perfection that is the kingdom of God. Your kingdom and mine. Okay … *your* kingdom!

But in order to do this, I must think and dream big. All I have to do is live my perfect dream, the dream You made for me, and for all your people. Open up the eyes of their hearts, Lord, to the beauty of Your kingdom, so all their dreams may come true.

(L-R): Ashley, Jenny and Pam surfing.

SIXTY-SEVEN

Heart Surfing

for Dale

(L-R): Colleen, John, Marty, Troy, Daniel and Patti just after Daniel got baptized.

> But Jesus insisted. "Do it. God's work, putting things right all these centuries, is coming together right now in this baptism." So John did it.
>
> MATTHEW 3:15

June 22, 2008

Dear Lord,

Thanks for yesterday. After last year's Surf Camp I just kept thinking about the baptism and how cool it would be. I dreamed about it, thought about it, and saw it as something that had already happened. I like it when I can climb inside Your vision and live there. Living inside a vision makes it real and makes me ready for the real thing, the thing we execute to complete the vision.

The funny thing is that doing it live can seem anticlimactic after already knowing how it will be. It has always been that way for me, which I suppose makes me lucky. It also makes me super impatient for the thing to happen. Like Surf Camp.

Friday afternoon I took off early and mowed the yard. I am actually blessed by mowing my lawn. No one can talk to me; no one can call me; e-mails are out of the question. There's just me, the mower, and the grass. I make a line and then make another. I walk around my yard and try my best not to step on dog poo. Not a problem if it's old and dry, but young and wet is another story—one you don't want to be part of.

After that I set up the tables. I love parties. The idea is to create a place, a setting, and an event where people can come, be themselves, and enjoy each other. The key is to welcome them in love. With Capernaum this is very easy as we all feed off each other. I don't mean like cannibals in the flesh, but in the Spirit! So for me just setting up tables is an act of love because I can imagine how everyone will feel. I imagine how I would feel and where I would sit. I see them there in my mind. I miss them ahead of time.

Pam and Mark Harmon arrived, and off we went for dinner with Tara, Rusty, Angela, and Jerry, Rusty's painter friend and a Capernaum buddy, a volunteer who is there to be a friend with our people. Jerry is standing on the end of God's diving board, ready to fall into Jesus, ready for someone to push him in. But not yet. Maybe he's near the end, but he's looking back to defend himself against any lunkhead who tries to come up behind him. He's a tough guy and has had a tough life. He cannot comprehend a God who loves him exactly as he is and who will forget his past. He can't forget, so why should God?

Saturday morning came, and I was ready to rumble. I was impatient, and, as always happens, time marched forward, and suddenly it was two o'clock and volunteers were arriving. Some prepared for the party, and others headed down to the beach to carry surfboards, set up tents, and prepare for the kids.

The official start was three o'clock, but it unofficially began at two thirty when Rusty took a bunch of kids into the water. Leave it to Rusty to break the rules! That's why he's such a good senior leader. Troy Smith, my big, bald-headed man-of-God friend, had once again brought a bunch of foam trainer boards, and other friends brought their long boards and tandems. Troy runs Titus International, a surfing company that includes Titus Surf School, which is an awesome way to learn.

Brandon is a huge, autistic black kid, weighing in around four hundred pounds. True to autistic form, he appeared frightened by the noisy waves, but he was obviously drawn to them as well, especially to the surf boards. We eased Brandon out in the water and worked to get him on top of Scott Cohen's tandem board, which takes two to carry all twelve feet of it. Huge!

By the time we finally got Brandon belly-down on the board, it nearly sank! Scott managed to turn it and positioned Brandon for a belly ride into shore. He did it! I could see Scott hanging on to the back of Brandon's life vest, then letting him go and watching his new little (ahem, huge) brother ride the wave in on his own.

Scott disappears but then runs back in to help Brandon get up. That's how it goes at Capernaum. We show them, we model the behavior, we teach them, we push and pull them, and then we let them go so they can do it on their own. Then we run back in to help them when they lie there completely shocked at what they've done. Scott provided the spirit and energy for Brandon on Saturday. Without him Brandon would not have done what he did. Scott is a hero. All of our buddies and leaders are heroes.

Page has Down syndrome and is proud of it. She will tell you about it and has written stories about it. Her parents are proud of her; God is proud of her; everyone in Capernaum is proud of her... so why should she not be proud of herself? Riddle me that!

Page is fearless, but when she first came to Surf Camp, she was frightened by the waves. After a while her fear evaporated. She started showing off and eventually managed to stand on a surfboard held in place by some of her new buddies. Capernaum is all about becoming instant friends. If you help me with my surfboard and make sure I'm safe and no sharks get me, then I will love you back. Any questions?

Page wound up winning the Most Outstanding Surfer award after receiving a lot of help from some outstanding leaders, including Jenn from Virginia Tech and Miss CNU.

A lot of people would prefer if folks with disabilities just stayed inside and out of sight. But we have just as much right as you to act like a wild woman or man, have ridiculous amounts of fun, and live life large and to the absolute max.

Those people would best be advised to stay out of our way because God has a plan for us, and no one will stop our relentless pursuit of our own perfection. The perfection God made in us. We rock!

The weather was stormy just to the west of us, so a lot of people didn't come. Even so we had about eighty folks there, including kids, family members, leaders, and buddies. We had about twelve trainer boards, plus a couple of long boards and tandems. Two tents, some beach chairs. A bunch of sand and a big old ocean!

Bobby and his twin brother, Earl, surfed. First Bobby and then Earl, drawn by the pull of his brother's courage. I walked Earl out with a board and cracked up when he screamed like a girl as the water hit his thighs. Every time a wave came up higher, he would scream just like a girl; I was dying, trying to continue talking to him without laughing out loud. It was really hard!

I got Earl on the board, turned him around, and pushed him into a nice little wave, which caught him and carried him in to shore, easy as pie. Meanwhile I looked to the left, and there was Bobby riding the same wave in to shore. It wasn't planned but just happened, maybe a nice little touch from God to show us who's in charge of twins and the rest of us.

Then the baptism happened. What can I say? It was huge. The beach became holy ground, and we were turned into God's holy people. Our three pastors—Marty, Patty, and Troy—were beautiful and perfect for the job. The twins stepped forward to be baptized—even Earl, the quiet brother. Back in December at our Christmas party, Marty, the senior pastor at Church of the Messiah, told Earl about giving his life away to Jesus and inviting Him into his heart. And so he did.

Then Pam Bolt stepped up to be baptized, and my spirit came up, and I cried. Not that the others didn't also make me feel huge and lit up like a Fourth of July fireworks display, but Pam's baptism was unexpected and a double scoop of blessing from God. She said that she had accepted Christ as her Savior a long time ago, but she had never been baptized. So she came forward and was baptized.

What a pleasure and honor to provide a chance for my friends to complete this outward symbol of their internal baptism.

We were nearly done when someone ran up to me and said that Brandon wanted to get baptized. His mom said he understood and wanted to do it. Meanwhile she was crying on the shore as we led the gentle Brandon down to the water and laid him back into the waves three times. Not once, as might have been preferable due to our people being frightened by autism, CP, Down's, and a host of other things. Pastor Marty said we would dunk them the Father, the Son, and the Holy Spirit trinity way . . . and so we did!

If I died today, I would go to heaven and tell You about Surf Camp. It makes me feel that some of my work here is done. Lord, I don't know about tomorrow or the day after. I don't know how much longer I have in this part of Your kingdom, this part of my life. But I want to thank You for the service You have allowed me to do thus far.

Surf Camp was a dream come true, and the baptism was a dream within the dream. I think everything that comes along now is just a bonus. Gravy. Extra stuff. I can't wait!

Local croaker fish and Jasper the dog. Image was originally part of Va. Beach SPCA's Scoop the Poop program.

SIXTY-EIGHT

Jasper the Amazing Dog

for Patty, Kimmi & Danielle

JOHN KÖEHLER

> We aren't immortal. We don't last long.
> Like our dogs, we age and weaken. And die.
>
> PSALM 49:12

July 3, 2008

Dear Lord,

I'm kind of shaky right now because my dog Jasper is dying downstairs. Patty is calling the vet to schedule a time when we can help Jasper finish dying. I feel a powerful emotion that is too big to describe or control. Let me tell You about my dog Jasper, as if you didn't already know. Let me tell you.

Jasper is the family dog and has been with us for the past sixteen and a half years, if You can believe it. Well, I reckon You can believe anything since You invented belief and stuck it in our hearts as a signature way for us to connect to You and to the world.

Patty gave Jasper to me as a birthday present way back in 1992. Probably the best present I've ever received, even if some folks yelled at me for getting a purebred dog instead of a shelter dog. To all those folks, I invite you to reconsider your ignorance.

I remember going to pick Jasper out of his litter. Since they were chocolate labs, I brought some white tape to mark the puppies I was interested in. They were all swarming together and play-fighting in a brown rugby scrum. I started putting on a few pieces of white tape, and then I noticed that one of the marked pups would play with his siblings and then leave the scrum and lie down and watch the others.

That's my dog! I loved his laid-back approach to life, and sure enough, he was the perfect dog for us and our laid-back family.

This morning Jasper was whimpering in pain. I comforted him, and when I was next to him, he quieted. Then when I was eating breakfast, he whimpered until I came over and petted him some more. So I dragged him (he can't get up anymore) over near the kitchen table so he could see me from where he lay while I ate. This quieted him down.

All his life he has just wanted to see me, Lord. Whether I was working up here in the studio, riding my bike, swimming in the ocean, or just watching TV. Jasper always needed to position himself so he could see me. I don't know if this was because I trained him or because we were, and are, best friends. Regardless, it is what it is, and I am thankful for his need to see me.

His need kept me here and made me realize how important I am to all God's creatures, great and small. Two legs or four. Sentient or not. Your creatures, Lord. I'm thankful for my brown-eyed friend; I really am. I'm having trouble writing this without crying. Dang it!

I hate funerals. I know the point of them, but the point sucks, and the setting and tone suck more. So sad and stupid, when the life of the dead one is anything but sad. Same with Jasper. I know I'm going to grieve—I already am—but I refuse to give in to too much of it, Lord. The whole thing going on inside me right now is nobody's business but my own. Why do I have to share that with anyone? I don't want to.

When we moved to the beach, Jasper was afraid of the waves. This seemed completely wrong to me since my dog, our dog, was supposed to love the water. He did love it, but the waves scared the poo right out of him. I wanted to *ease* him into it, so I picked him up and threw him into a wave. He learned how to ride the waves pretty quickly!

One of my favorite memories of Jasper is when we first moved here. Patty was living up in Maryland with Danielle, finishing out the school year as a teacher. I was down here with Kimmi. Jasper and I would meet Kimmi at the end of the street every day when she got off the bus. Then we'd hop on our bikes and ride back into Seashore State Park. Jasper would trot along beside us, then race off after something, and eventually catch back up to us.

He became a true North End dog by wandering all around the area. He'd always come back, sometimes covered in mud from the marshes he'd walked through. He'd come back home and rest a bit, happy to get the biscuit we gave him whenever he came back. When he was much older, he would walk outside, down to the yard, make a hard U-turn, and scratch on the door to come back in. For a biscuit. He would do this over and over again until we wised up. But I was happy to pay him back for all the joy he brought us, and if getting a little bit of biscuit fat was part of the price, so be it.

Jasper became the Dog of the Street after Buddy died. Buddy was a big, old, ornery Wolfhound, scary and crotchety. The rule for the Dog of the Street is that he can crap anywhere on the street with impunity. That's the rule—even if some folks never got a copy of it, much less agreed to it. Now that Jasper is leaving the planet, Bianca will assume the title. Thing is, she already craps in my yard with impunity. Maybe she assumed her title a little early. Long live Bianca!

Sixteen years is a long time for any dog to live, much less a big dog. Twelve is the average number. This makes Jasper exemplary in age as well as behavior and style. Everyone loved him, and he loved everyone. All except for the black dude who was walking down our driveway to put something on our doorstep just as Jasper and I walked outside.

Jasper's hackles went up, and he started doing that crazy, stiff-legged running/hopping/barking strut that dogs do to tell you to get the heck off their yard. The dude did a perfect cartoon arm windmill with his legs running in place on the gravel. He went down hard, left a big rut in my driveway, got up, and took off running. I could not help myself: I laughed out loud while also yelling an apology to the rapidly retreating dude.

Since Jasper is a dog of color, I'm quite positive that this was not discrimination. He just sensed something bad in the dude, and maybe he also wanted to impress me. Well, he did.

Jasper slept with our girls, hid under my desk during thunderstorms, and kept constant and vigilant watch as we slept—unless he was chasing rabbits in his sleep, in which case, forget it. Jasper was and is as much a part of our family as we are. We are about to lose a family member, and that just hurts badly. It sucks big-time.

Jasper is going out, and Lilli is coming in. Thanks for the coming and goings, Lord. Thanks for emptying our tanks and filling them up. Thanks for new life and the end of life. Thanks for everything. Thanks for Jasper.

Thanks for my best-friend dog. My dog (our dog) Jasper.

JOHN KÖEHLER

John giving Angela a reflex test as part of her Intern Training. She bit him back.
Photo by Glen McClure.

JOHN KÖEHLER

PART EIGHT

NEW SONGS

for Elaine

MY INFLATABLE HEART

Publishing poetry opens me up to charges of vanity, and if they come I will plead guilty as charged. Poetry is simply another media that can be used as a form of self-expression. Nothing more and nothing less. These poems are all about me, therefor inherently prideful. So why share them?

I have always put down my poems, partly because I am not a poet, partly because my style is akin to Dr. Seuss and because for some reason it still feels strange to me when I offer my poems to the world. I really don't write poetry often (thank the Lord!) and usually I write them when I'm going through a tough time. When I write poetry you know I'm in the big surf, getting beat up.

I think that poems provide another type of window, another glimpse into my world, my life and my beliefs. They are personal.

I shared some in my first book and they proved more popular than I imagined they would. Some of them have been turned into songs, which is super cool for me. Like having a son get called up to the majors.

So now I share – with apologies to the real poets out there – these silly poems for your enjoyment. Or not. Bon apetit!

JOHN KÖEHLER

My Busted Heart

Take your righteousness and shove it.
Take my busted heart and love it.
Take a snapshot of my face.
Take me out of this stinking place.

Make yourself at home in my pain.
Make me go completely insane.
Make me some wings to fly away.
Make me remember all the things you say.

Give me a chance to prove that I'm true.
Give me a little time to get next to you.
Give me your love in a coonskin cap.
Give me a way to get out of this trap.

Show me the way to the front of my life
Show me a place without any strife.
Show me the how and the why it will end.
Show me the beginning all over again.

Refrain:
Take my busted heart
Make me remember
Give me another start
Show me December

MY INFLATABLE HEART

Outside In

You asked me how I'm doin',
I told you pretty good.
I didn't think you'd want to know
My heart was made of wood.

You asked me where I'm goin'
I said I'm on a roll.
I didn't think you'd want to see
The colors of my soul.

On the outside I am healthy
Wealthy wise and cool.
But on the inside I'm just busted
Adjusted like a fool.

If you can love me outside in,
Dreams and nightmares too.
Then I will let my heartstrings play
A love song just for you.

There's no mistaken that I'm achin'
Fakin' my way through life
Filled with contrition and blind ambition
I'm just hopin' for your permission.
I'm just hopin' for you
Just hopin.'
For you.

JOHN KÖEHLER

Butterfly Dream

The sound of waves on the ocean floor
A good friend knocking on your front door
What's the point in looking for more
When it's all right here.

A baby's laugh and a butterfly dream
The winning goal for your home team
Sometime life is more than it seems
If you don't try so hard.

Breath in, breath out
Eyes closed to see
There is no doubt
Just you and me

A kitten plays with a ball of string
Walking tall with your new bling bling
Livin' life ain't nothin' but a thing
At the top of the world.

A really good book and a sweet sunset
The perfect wave you won't ever forget
So much world for you to get
If you leave it alone.

Slow down, give in
Rhythms of your heart
Losing creates the win
Soulful engines start.

MY INFLATABLE HEART

Puttin' On The Fool

Well I'm a medium hot
I'm okey dokey fine
And you better believe
I get better all the time.

Yeah I'm lickety split
I'm keepin' it in line
Not tryin' to make a fuss
But I'm feelin' pretty fine.

When Monday looks my way
I'll be ready to cool
But it's Saturday night and
I'm puttin' on the fool.

Cause I'm a ready to boil
And I'm ready to rock
I'm puttin' it in drive and
I don't know when I'll stop.

Hitch a ride on my caboose
Jump in and strap 'em down
Cause now I'm on the loose
Gonna liven up this town.

When Monday looks my way
I'll be ready to cool
But it's Saturday night and
I'm puttin' on the fool.
Yeah I'm puttin',
Puttin'....
On the fool.

One Foot in Heaven

I got one foot in heaven,
And another foot below.
I'm a little bit conflicted
About which way to go.

I got an angel on my left,
And a devil on my right.
They try to make me listen
And they try to make me fight
For the right way to go.
Well, how's a guy to know?

Well I'm readin' good books,
Most every day.
But the story of my life,
Still gets in my way.

I got friends that are saved,
And friends that don't care.
Which ones should I pick,
Which ones to beware?

There's just so many ways,
And so many choices.
How must we behave,
To make heaven rejoice us?

I know Goody Two Shoes,
And her brother Steel Toe.
Will one go to heaven,
And the other below?
How's a guy to know,
The right way to go.
Yeah, how's a guy to know,
The right way to go.

MY INFLATABLE HEART

Kneel Upon My Life

Just when I
Think my life is over
That's when you
Find a four-leaf clover
Over

Just when I
Want my life to end
That's when you
Teach me to begin
Again

You lift me up
From all the pain
You set me free
Show me that
I'm not done again

It doesn't matter
How much I falter
You gave your life
As my own alter

So I kneel upon my life
And I sing upon my soul
I execute my strife
Your love makes me whole
Yeah, your love
Makes me whole

Symphonic Life

If life is a song
Perfect and true
What if I'm wrong
What if I'm blue

I'd like to be jazz
Amazingly magical
But it's too razmataz
And I'm just too practical

The blues of the night
Turn to daytime love songs
Dreams filled with fright
Day proves them wrong

A symphonic life
Isn't possible for me
Discordant strife
Turns to asymmetry

But there in the midst
Of the chaotic sounds
The heavens exist they're
Just waiting to be found

Moments of madness
Become angelic rhythm
Fear becomes gladness
Singing we're with him

MY INFLATABLE HEART

Top Of The Hill

Three men standing on the top of the hill,
Black bird flyin' 'cross the sky.
One man waiting for his father's will,
Two men learning how to die.

Three men rolling for the pick of the king,
Spear tips gleaming in the sun.
One man listens to the angels sing.
One Dad weeps for his son.

One thief spits across the royal tree,
A donkey brays behind the hill.
Second thief wants forgiveness for his fee
Third man pays for his bill.

Two men die and nobody cares,
A soldier wears a new shirt.
One man alive and everybody stares,
His mother weeping in the dirt.

One man living on the top of the hill,
Blue bird flies from his heart.
Three men their trees so still,
Dead men laying on a cart.

Refrain:

The things you did for me
Will last beyond eternity
Regardless if I ever see
The beauty of your face.
Your everlasting grace.
You did it all for me.

JOHN KÖEHLER

Dad's Prayer
(after the Lord's Prayer)

He's your Dad and mine,
He's right here beside us
All of the time.

You make us feel loved,
Whether visiting with us
Or living above.

Your name is so glorious,
We love saying it
Like a story to us.

Come and light up our hearts,
Show us how to live
So our life is your art.

Paint our souls with mirth,
Rainbows that connect
The heavens to the earth.

We eat your holy seeds,
To lives our lives today
You know what we need.

Forgive me for hurting you,
Help me to forgive them
When I am torn in two.

Lead me away from the call,
Of the beautiful doom
Awaiting my fall.

Your place is all powerful
It is forever and ever
Bountifully beautiful.

I am there now and again
I will be there with you
Remembering when.

MY INFLATABLE HEART

Stopped at a Green Light

I was stopped at a green light
Didn't know what to do
And all the other traffic was
Barreling through

Took a left at a right turn
And I stepped on the gas
What's wrong with these people
They won't let me get past

Made a Y at a U-turn
It seemed natural to me
You're not going the right way
I don't care if you agree

I went straight on an S-curve,
Went off of the road
I wish someone would take
My three-quarter-ton load

I pulled over for a cop
But he blasted past me
I followed in front
So I could pay the fee
For just being me
Please let me pay the fee

JOHN KÖEHLER

Abundant Light

The seasons of my soul reflect
The reasons for God's intellect
But reason can not soothe my pain
When darkness covers me again

In Summer time the darkness flees
No slumber time, get off your knees
And celebrate the glorious light
That God has given forth to please

The Fall of man and harvest bells
Recalls the land of bounteous smells
Shorter days and longer nights
Call you below to Winter's hell

Darkest days of Winter's crumbs
Hark the ways of kingdoms come
Veil the beauty of wondrous life
Behold his heart so dead and numb

But wait, the Spring of God above
The gates of hell fall with his shove
The light has come for you to claim
Another victim of his love

Whether long or short the days I live
Another song of praise I give
No matter how the darkness reigns
Abundant light calls me again

Abundant light shines in my soul
Provides the sight to make me whole
Abundant light my hopes within
Lift me beyond my heart's console

MY INFLATABLE HEART

Pigman & The Prince

Pigman stinks but can not smell
The odious stench that covers his heart
He wonders how it was he fell
What caused his world to tear apart

He remembered when his riches flowed
Inherited from the man he adored
But money proved a painful load
And pigs became his just reward

He dreamed a place where honey flowed
And he was crowned beloved prince
Pigman looked at his abode
And jumped across the pigsty fence

The road was long and long he cried
He feared the retribution place
Ashamed he finished off his pride
From strangers Pigman hid his face

A father waits far down the road
His tears make lakes for ants below
His son is dead, his heart is bowed
Why did he ever let him go

A son has come with nothing left
And sees his father weeping still
The father spies him in the cleft
And soon is running down the hill

JOHN KÖEHLER

A strong embrace between two men
Who look alike and sound the same
A son who is consumed with sin
A father's heart now beats again

"Forgive me father, for I have sinned
They call me Pigman where I lived
I gave my riches to the wind
And now have nothing left to give"

The father picked him off the ground
And led him through the golden fence
"My son was lost but now is found
No Pigman here, I see a Prince"

MY INFLATABLE HEART

Oasis

I walk the dessert of my life
Filled with emptiness and strife
A mirage that I just can't afford
I'm so thirsty for you Lord
Let me drink your life

I see a garden of life ahead
Doesn't matter that I feel dead
Can't feel my feet, I'm torn apart
Let me drink from your heart
Let me eat your bread

I hear your water flowing near
Can't see you but I know you're here
The new oasis of my death
Living waters from your breath
Wash away my fear

I step into your moonlit pool
See reflections another fool
White Water washes my sin away
While angels splash baptism day
Across the meadow clean and cool

I'm drowning Lord and I can see
A dream filled with serenity
Moonlight fills a newborn's face
Swimming in your awesome grace
He looks at my eternity

Desert oasis for us to find
Discovered even though we're blind
Miraculous waters fill us there
We will serve you without care
Broken hearts you'll soon unbind

Beach Angel

I saw an Angel at the beach
You'll think that I'm not serious
I saw her sitting there in reach
My heart beat so delirious

A Rusty friend said she was there
But I was heading off the sand
I turned and saw her sitting fair
Waving with her broken hands

Across the beach I walked into
Beach Angel's life of hope and love
My day was done, my minutes few
My Angel came down from above

She spoke but I could not pretend
The things she said I did not hear
Nor with my ears could comprehend
Within my heart the meaning clear

She stayed an ocean of her smiles
The sunset moved across the sky
Please let me stay and talk awhile
Beach Angel teach me how to fly

She fills a space within my heart
A special place where few can go
Loving Angels is an art
For mortals living here below

Refrain:
Beach Angel, light me up inside
And fill my heart with your love song
Beach Angel will you provide
Another heaven where I belong

MY INFLATABLE HEART

Shooting Star

If pigs can fly then why oh why
Can't I just make her mine?
If dogs chase cats, whose keeping the stats
In the middle of time. All time

I don't understand how the world
Keeps turning away from my view
No matter how hard I put myself down
I get torn in two. Torn in two

Why won't she let me in to her heart?
Why won't she let me belong to her?
I don't believe that she knows I'm alive
I think it's high time I learned to survive
Without her. Without her

If flowers can bloom then why can't my heart?
I probably lost her but hey, that's a start
Will she run from me when I tell her that I
Love her and shove her to the top of my heart?
Will she love me? Love me?

Or will she come to me when I show her the size
Of my daffodil soul and give her the prize
For winning, and spinning her beautiful eyes
Oh say, can you see if she noticed it was me?
Did she notice it was me?

If magnets lift cars and I can see stars
Then why can't I find my way home to her
Heart that is sounding, another man drowning
The life raft is thrown, I don't' think I'll go far
I don't think I'll go far
With my shooting star
Don't think I'll go far
Shooting star, shooting star, my shooting star,
Shooting star, shooting star, my shooting star

www.ingramcontent.com/pod-product-compliance
Lightning Source LLC
Chambersburg PA
CBHW031229290426
44109CB00012B/219